Research Methods in
APPLIED BEHAVIOR
ANALYSIS

To Mont Wolf, mentor and the
"founder of applied behavior analysis"

Research Methods in
Applied Behavior
Analysis

Jon S. Bailey • Mary R. Burch
Florida State University   *Behavior Management Consultants, Inc.*

Sage Publications
International Educational and Professional Publisher
Thousand Oaks ■ London ■ New Delhi

For information:

Sage Publications, Inc.
2455 Teller Road
Thousand Oaks, California 91320
E-mail: order@sagepub.com

Sage Publications Ltd.
6 Bonhill Street
London EC2A 4PU
United Kingdom

Sage Publications India Pvt. Ltd.
M-32 Market
Greater Kailash I
New Delhi 110 048 India

Printed in the United States of America

Library of Congress Cataloging-in-Publication Data

Bailey, Jon S.
  Research methods in applied behavior analysis / Jon S. Bailey
and Mary R. Burch.
      p.   cm.
Includes bibliographical references and index.
  ISBN 0-7619-2556-2 (pbk.)
    1. Psychology, Applied—Research—Methodology.   I. Burch, Mary R.
II. Title.
  BF76.5B35   2002
  150´.7´2—dc21   2001005394

06   07   10   9   8   7   6   5   4   3

Acquiring Editor:	Jim Brace-Thompson
Editorial Assistant:	Karen Ehrmann
Production Editor:	Denise Santoyo
Copy Editor:	Elizabeth Magnus
Typesetter/Designer:	Janelle LeMaster
Cover Designer:	Michelle Lee

CONTENTS

PREFACE

Our goal in writing *Research Methods in Applied Behavior Analysis* is to provide the beginning researcher with a how-to text for designing applied behavior analysis research. This text covers all of the elements of single-subject research design, and it provides practical information for designing, implementing, and evaluating studies. The researcher who is a Certified Behavior Analyst will hopefully recognize many of the field's behavior-analytic principles and procedures from which the Board Certified Behavior Analyst's Task List was derived. The earliest version of this book and its original outline were written by the first author in 1977. Since that time, the book has been used to teach beginning researchers and behavior analysts in both undergraduate and graduate programs across the country.

Applied Behavior Analysis

Applied behavior analysis is the name given to a specific psychological approach to the study of behavior. The term evolved from an earlier expression, behavior modification, that was popularized in the early 1960s and is still in use by some today. Behavior modification expressed an orientation to behavior that assumed that behavior was quite "plastic" or malleable and controlled primarily by consequences. The earliest "behavior modifiers" were, for the most part, laboratory-trained experimental psychologists who, through a variety of circumstances, became interested in distressed and often disenfranchised clinical populations. Other early pioneers in this field had their initial training in traditional clinical psychology. Usually through some strange twist of fate, many of these clinical psychologists came into contact with an enthusiastic behavior analyst and became fascinated with the field and its unique potential to improve the human condition.

Applied behavior analysis strives to develop empirically based treatments and interventions that can be demonstrated to work at the level of the individual. Behavior analysts are not usually interested in making general statements about populations; rather, in the tradition of B. F. Skinner, they are primarily interested in understanding individual human behavior. Whereas some psychologists are concerned with testing theories or describing trends in populations, behavior analysts are fascinated with why a person engages in a certain behavior. Furthermore, behavior analysts attempt to take this knowledge and use it to produce effective interventions in educational, treatment, rehabilitation, or corporate settings. In a time when health care costs are skyrocketing, there is a desperate need for therapeutic treatments that can demonstrate results (Berman, 2000), and some independent observers see single-subject design research as the vehicle for producing basic research that will actually benefit applied practice (Morgan & Morgan, 2001).

To date, a broad, empirically based approach to effective treatment has emerged from over 40 years of intensive applied behavioral research with a range of participants from autistic children to corporate executives (Austin & Carr, 2000). Applied behavior analysis has been empirical from the outset—the sole purpose has been to develop procedures that are experimentally derived, clinically useful, and ultimately accountable. It appears that the value of the single-participant experimental approach is just now being recognized by professions such as psychiatric nursing, rehabilitation, physical medicine, and the care of the elderly.

We assume that those wishing to embark on their first research project are thoroughly acquainted with the field and have had one or more basic courses in applied behavior analysis. There are several standard texts that cover this material quite well, and we recommend several to the interested reader:

- Behavior Modification: What It Is and How to Do It (Martin & Pear, 1999)

- Behavior Modification in Applied Settings (Kazdin, 2001)

- Behavior Modification: Principles and Procedures (Miltenberger, 2001)

- Applied Behavior Analysis (Cooper, Heron, & Heward, 1987)

- Handbook of Applied Behavior Analysis (Austin & Carr, 2000)

ACKNOWLEDGMENTS

We would like to thank Jeannie Plowman, Niki Thurkow, Dawn Bailey, Mae Barker, Christine Ratcliff, Colin Peeler, and Tom Welsh for their helpful comments on the initial drafts of this text.

1

WHAT IS APPLIED BEHAVIOR ANALYSIS RESEARCH?

MAIN TOPICS

The Operant Research Model

Important Methodological Milestones

Measurement of Significant Behavior

Science and Clinical Success

A Paradigm Shift

The Dimensions of Applied Behavior Analysis

LEARNING OBJECTIVES

We first consider the operant research model of behavior and review observation and measurement procedures from a historic perspective. Next, we review the seven dimensions of applied behavior analysis. After studying this chapter, you should be able to

- Describe observation and measurement methods and tell when they were first used.

- Discuss the history of the *Journal of Applied Behavior Analysis* and its role in promoting quality methodology for applied behavior analysis.

- Describe the paradigm shift that occurred in 1982.

- State and give examples of each of the seven dimensions of applied behavior analysis.

The field of applied behavior analysis has attracted a great deal of attention in recent years as the promise of an effective technology based on the products of an experimental analysis of behavior (Morgan & Morgan, 2001; Skinner, 1974) has begun to emerge. The contributions of the field are well documented in several journals now specifically devoted to the topic and in numerous excellent texts and collections of readings (see the suggested list of readings at the end of Part I). This extensive literature describes the important contributions that have been made in mental retardation, rehabilitation, delinquency, mental health, counseling, education, business and industry, and many other fields. It represents the development of procedures for behavior change arising from the experimental analysis of behavior with lower organisms.

Applied behavior analysis has attracted many enthusiastic participants, in part due to a kind of deceptive simplicity. Socially significant target behaviors are identified, an intervention is devised and put in place, and the resulting data show convincingly that it was effective. This apparent simplicity of the methodology may actually be a function of a limitation on journal space that prevents researchers and authors from fully describing the extensive efforts necessary to accomplish the behavioral changes that were achieved. Research articles almost never describe how a researcher came up with the original idea, nor do they trace the modifications in thinking that occurred through stimulating brainstorming sessions, sharing data with colleagues over coffee, or the pure dumb luck of being in the right place at the right time. Published articles rarely detail how the researchers happened to locate the particular environment where they work, gained the confidence of the established authority, and finally obtained permission to carry out their study. The specific details involved in the moment-to-moment conduct of the research once it is under way are simply never discussed in the text of an article. Such statements as "five preschool children were chosen" or "the study was carried out in three nursing homes" simply do not properly describe the extensive planning, intensive strategizing, and diplomatic behavior required from the applied researcher. This public abridged version is driven by the cost of journal space but grossly misrepresents the sustained effort and finely tuned skills researchers must acquire to conduct quality experimentation in applied settings.

Novice researchers, without the advantage of having apprenticed with established researchers, must often engage in extensive, frustrating, and wasteful trial-and-error activity. Applied behavioral research most often is exceedingly difficult to accomplish, often much more so than basic laboratory research where the subjects come in packing crates from a breeding farm, the measurement equipment is readily available, the experimental protocols are already established, and the research questions are derivative. The careful preplanning, eye for detail, compulsion for precision and consistency, and ample persistence required of all good researchers are obviously necessary. However, the creative, managerial, and administrative skills needed to conceptualize a unique applied problem and orchestrate the applied research are not obvious to the casual observer.

The present text is an effort to fill this void in the applied analyst's repertoire. Over the years, it has become clear that there *is* a proven formula for successful research. A major goal of the present book is to describe that formula for aspiring researchers and practitioners in the form of helpful hints, specific steps, suggested guidelines, and rules of thumb that may be followed. The intent of this text is not to review the literature or prescribe treatment procedures but rather to give eager new researchers a set of guidelines by which they may carry out their own initial research and hopefully contribute to the science of behavior. Before we proceed, however, a brief review of some basic features of operant research and a few landmark studies that have contributed to our current methodology seems to be in order.

The Operant Research Model

The earliest applied research studies were patterned in many ways after the style of research developed by B. F. Skinner and his students (Ferster & Skinner, 1957; Skinner, 1938) as they worked with rats and pigeons. A fundamental feature of the methodology is the detailed analysis of the behavior of the individual organism. As was the case with the original laboratory studies, a small number of individual subjects (very often only one subject) were observed for extensive periods of time. In these early applied studies, the "free-operant," ongoing behavior (frequently deviant in nature) of one or at most a handful of human subjects was measured during an initial baseline condition to determine the operant level of performance. Subsequently, some type of intervention procedure was systematically brought into contact with the target behavior, and the procedure's effects were noted. At some later point in these original studies, the contingent procedures were withdrawn to provide further evidence of the procedure's functional relationship to the target behavior.

Although this seemingly simple extrapolation of a kind of "case study" methodology would seem to be an easy extension, the task required some adjustments in experimental methods. New data-recording techniques had to be developed in the transition from laboratory to field research environment. Experimental subjects were humans with broader behavioral repertoires and larger environments. Manipulated consequences were more than food pellets and 2-second presentations of food hoppers. Target behaviors having social importance were usually not amenable to measurement with automated devices. Instead, human observers had to be extensively trained, and ways of ensuring the objectivity of measurement procedures were necessary. The reintroduction of the human observer into experimental analysis brought with it a host of logistical and methodological problems. These concerns were added to the difficulties associated with attempts to stabilize experimental environments in field settings. All of this contributed to the difficult early development of the emerging field of applied behavior analysis.

Important Methodological Milestones

Although it is often taken for granted, systematic observation procedures for collecting data on significant human responses in natural settings are a relatively recent development.

Measurement of Significant Behavior in Applied Settings

The seminal article "The Psychiatric Nurse as a Behavioral Engineer" by Ayllon and Michael (1959) represented a major contribution to applied behavior analysis. In this case study, problem behaviors of chronic psychotic patients were selected, defined, and measured systematically. In addition to the straightforward counting of such behaviors as "number of entrances to the nurses' office" or "number of magazines hoarded," Ayllon and Michael employed time-sampling recording procedures to evaluate "psychotic talk" or the presence of nonviolent behavior at 15- to 30-second intervals during the experimental sessions. The application of this efficient and accurate method of behavior measurement represented a major innovation in applied human research. Various aspects of this method of behavior measurement were, of course, part of human factors engineering in industrial psychology, but the more precise application of regular observation techniques to applied human research represented a largely new development. The reversal design that is described in detail in a later section of this text was also successfully applied by Ayllon and Michael to the hospital ward environment. Figure 1.1 is taken from this published report.

This graph reveals that an initial pretreatment condition consisting of one session was subsequently followed by a reinforcement condition and then later by a return to the pretreatment situation—the original ABA design.

Refinement of Observation and Control Procedures

Over the next few years, applied researchers began applying this new technology more extensively to modify deviant child behavior. During the

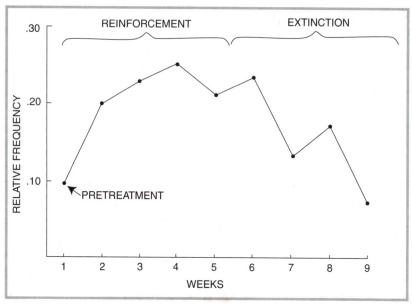

Figure 1.1. Reinforcement and subsequent extinction of the response "being on the floor"
SOURCE: From "The Psychiatric Nurse as a Behavioral Engineer," by T. Ayllon and J. Michael, 1959, *Journal of the Experimental Analysis of Behavior, 2,* pp. 323-334. Copyright 1959 by the Society for the Experimental Analysis of Behavior. Reprinted with permission.

1960s, researchers such as Don Baer, Mont Wolf, and Sidney Bijou, who were all at the University of Washington at the time, made significant advances relative to changing the behavior of "deviant" children. One of the first refinements came in the area of observation procedures, where a more intensive analysis of moment-to-moment changes in behavior was needed. The 10-second-interval recording method evolved and was an important advance in the precision of behavior observations (see Allen, Hart, Buell, Harris, & Wolf, 1964). Figure 1.2 shows one of the first widely distributed descriptions of this kind of observation technique.

Allen et al. (1964) employed other important advances in data analysis and methodology. Their study elaborated the use of the reversal design by extending the original baseline period over several sessions. This allowed for a better analysis of the inherent variability of preintervention behavior and also made possible an analysis of possible trends in the performance from day to day. In addition, the added refinement of posttreatment checks

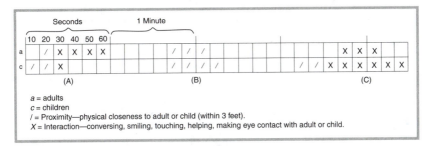

Figure 1.2. The original 10-second interval observation form and code
SOURCE: From "The Effects of Social Reinforcement on Isolate Behavior of a Nursery School Child," by E. Allen, B. Hart, J. Buell, F. Harris, and M. Wolf, 1964, *Child Development, 35,* pp. 511-518. Copyright 1964 by the *Child Development Journal.* Reprinted with permission.

gave evidence of the durability of behavior change (Figure 1.3). The Allen et al. study also presented evidence of observer reliability to demonstrate that the definitions of behavior were clear and that the features of behavior that were selected by the investigators were, in fact, the major controlling stimuli for the observer. Although today reliability procedures are taken for granted, the implementation of their use in studies such as the one by Allen et al. (1964) typified the movement toward greater precision in behavior analysis in its early years.

The mid-1960s represented a period of exciting advances in the infant technology of applied behavior analysis. The Allen et al. study was accompanied by several other important publications that used similar methodological refinements (see Harris, Johnston, Kelley, & Wolf, 1964; Hart, Allen, Buell, Harris, & Wolf, 1964). These and other studies were the outgrowth of the laboratory-based child research programs described by Bijou and Baer (Bijou, 1961; Bijou & Baer, 1961; Bijou & Orlando, 1961; Bijou & Sturges, 1959) and verified the approach to child development taken by these researchers.

Science and Clinical Success

Perhaps the most dramatic and well publicized of this early series of applied studies involved a 3½-year-old autistic child named Dicky. Dicky had surgery to remove the cataract-clouded lenses of his eyes, and he was in danger of losing his vision if he did not begin wearing prescription glasses

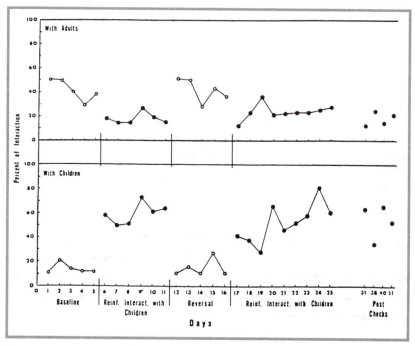

Figure 1.3.   Percentages of time spent in social interaction during approximately 2 hours of each morning session

SOURCE: From "The Effects of Social Reinforcement on Isolate Behavior of a Nursery School Child," by E. Allen, B. Hart, J. Buell, F. Harris, and M. Wolf, 1964, *Child Development, 35,* pp. 511-518. Copyright 1964 by the *Child Development Journal.* Reprinted with permission.

(Wolf, Risley, & Mees, 1964). This research program clearly revealed that scientific rigor need not be sacrificed during design of the successful treatment of severely deviant behavior. The program involved the strategy of breaking a complex repertoire into smaller components (tantrums, self-destructive responses, bedtime problems, wearing glasses, throwing glasses, eating problems) and gaining control over each one separately. The result was that the previously hospitalized child was eventually discharged to his parents and was reported to be "a new source of joy to members of his family" (p. 145). These early systematic applications of behavioral principles, together with more refined data measurement and analysis techniques, ushered in a new and exciting era in applied psychology. The well-documented and substantial changes in behavior reported in the early published studies suggested that operant methodology would ultimately play a major role in the development of a behavioral technology for treating psychopathology.

As we have noted earlier, by 1968 the field known as the experimental analysis of behavior contained many active and enthusiastic researchers. Major advances arising from the application of behavioral principles to programs for precomputer teaching machines were heralded by Skinner in his *Technology of Teaching* (1974). Skinner's colleagues (notably Sidney Bijou and Fred Keller) were studying behavior of more clinical relevance. Bijou and a number of his students and associates at the University of Washington were engaged in research that applied operant conditioning principles with children. At the same time, Fred Keller at Arizona State was developing features of his "personalized system of instruction." Important concentrations of applied behavior analysis developed at the University of Kansas, Western Michigan University, Southern Illinois University, and the Institute of Behavioral Research in Silver Spring, Maryland, to mention only a few. By 1968, there was a sizable corps of investigators throughout the United States who were engaged in the formulation of a more systematic technology of behavior.

A Journal Is Born

The mixed reactions from editors of the then-available applied research journals, together with the rapidly increasing research activity in the applied analysis of behavior, led the Society for the Experimental Analysis of Behavior (SEAB; this group is the publisher of the *Journal of the Experimental Analysis of Behavior* [*JEAB*]) to create the *Journal of Applied Behavior Analysis* (*JABA*). JABA started in 1968, with Mont Wolf, described by Todd Risley as the founder of applied behavior analysis, was the first editor (Risley, 1997). The birth of this journal and the assembling of its editorial staff represented a more unified thrust in the field and called for a clearer description of the identifying characteristics of this totally new field. Baer, Wolf, and Risley's (1968) article "Some Current Dimensions of Applied Behavior Analysis" appeared in the first issue of *JABA* and remains to this day a keystone article in the field. This most influential article set forth a number of fundamental characteristics of applied behavior analysis that we will consider shortly.

A Paradigm Shift

Something of a paradigm shift in behavior analysis methodology was to take place in 1982. Brian Iwata and his colleagues at the John F. Kennedy Institute and the Johns Hopkins University School of Medicine published a study titled "Toward a Functional Analysis of Self-Injury" (Iwata, Dorsey, Slifer, Bauman, & Richman, 1982/1994). This paper outlined a completely new method of analyzing human behavior that could lead directly to effective treatment. Whereas previously the search for treatments had been rather hit-or-miss, Iwata et al.'s functional analysis sought to directly determine the variables responsible for the behavior in question. By alternating various likely controlling variables, it was possible to directly analyze the data and determine that one child's self-injuring behavior might be "caused" by academic demands (i.e., escape from demands), whereas another's might be the result of social disapproval. In hindsight, this methodological development seems obvious, but at the time it was a major breakthrough in our thinking. The multielement design data are shown in Figure 1.4.

Because of this one study, the entire focus of behavior analysis shifted from simply "modifying" inappropriate or deviant behavior to understanding causal variables and then developing appropriate treatments to match them. Subsequently, hundreds of replications of this basic design have been used in research and clinical settings, and the result has been a new generation of treatments that are far more humane and more likely to be adopted by consumers.

The Dimensions of Applied Behavior Analysis

By the 1970s, Mont Wolf, Don Baer, and Todd Risley had all joined the faculty at the University of Kansas. They were preparing to publish the first issue of *JABA* when it dawned on them that they should probably have some kickoff article to inform readers about the future direction of this new endeavor. All had been involved in the early attempts to analyze and modify

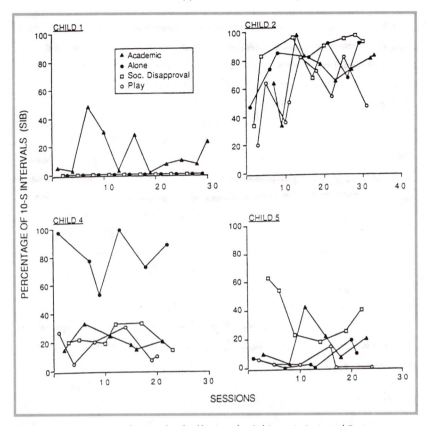

Figure 1.4. Percentage of intervals of self-injury for Subjects 1, 2, 4, and 5 across sessions and experimental conditions
SOURCE: From "Toward a Functional Analysis of Self-Injury," by B. Iwata, M. Dorsey, K. Slifer, K. Bauman, and G. Richman, 1994, *Journal of Applied Behavior Analysis, 27,* pp. 197-209. Copyright 1994 by the Society for the Experimental Analysis of Behavior. Reprinted with permission.

child behavior. They knew that some features of this approach differentiated it from applied psychology, clinical psychology, experimental psychology, and child development. Applied behavior analysis research was unique in several respects.

Applied Focus

The term *applied* implies that a technology is being used to achieve a practical effect of more immediate social value. Prior to the 1960s, behavior analysis more frequently than not employed behavior that was convenient for the investigator. Scientific rules were being identified that applied to all operant behaviors. Processes that were common to all learning situations were first identified. But the pressure from society to produce techniques that would ameliorate social problems increasingly induced researchers to select behaviors for analysis that were of social importance. The experimental subject, behavior, and procedures were to be studied because of "their importance to man and society" (Baer et al., 1968, p. 92). Although this was not always an easy task, as Wolf (1978) has noted, the selection of behavior having immediate or at least close-to-immediate social importance clearly distinguishes the field of *applied* behavior analysis.

For the beginning researcher, the applied dimension provides a starting point for thinking about possible areas to research. Applied problems are all around us. One can simply pick up a local newspaper or check the evening news to have them dramatically presented. Violence in the schools, crime in the streets, "road rage" on the highways, and injuries on the job, to name just a few, are all areas where an applied behavior analyst could have a fine beginning as a researcher. An *applied* problem is one that has immediate face validity; it is something that almost any citizen would complain about if asked. Editorial writers pick up on applied problems, as do politicians and city planners, school principals and middle managers, public health nurses and traffic engineers. Applied problems are all around us and often jump out and grab us. This was the case when one doctoral student came into the office complaining about middle school students on a bus pelting him with trash as he stood on a street corner waiting to cross. We will discuss this in more detail in Step 2.

Behavioral Focus

Applied analysis places a premium upon the objectivity of its data. The primary focus of measurement procedures is *observable behavior*. Phenomena that are inferred, such as states of mind, feelings, and events with which only an individual person is in contact (private events), are not usually selected as primary data. Instead, the focus is to be upon what the person actually *does*, as observed and recorded by a second person. Clearly implied in all of this is the necessity of sophisticated observation systems that can be used in field settings. Furthermore, the behavior that is changed as a result of certain procedures must be that of the participant and not the observer. That is, we must be sure to eliminate or control for observer bias. Baer et al. (1968) stressed the need for procedures that give powerful evidence of the validity and reliability of observer-generated data. Although the precise criteria for acceptable kinds of data cannot at this point be described by any single rule, we shall later see that observer reliability procedures have been and remain an important aspect of the field of behavior analysis.

The behavioral focus of applied behavior analysis makes it necessary for the fledgling researcher to be careful in selecting dependent variables. For example, the school behavior analyst is interested in actual observable aggression on the playground, not the hastily written reports of teacher aides. The industrial behavior analyst is interested in safe *behaviors* on the job, not employees' "recall" of a safety poster or short-run safety campaign.

Analytic Approach

This dimension requires that research give a "believable demonstration of experimental control over the behavior" in question. That is, the researcher must show a functional relationship between the procedures implemented and the behavior changed. Being analytic means being systematic and orderly in designing and executing the study so that we can say with some degree of credibility that a certain condition was responsible for some specific change in behavior. It is not sufficient to simply implement an intervention and try to claim some dramatic results—as happened recently when D.A.R.E., a national program to educate children about the negative effects of using illegal drugs, was implemented in several elementary schools in Florida and later took credit when no drug arrests were made in the schools that year. In behavior analysis research, even a baseline followed by an intervention is not sufficient to meet the analytic standard because other possible variables could account for the change. To produce a "believable" change in behavior, baselines and interventions must be repeated or replicated. The replications that form a fundamental part of *analysis* must therefore be minimal but enough so that, in the judgment of the critical scientific audience, assertions by the investigators are believable.

The criterion of believability is often very difficult to identify and cannot usually be specified in terms of statistics or strict rules. Judgments of the data by colleagues and consumers are necessary to determine if they "buy" the results. "Has a convincing demonstration been made?" is always the basic question. A journal reviewer may be unconvinced, but a third-grade teacher may find the results compelling. In either case, the judgments of the data are necessarily subjective in that they involve bringing the past experiences of the judge (e.g., the journal reviewer or the teacher) to bear upon the evaluation of experimental effects.

Baer et al. (1968) described two major experimental designs commonly used in the field of applied behavior analysis: the *reversal* and *multiple-baseline* designs. Further variations of these designs have been developed since, and all of these will be more fully discussed later in this book.

Students just designing their first study might be advised to keep the analytic aspect simple by starting with a simple multiple baseline across behaviors or A-B-A-B reversal. Make sure that the baseline is quite stable so that the effects of the intervention can be easily seen, and design an intervention that is likely to have optimal effects the first time it is implemented.

Technological Approach

As used by Baer et al. (1968), the term *technological* refers to the degree of specificity involved in the description of procedures used as independent variables in behavior analysis. This is an especially difficult area for novice and seasoned researchers alike. Behavior has been shown to be under the control of environmental variables that are often very subtle. Most behavior is a complex product of a myriad of variables (i.e., it is multiply caused), and determining which variables are significant contributors is often a difficult task at best. It is probably safe to say that the researcher simply selects one or only a few of the truly controlling variables as the independent variable procedures, leaving others undetected or momentarily ignored. However, the development of a technology of behavior that can be immediately applied to social problems demands that procedures alleged to be successful must be described with enough accuracy so that they can be replicated by other researchers and practitioners and prove acceptable to consumers (Wolf, 1978). Procedures must be described in clear terminology with exact referents. They must be detailed enough so that they can be duplicated. All of this requires an objective vocabulary that refers to publicly observable processes.

Researchers who are just starting out are advised to focus their efforts on this dimension by putting all interventions to the writing test. That is, once they have designed their treatment or intervention and tried it out themselves, they should prepare a written description, give it to a colleague or assistant, and ask this person to follow the directions. The researcher takes notes during the demonstration and determines if there is a match in procedures. If not, the necessary corrections are made to the instructions, and a second colleague is asked to follow the directions. This is continued until an associate is able to produce the therapy or intervention as originally designed. This description then becomes the basis for the description used in the Method section of the paper.

Conceptual Systems

Much of what passes for advice in the realm of human behavior is very particular and possibly idiosyncratic. A parent may recommend "Crispy O's" as a "treat" to get a child to put her toys away, or a teacher may be convinced that sitting alone for 30 minutes is a good "lesson" for a child who engages in disruptive talking in class. We need to find consequences that can be counted on to increase behaviors in a reliable fashion. Those consequences that increase behavior are labeled *reinforcers*. Consequences that decrease behavior when made contingent fall into a class referred to as *punishers*. The behavior-analytic researcher is charged with looking for commonalities in procedures that allow for some common conceptual language to emerge and to show the consumer "how similar procedures may be derived from basic principles" (Baer et al., 1968, p. 96).

Effectiveness

The primary goal of behavior analysis research is to discover procedures that can reliably produce socially significant behavior changes. The determination of social significance is made by the consumer rather than the researcher and may involve comparisons or expectations that researchers may not encounter unless they specifically seek them out (Wolf, 1978). Effectiveness in behavior analysis research is measured not by statistical tests but rather by questioning those directly involved as users or consumers of the findings in order to determine the *social importance of the effects* (Wolf, 1978). This is not to be confused with the previously described "analytic" dimension. In behavior analysis research, decisions about causality (analytic) are separated from those about benefit (effective). Using a reversal design, one might clearly show experimental control and have it recognized by research colleagues as a clear demonstration of a procedure. However, the consumer could very well say, "Sure, I see that you can produce a change in behavior, but it is so small I don't see the value in it."

A tip for new researchers, then, is to determine in advance who the likely users are and to probe them for information on desired effect size: that is, to determine the *social significance of the goals* (Wolf, 1978). This can be done via survey, via focus groups, or informally as the study is being formulated. It is advised that several consumers be polled during this exercise, for you may discover that there is considerable variability in their responses. We will discuss this in more detail in the section on *social validity* in Step 4.

Generality

The generalization of responses acquired in a behavioral framework is usually seen as a plus for the researcher. A child who acquires social skills in a classroom may "generalize" them to the playground or school bus (stimulus generalization) or to other school-related *behaviors* such as study or homework skills (response generalization). If this generalization does not occur during the study in such a way as to confound the research design, most researchers will be delighted, as will the consumers. How and why such generalization occurs, however, is largely a mystery to the field and constitutes an important area of research that should be pursued. It should also be noted that generalization is not always a positive. A child who acquires social skills in a classroom and then begins using them with strangers in the neighborhood (stimulus generalization) is now at risk. If the social skills generalize to less desirable forms of social manipulation (response generalization), parents and teachers will disapprove.

New researchers should be prepared to detect any forms of generalization that may occur as a result of their work and to take the necessary steps to prevent harm. Additionally, generalization per se may be an extremely valuable area to study.

The above-mentioned dimensions of applied behavior analysis have particular importance for the study of research methods, which is the focus of the present book. *To summarize, the field of applied behavior analysis stresses the study of socially important behavior that can be readily observed, and it uses research designs that demonstrate functional control, usually at the level of the individual performer. The procedures developed by this field must be replicable, and the extent of the resulting behavior change must have important practical significance for the social community.*

The Baer et al. (1968) article served as a powerful guiding influence upon the field of applied behavior analysis. Applied behavior analysis has rapidly developed following its publication. Only one decade after the publication of this landmark article, the energies of a considerable number of researchers were devoted to the development and refinement of an effective technology of behavior change. The trend continues.

How to Use This Book

This brief discussion should give you an overview of the goals and purposes of the field of applied behavior analysis. Before embarking on a research project of your own, you should have one or more basic classes in applied behavior analysis. If you are a student or professional not enrolled in a graduate program in behavior analysis, you might consider finding a mentor to guide you through the steps that will be described in Part II, "Research Methods in Applied Behavior Analysis."

The methods by which the research is actually carried out have been left sketchy by design because the purpose of the next major section, Part II, is to take you through the detailed steps necessary to actually complete a study. The best tactic is to read through all of Part II before you begin your research project. Then it is advisable to review each step as you progress to make sure that you do not overlook any relevant detail or fail to consider some key issue as you proceed.

A general handbook such as this is, of necessity, not overinclusive with cautions and queries that may not pertain to each reader. An attempt was made to reach as wide an audience as possible. Thus, you may find many of the questions or recommended substeps irrelevant to your purposes; in such cases, follow your natural inclination to skim over these passages.

RESEARCH METHODS IN APPLIED BEHAVIOR ANALYSIS

Ten Steps for Successful Research

SELECT YOUR GENERAL TOPIC, FIND A GOOD SETTING, AND CHOOSE APPROPRIATE PARTICIPANTS

MAIN TOPICS

How to Come Up With a Good Idea to Research

Finding Just the Right Setting

Determining Who Your Participants Will Be

Gaining Access to a Great Setting

Cultivating a Research Setting

Doing Your Own Research

LEARNING OBJECTIVES

In Step 1, we present a strategy for finding a good research setting and participants that are appropriate. We show you how to gain entry to just the right setting and how to cultivate a research setting. After studying this step, you should be able to

- ▶ Describe the necessary characteristics of a good setting.

- ▶ Discuss the characteristics of participants that make them suitable for research.

- ▶ Specify how entry into research settings is typically gained.

- ▶ Explain how to cultivate a research setting.

Coming Up With a Good Idea to Research

One of the most attractive features of behavior analysis research is that good ideas for research can come from almost anywhere. You might be talking to a neighbor or colleague and hear of a serious problem in a school or the local community. Modern problems faced by communities everywhere include teenagers who are bringing guns or other weapons to school, children who are becoming couch potatoes, and citizens who are littering in the parks or are loitering there after dark. You might see a fascinating story on the nightly news or a feature story in the Sunday paper that gives you an idea for behavioral research. On any given day, examples of potential research ideas from your local headlines could be the problems encountered by people with disabilities when people park in their designated spaces at the mall or children who are at risk in supermarkets from falling out of the baskets because they are not buckled up. For many new researchers, ideas for problems to research might come from their own personal experience. You might encounter a behavior problem in the context of one of your hobbies or leisure activities, for example, new members signing up at the gym and then dropping out soon afterwards. You could learn that volunteers are needed to donate blood or volunteer at the neonatal unit and that strategies are needed to encourage participation. Finally, you might have the good fortune to live near a unique and interesting setting, like a zoo or marine mammal park, where applied behavioral research is clearly needed and appropriate. Interesting and worthwhile behavior problems are all around us—problems that need solutions and for which a behavioral resolution is the best. And you are likely to discover, after doing a little digging, that no research exists on that particular topic. You may, of course, develop an idea for your first research project in a more traditional way from a class you are taking, an assigned article you are reading, or a seminar you are attending. One strategy, then, is to start with an interesting idea or compelling problem and then look for a good setting where you can begin to explore it. This is not as easy as you might think.

The Importance of a Good Setting

Although the primary focus of behavior analysis research is human behavior, a moment's reflection will indicate that the behavior we are interested in must occur in some setting. Because environment-behavior relationships are determined by manipulating contingencies in these settings, the first step in conducting a study should be the selection of a setting where research is most readily accomplished. Because the core of sound applied research is tight experimental control, any setting under consideration must guarantee *this* requirement at a minimum. The researcher will need to schedule observations at specific times, post signs in a certain place, have announcements made in a consistent manner, have staff carry out procedures in a special way, and so on. If such operations are carried out haphazardly or inconsistently, the confounding of variables will be such as to preclude any definitive research findings. The problem for the applied researcher, of course, is to find settings in which experimental control is possible. Ideally, once found, a good setting can be used for more than one study; the results of each study can be adopted, and the effects can be cumulative. However, for the beginning researcher, finding just the right setting may take the better part of a semester. The time spent is clearly worth the effort down the line in fewer headaches and less heartburn.

Necessary Characteristics
of a Good Research Setting

All settings are *not* created equal when it comes to research. Some provide a rich proving ground for testing new ideas; others are just plain frustrating and ultimately may defeat your primary purpose. Finding just the right location is a matter of asking the right questions, having high standards, and being persistent. Here are some specific characteristics for which you should look.

Face Validity

If your research is to have meaning for practitioners or other applied researchers, the setting in which you work must have many characteristics in common with theirs. If you are doing research in a halfway house for vocational rehabilitation clients, it needs to be operated and funded like other such programs, and it needs to serve the kind of clients likely to be found in other such programs. If your clients all have the same handicap or are of the same race, then your results may not be useful to others who work in similar settings but who serve the heterogeneous population common to such programs. If your program requires special grant funds unavailable to most other programs or is organized in some unusual fashion, then it seems obvious that others will be unable to use or replicate your findings. *Your research will generate the most interest if your physical plant resources and clients closely resemble those to be found in similar settings across the country.* If the setting in which you want to work has some peculiarity, you may be able to modify it so there is more face validity. You might work with the administration to have a different or more common type of patient admitted, or you might arrange for the funds needed to support your part of the program to come from the standard operating budget.

In a recent study (Barnette, 1999), for example, the researcher was interested in improving occupational safety behaviors of workers and testing for generalization of those behaviors once modified. To meet the requirement of face validity, a setting was needed where accidents occurred and where the documentation was systematic. An interview with the chief safety officer at the university yielded a rank-ordered list of occupations that had the most accidents. From this list, the researcher was able to gain access to workers of two occupations that are common in the culture, painters and electricians. Informal observations led to the conclusion that their work practices appeared to be identical with standard work practices in the local community. By selecting a setting that appeared to present the same safety challenges that might be found in almost any industrial setting, the researcher anticipated that the findings would generalize to other similar sites.

Flexibility

Because most behavioral research relies on participants' exposure to different experimental conditions over time, the setting must be designed to allow for such changes to take place smoothly, easily, and with little disruption to staff or other ongoing programs. Strict rules concerning when and how certain activities are carried out regulate many potential settings. Common examples of settings tightly bound by rules include special types of educational settings and health-related institutions. The notion of stopping a program for a short period and then restarting it may be totally inconceivable to the administration or staff, even if you have the best of experimental reasons for doing so. If a central manager or administrator who is sympathetic to your needs functions at a sufficient level of authority, generally you will be guaranteed the needed flexibility to conduct your study. However, it is wise to explore in advance with this person, as a form of insurance, the type of freedom you will need to make on-line decisions. "I was thinking of starting this training program on Unit A and letting it run for 2 to 3 weeks. If it works, I would like to start it immediately on Unit B; if that's not possible, I would like to try something else on Unit A before we proceed further with Unit B. Do you think we can arrange to do it that way? Do you see any problems?" Seeking permission, agreement, and advice from the department head, nursing supervisor, or curriculum coordinator is a necessary part of maintaining your control of the setting throughout the period of research. Of course, gaining initial consent to future procedures does not guarantee cooperation. Experience has shown that the successful behavioral researcher stays in close contact with the key person in the setting. Regular meetings, usually two to three times per week, are necessary to maintain a close bond with the person who can make or break your study. By showing your key contact people the information as it flows in and by sharing your concerns with them, you will find that they become almost as vested in the project as you are and that their willingness to provide the flexibility that you need to be successful will be assured.

In a recent project in a major supermarket chain (Barker, 2001), the general manager initially gave the researcher strict company guidelines for interacting with customers, the goal of which was to make sure that customers would not be scared off or offended in any way. Over a 10-week period of taking observations and trying various interventions, Barker shared the data with him, and his interest changed from passive agreement to active participation. After seeing the data repeatedly over time, he suggested an intervention that would have initially been disallowed. It was this intervention that ultimately made the project a success. The general manager's "buy-in" extended to the sharing of "his" results with the district manager who had the ability to affect company policy. Having the flexibility to adjust and modify procedures as an experiment unfolds is extremely important in almost any applied behavioral study.

Stability

Many applied studies take 6 to 9 months from start to finish, and some will run much longer. For this reason, a significant degree of stability in the setting is required for the researcher to arrange for contingency changes to take place on time and in special ways. Stability of four types is important: administrative, staff, program, and financial.

Administrative Stability

If the key administrator of the site where you plan to conduct your research is brand new or is inconsistent or disorganized, then research success is unlikely. If the general manager who is about to retire or move away operates on the basis of whim, caprice, or emotional response rather than calm and reasoned management principles, you may find your program modified beyond recognition or scuttled altogether without your input. Horror stories abound of well-planned research gone awry because of administrative instability of one sort or another. In one case, we were 6 months into baseline and were ready to begin the first intervention when the general manager of a large national chain retail store announced that he was being promoted and was leaving almost immediately. He introduced us to his replacement, who made it abundantly clear that she had no interest in supporting "his little project" and in fact planned to eliminate the problem we were studying by reorganizing that department entirely. In a study we conducted at a local chain of a national gym (Nicolson, 2000), there was a major shift in management philosophy soon after we began the first intervention. Countless hours of meetings with the owners and managers were necessary to protect the project. As a new researcher, you can't overestimate the importance of "qualifying" the management of the setting where you plan to do your study. Just as real estate agents "qualify" potential buyers before they exert much effort to find them a property, you will need to determine if the person you will be working with for the next 6 to 9 months is solid enough to see you through.

Staff Stability

If staff morale is low, if discipline is poor, or if personality conflicts among employees have the staff in turmoil, then it will be naive to expect full attention and cooperation from staff. Check around to be sure that the staff with whom you will be working do not plan to leave or retire soon and that they are not about to be fired or transferred. If absenteeism is high, or if there is a high staff turnover, it will be almost impossible to have behavioral interventions carried out with precision for the duration of a study. In some cases, you may be able to compensate. For example, if there is consistently high absenteeism on certain days of the week or on weekends, it may be better to simply eliminate those times from your study. As you investigate possible sites for your research, you may want to inquire about management programs that reinforce employees for coming to work on time or for reducing absenteeism. Of course, staff instability can itself become a target for research. Only a few such articles have been published to date, and there is a clear need for work on these persistent personnel issues. Because the process of systematically analyzing and implementing effective interventions for problems such as absenteeism can easily take 2 or more years, it is recommended that projects such as these be undertaken by those prepared to work on long-term studies.

Program Stability

Obviously, if the setting you are considering is in flux and the program is being redesigned or reorganized, you will not be able to count on your research being carried out according to your specifications. In such cases, it is usually best to simply choose another site or wait until the changes are completed. As a general rule, new settings do not make good research sites. During the first 3 to 6 months following the opening of a preschool, restaurant, or retail outlet, for example, routines and work assignments are usually still being determined. You will want to "wait until the dust settles" before seriously trying to collect any data. This may be an opportune time, however, to try to influence a program so that it will make an acceptable setting later.

Financial Stability

Nothing leads to instability in a setting more than a shaky financial base. If there are rumors of budget cuts, the elimination of some program, or layoffs of staff, you can count on a negative impact on your research plans. If your research relies on any financial support from the facility, be wary; research is usually the first to go in a tight money situation.

Qualifying a setting for its stability can be done only through contact with key personnel in the site. As will be recommended later, you should plan on spending some—perhaps a considerable—amount of time in the setting, perhaps as an observer, volunteer, or intern, before deciding that this is *the* site for you. Make sure that the key person—usually an administrator or manager of some stature—is friendly, available, and effective. Once this is established, you will need to make sure that the mission of the site, organization, or company matches your research objectives.

Cooperation and Continuity of Goals

For almost any research endeavor, you will require the almost complete cooperation of the staff and the administration. This will be more likely if your goals and theirs are the same. However, similar goals alone will not guarantee cooperation unless the staff and administration are part of the decision-making process. The most cooperation is achieved when the staff *wants* to participate rather than having been coerced into helping. If you show staff members the data and ask for their opinions and recommendations (and give serious attention to their advice), they will begin to see themselves as a part of the research team.

In one safety study (Barnette, 1999), it was discovered that a safety committee that included a union steward would have to approve any research proposal. The researcher determined that it would be a good idea to approach this committee early in the process to determine their willingness to participate. Special effort went into the introductory presentation to assure them that the study's objective in making repeated, unannounced observations was simply to give a valid picture of the safety behaviors and to assure them that none of the data would be used against any worker. Safety committee members were kept informed as each phase was completed. They ultimately provided the necessary support to complete the study successfully. Subsequently, the safety director recommended the research team to another unit on campus on the basis of their "openness and willingness to share their findings."

Things do not always go so well, of course. In one setting, where we were interested in measuring and ultimately improving suggestive selling by waitstaff, we thought we had a clear agreement from the restaurant manager on the nature of the data we were taking. But after a few weeks of baseline, the manager began asking for the names to go with the coded data. When we declined to give them, he became irritated and indicated that he "only let us take the data so he would know who to let go." After a short meeting, we decided to terminate the project and move to another setting.

Few settings will meet all of these characteristics, and the intent of this discussion is not to turn you away from any setting that is not "ideal." Rather, we hope that seeing various common deficiencies from a research perspective will make you aware of the problems in applied settings and thus able to take the necessary precautions and corrective action. In addition, some of the "deficiencies" may actually make good research projects themselves if approached correctly. Is there, for example, a way to modify the behavior of administrators in a particular setting so that they operate less on whim and more on data? Can a method be developed for reducing staff turnover or improving "morale"? As you examine various potential settings, you will, no doubt, also need to analyze certain subject characteristics that can affect the viability of your project.

Necessary Characteristics of Participants

Representativeness

As previously discussed, it is important for your participants to be appropriate for the behavior you wish to study. If your research is of the problem-solving variety, this will be taken care of automatically. If you are doing demonstration research, however, make sure that your participants are appropriate in that they represent a more general population. For example, if you want to demonstrate an instructional program to teach safe street crossing, you will want to choose participants who have the highest rate of pedestrian accidents (either children or senior citizens) rather than teenagers or normal adults. If you want to study job interview skills, you should work with people who are chronically unemployed rather than those who have jobs.

There is a strong custom in traditional psychological research to use participants who are convenient, such as college sophomores, rather than participants who are relevant. For example, one recent study of "executive decision making" was carried out using college students who were asked to "play the role" of a business executive, and another study asked college students to read a scenario describing a person with an eating disorder and then tell how that person would act in certain situations. This, of course, is entirely inappropriate in behavior analysis research. A behavior analyst who was studying eating disorders would use study participants who actually had eating disorders. The work of a cognitive research colleague who is interested in the decline in visual acuity and memory in senior citizens illustrates how relevant research participants should be chosen: He is using senior citizens recruited from the local community, and some of the work with lighting is actually being done in their homes. The research would not be as practical or the participants as relevant if this researcher used college students who wore shaded glasses to study problems with visual acuity in senior citizens.

Availability

Your participants will need to be regularly available over the course of the study; usually you will require their participation daily and perhaps on weekends. It is wise to be sure that they *will* be available. You will want to make sure that the participants you have selected are not dropping out of your setting, being transferred, or leaving town for the holidays. You will also want to make sure that they do not anticipate taking college courses, getting a job, or otherwise changing their routine in a way that would interfere with your study. On occasion, you may want to get them to sign a "contract" agreeing to a certain amount of participation in your research. Paying participants for their time is another good way to guarantee availability. In one study (Briscoe, Hoffman, & Bailey, 1975) in which we taught rural members of a community board to engage in problem solving, we noted an attendance problem at the meetings. A flat participation fee of $4.00 per meeting produced about 90% attendance at each meeting, thus ensuring that participants would be present for baseline and training sessions.

Stability

Several kinds of participant stability are necessary for successful applied research.

Health

If your participants are ill or subject to periodic ill health, they may not serve well unless you are studying this population deliberately (e.g., you are studying the effects of incentives on attendance of diabetics at a health clinic). If a potential participant is undergoing a change in medication or has recently suffered some trauma, it would be wise to wait a while before working with this individual. In some cases, the best option would be to simply select another participant.

Cooperation

When you are working in developmental disability, mental health, or geriatric facilities and you find that some of your chosen participants are recalcitrant, moody, or subject to bouts of stubbornness or depression, you may want to be more selective. Unless these behaviors are the target of your intervention, they will greatly impede your progress, and you will quickly discover that you are missing more days of data than you are getting. Because the nature of your selection process must be outlined in your Method section, you should have an opportunity to think carefully about the procedures you will use to select participants. It is best to choose participants who wish to participate in the study. Your participants should indicate during your screening that they find nothing objectionable about being observed, answering questions, or possibly being videotaped. Depending on the study, you will want all your participants to be about equally responsive to instructions and perhaps to reinforcers that will be made available during certain conditions. Having participants who refuse to cooperate further in a study once it is under way can be avoided by careful selection procedures. These selection procedures should include an examination of available records on participants, interviews with potential participants, and interviews with relevant staff.

Attendance

Because you want them to participate with great regularity, try to select participants who are not inclined to take unexpected leaves, run away from the facility, take illicit drugs, or become incarcerated because of illegal activities. In a study conducted in a hospital (Thurkow, 2001), the last condition was barely finished when two key employees left the unit via transfers. This circumstance was lucky for the researcher: If they had left 2 to 3 weeks earlier, the study might have been severely compromised.

It is almost impossible to find participants who will meet all of the requirements all of the time; however, simply being aware of some potential subject-related difficulties (e.g., ill health or regular attendance) should cause you to take precautions. It may be advisable to start out with more participants than you actually need or to have backup individuals available. The addition of participants assumes that your experimental design will permit this. Or you may find yourself providing a personal messenger, prompting, or taxi service for participants with poor memories or transportation problems. As long as you are not naive to these potential pitfalls and are prepared to compensate, you should be able to find an adequate number of participants to meet your needs in almost any average-size community.

How Entry Into Settings Is Typically Gained

Because so much depends upon the quality of the setting, it may be useful to discuss the ways most researchers typically make entry into a setting.

Employment

The most frequent way that beginning researchers gain access to a research site is through their own employment in some organization, business, school, or facility. The *type* of employment you have there will be critical to your ability to carry out research. Generally, the closer your position to a key position (e.g., principal, coordinator of psychological services, assistant director of education and training, supervisor of nursing personnel, general manager), the more likely you are to gain the cooperation necessary to successfully execute your study. If you are employed in a lower-level position (e.g., as a nursing aide, cottage worker, or assistant manager), you will generally find it more difficult, although not impossible, to garner the resources necessary to carry out a research project. In some cases, a facility may have a position (e.g., director of research or coordinator of evaluation services) created specifically to promote research. Although the facility's research may not always be behavioral, the research director has the needed authority, resources, and manpower to assist you in carrying out your study.

Students may find themselves working part time as a behavior technician or behavior specialist in a special school or residential facility. Such a position gives direct access to problem behaviors presented by likely participants. If you have a job in a setting where you would like to conduct your research, you should establish good working relationships with key administrators to make the necessary arrangements to conduct a study. In one research project that we implemented in a health club, the student researcher worked part time as a fitness instructor. She was able to become thoroughly acquainted with the owners and managers of the gym so that a later proposal to do research there was not seen as any threat.

If you are working in a nonkey position, you will want to become acquainted with whoever is in a position to permit research to take place. Often, you must make these contacts weeks or even months before the time that you approach the person with a request for permission to do research.

Friends, Neighbors, and Relatives

Although it is rarely discussed and never mentioned in published articles, access to applied settings is frequently obtained because the applied researcher has a close friend or relative who works (probably in a key position) in some setting. In many of the early classroom management studies, for example, the teacher who identified the problem behaviors and gave the initial permission for research to be carried out was, in fact, the spouse of the researcher.

Apart from such accidents of acquaintance, beginning behavior-analytic researchers can increase their likelihood of finding appropriate settings by perfecting the art of networking. Graduate student colleagues, friends of your faculty advisor, neighbors, and friends of neighbors all can provide leads in finding a quality setting. Your first step is to start talking to all of your acquaintances about your interest in a certain population or type of setting. Indicate that you would like to do a project, and perhaps tell a little about what you would like to accomplish. "I'm really interested in safety, and I'd like to find a company that is having some safety problems" is a good lead-in. Experience has shown that if you are diligent about bringing this up in most of your conversations over the next few weeks, someone will have a lead for you.

Cold Calling

If nothing pans out from networking or you are new in town and have no connections, you can always try "cold calling." In a recent instance, a student researcher made cold calls to the general managers of a dozen retail, home improvement, and grocery store chains, only to be turned away again and again. Some had policies against any outsiders doing any surveys in their stores. Others appeared apprehensive about the idea of "research" going on with their customers. Finally, one manager was receptive and allowed an interview. The researcher and store manager became fast friends when he learned that she had worked for the same chain as an undergraduate student and that they were both from the same town and actually knew some of the same people. If you are trying this strategy, expect to be turned down a high percentage of the time. Try to learn from each rejection, and work to perfect your pitch for the next location.

Public Lectures

In some cases, a facility will initiate a request for someone to do applied research based on a story in the paper or a public appearance. In one case, I (JB) was asked to conduct some research as a result of a public lecture on performance management with a local training organization. A person in the audience came up after the presentation and wanted to know if any graduate students were available who might be interested in a project with her organization. This led to a series of meetings with the staff of the county library and the subsequent investigation of service quality and a proposal for ways to improve it with behavior analysis procedures.

Internship

Some graduate programs require that students complete one or two practica or internships. Although these are seen primarily as opportunities for students to gain hands-on experience, they can sometimes lead to research opportunities. In a recent instance, a doctoral student was completing an internship in a large mental health facility. His primary responsibility was to work as a consultant on performance management projects. In the course of providing the assistance, he uncovered a project with great potential that was clearly beyond the scope of the skills and time of the normally assigned individuals. He was able to adopt this difficult project for his research project. We should add that this venture was not the first for the graduate student but was the fourth or fifth that he had explored. Persistence counts.

Specifically Designed Research Environments

For those behavior analysts who have become well-established researchers and who have a long list of publications to their credit, the dream of a specially constructed environment that is designed and operated primarily for research purposes can be a reality. Such settings are usually built with funds from granting agencies. Most typically, these settings are dedicated to advancement of a whole line of research in a particular area, such as head injury. Most often, a team of behavioral researchers, graduate students, and assistants will be involved in the endeavor. Such settings are maximally efficient and highly effective at producing research findings. It is not unusual for these research settings to produce 6 to 10 publications per year in a virtual assembly-line fashion. Students working in such labs are often assigned to projects that can evolve into a thesis or dissertation. Because many of the complications arising from having to find participants and settings and determine significant applied problems are eliminated, these settings are obviously ideal for students wishing to quickly acquire research experience.

Cultivating a Research Setting

If you are a newcomer to a community (e.g., you are a new assistant professor or graduate student at the university) and you wish to establish a research base, there is a specific plan to follow. Basically, it involves establishing yourself in the community and gaining some visibility, developing professional contacts, and employing well-polished public relations skills. Because you may have been preceded by others who left a bad impression, particular care must be taken to establish yourself as a low-key, nonabrasive, responsible professional who has respect for community leaders, is trustworthy, and has a serious desire to contribute to the welfare of others. Building this reputation can take months, and there are few ways to speed up the process. Essentially, this method goes as follows.

The Importance of Community Contacts

Before you directly approach any setting, it is advisable to gain some informal contacts and visibility in the community. This serves the function of establishing yourself as a potential resource person and gives you time to learn who the community leaders are. You can do it by attending open meetings of the city or county commission or the school board and becoming a member of any local associations or volunteer groups related to your particular interest (parent-teacher organization, local agency for aging, county association for retarded citizens, etc.). Once you become known and have a few professional contacts, later inquiries regarding research will be much better received.

Evaluating Potential Settings

In the process of establishing community contacts, you will come to know people who can give you information about certain settings. You will want to know how long the facilities have been in operation, how they are funded, who the key people are, the types of clients served, and so forth. You will want to eliminate settings that appear to be floundering or fly-by-night operations and those where the administration is ineffective, hostile, or capricious. Without appearing to be conducting an investigation, you will want to inquire about the key people: what interests they have, where they worked before, and so on.

Brushing Up on Your Public Relations Skills

Most often the person you will be dealing with will have considerable expertise in meeting the public and will expect you to have comparable diplomatic ability. If you are abrasive, demanding, or overbearing, the door to community research opportunities will quickly close, and your reputation will travel fast. If you feel inexperienced, a couple of days spent closely reading a book such as Dale Carnegie's *How to Win Friends and Influence People* (1981) or Leil Lowndes's *Talking the Winner's Way* (1998) may serve you well.

The Important First Meeting

Armed with your background information on the setting, the name of a referral person, and your best positive attitude, you are prepared to ask for an appointment with the key person at your first-choice site. Depending upon protocol, you may either phone the person directly and ask for a meeting or work through the secretary of your contact person. In either case, use whatever titles and affiliation you have accumulated to date. "Hello, this is Dr. Smith from the Psychology Department of Suburban University. I would like to have an appointment with Ms. Brown at her convenience" is much better than "Hello, this is Joe Smith and I would like to see Ms. Brown." If you can, keep the meeting short and make it a get-acquainted session. Be sure to use the name of the person who referred you to this organization. It will help break the ice and give you some automatic credibility.

A typical scenario is: You have recently moved to the community, you are interested in developmental disabilities, and you would like to find out about their program. Do not make demands, do not rush things. Do offer service or assistance if you see the opportunity. "I have had some experience in setting up motivation systems for children with behavior disorders and would be willing to volunteer my time to work with your staff." It is best not to mention your research interest at this point. You are not being dishonest by not mentioning an interest in research at the first meeting. At this point, you may hope that the setting will be suitable for research, but you won't know for sure until you spend some time there. The beginning researcher who is too aggressive when meeting with facility administrators can end a potential project before it starts. Starting a "Let's get acquainted" meeting by describing how you intend to publish your work at the facility can intimidate administrators so that they don't feel comfortable dealing with you.

At the end of the initial meeting, leave your business card and request one from the contact person. Suggest lunch on a later date. If the individual doesn't contact you in 2 weeks, call back and ask about setting up lunch or another time if lunch is not convenient. Sometimes people are simply busy and they may not get back to you. Judge your reception by this second contact. It's possible that this agency or organization is just not interested; if so, move on to the others on your list.

Mutually Beneficial Research

It may take you from 1 to 6 months to become well established in a particular setting. Once you are established, you may discover ways that you can perform some service or, hopefully, research that will aid the facility in some way. After you have been connected with the setting for a while, you should begin to pick up on problems that look like they need solutions. Without a lot of fanfare and in an informal situation (e.g., over lunch), you may want to describe to the key person the idea you have that may help them in some way. If you work with children with disabilities and have been observing or volunteering for a while, you might try something like "I have an idea about how to motivate them," or "You know the problem we have [note the use of "we"] with the children who will not take their naps; well, I was reading an article the other day and . . ." Remember, go easy, be low key, and be responsible about what you suggest or promise to do. If you follow through, you will be sought out; if you make promises and do not keep them, you will lose credibility fast. Discover ways of involving the staff and key administrative personnel in the various facets of the experiment. This can be done by asking their opinion about how certain kinds of data might be collected, inquiring as to their suggestions for possible treatments, and so on.

Doing Your Own Research

This is the last step in the sequence and usually comes after you have gained a solid reputation and are considered a part of the organization. By the time you get to this stage, you will have an excellent idea of what kind of research is needed. As in the previous stage, it is important to keep the staff and administration involved in what you are doing. Have periodic meetings with the relevant people, show them the data, discuss the options, ask for their advice, project possible outcomes, and go out of your way to help them understand the importance of your study to the setting and to the field. Letters to key administration personnel praising the work of staff who helped you will keep morale high and ensure future cooperation. Depending upon local conventions, giving small tokens of appreciation or offering to take a person out to lunch may be appropriate. If a publication should come out of your research, remember to acknowledge the administration and staff in a footnote. When the thesis or dissertation is completed or the article is accepted, send them a copy for their files with a note attached, thanking them again for their assistance.

Once you have become affiliated with some setting and are acquainted with the operation, you should begin to have some ideas for potential future research topics. You are now ready to examine each of the possibilities in detail so that you can select and formulate the one that is the most likely to pay off.

NARROW DOWN YOUR RESEARCH QUESTION

MAIN TOPICS

How to Review the Research Literature

Deciding on the Specific Behavior You Want to Study

Deciding on the Type of Change to Study

Determining the Resources Necessary to Carry Out Your Study

LEARNING OBJECTIVES

In Step 2, we suggest ways of narrowing down your topic to a specific question. You will learn how to effectively review the relevant literature and decide on a specific behavior to study. Finally, we take you through an assessment of the resources necessary to carry out your study. After studying this chapter, you should be able to

- Quickly find the relevant research literature databases for your question.

- Determine whether you will be attempting to change the rate of a behavior, foster the acquisition of a behavior, or change the stimulus controls for a behavior.

- Discuss possible relevant methods of behavior change such as instructions and shaping.

- Decide if you will be including generalization of behavior as part of your study.

- Ascertain the resources necessary to carry out your study.

In applied behavior analysis, one of the primary reasons that behavioral research is carried out is that a problem of some sort presents itself: Drivers are not buckling up or they are talking on their cell phones while speeding down the highway, children are disruptive in a classroom to the point that no learning is taking place, a person with developmental disabilities has bizarre speech at work and is in need of treatment, or emergency room nurses aren't wearing gloves to prevent AIDS infection. There are literally thousands of fascinating behavior problems out there that have never been researched, and behavior analysis can probably make a significant contribution with each of them. Needless to say, it is not usually necessary to go to the library or log onto the Internet to find a problem on which you can work. Nonetheless, it would be sheer folly to begin your study without having discovered if someone else has already solved the problem. Thus, contrary to most of the textbooks on how science is done, the preliminary review of the literature is often carried out *after* a decision has been made about what the general research topic will be. Conducting a preliminary review of the literature can spare the researcher from months of designing research and collecting data for research that has already been done.

Often one of the most important decisions in formulating the research question is determining the type of behavioral change that is of interest to you: for example, whether you are interested in changing the rate of an existing behavior or in producing a totally new behavior. You will also need to determine whether you will study generalization and maintenance of behavior change. Finally, and perhaps most importantly, you will need to work and rework your research plan to make sure that you have sufficient resources to cover the scope of the question. All of these concerns are covered here in Step 2.

Reviewing the Literature

Behavior analysis is new enough so that reviewing the available research literature is not the arduous, time-consuming task that it can be in the humanities or some other social sciences. Furthermore, only a few journals publish the bulk of applied research, and modern referencing systems (e.g., computer search capabilities available at most large university libraries) make the task of finding studies related to your interest relatively straightforward.

Where to Look

Perhaps the most effective strategy is to use the Cumulative Index of the *Journal of Applied Behavior Analysis (JABA)*. This useful tool is found in the *fourth issue* of every volume and is cumulative across years. Every article is cross-referenced by subjects, behavior, various procedures used, and often setting or other characteristics of the article. Because the index is cumulative across years, you can, for example, by examining Issue 4 of Volume 33 for the year 2000, discover any article published in the previous three years. Such a search will turn up any *JABA* articles related to your topic, and by examining the references cited at the end of each article, you will gain a pretty good grasp of the state of the art. A second extremely useful way to research your topic is to use the *JABA* Web page. If you point your browser to <www.envmed.rochester.edu/wwwrap/behavior/jaba/jabaindx.htm>, you will discover that you can search very quickly for any key words that appear in the author listing, title, or abstract of an article. As long as the authors used certain words to describe their study, you will be able to find it.

Using the Internet as a tool has changed everything about the way that traditional "library" research is done. By using LexisNexis Academic Universe, you can search hundreds of newspapers and general periodicals in business and medical areas. For specific searches in psychology, the PsycINFO database is invaluable. You should be able to access this database through your university library Internet services. A fairly new, related hard-copy resource is *PsycScan: Behavior Analysis and Therapy*, which is produced quarterly by the American Psychological Association. PsycScan publishes approximately 2,300 abstracts each year from nearly 40 selected behavioral journals and is very likely available at your university library.

A final strategy is to begin with the most recent issue of those journals that are the most relevant to your topic. Simply scan the table of contents and look for relevant articles. This low-technology procedure can be time-consuming and somewhat tedious, but it will put you in closer touch with the field than using any of the index or abstracting systems. Listed below are the journals that regularly publish applied behavioral studies:

- *American Journal of Mental Deficiency*
- *Analysis of Verbal Behavior*
- *Behavior Change*
- *Behavior Modification*
- *Behavior Research and Therapy*
- *Behavior Therapy*
- *Behavioral Interventions*
- *Education and Treatment of Children*
- *Journal of Applied Behavior Analysis*
- *Journal of Behavior Therapy and Experimental Psychiatry*
- *Journal of Behavioral Education*
- *Journal of Organizational Behavior Management*
- *Journal of Positive Behavior Interventions*
- *Journal of School Psychology*
- *Psychology in the Schools*

Three other journals occasionally publish behavioral studies:

- *Environment and Behavior*

- *Journal of Experimental Child Psychology*

- *Psychological Record*

What to Look For

In reviewing the literature, you are basically trying to (a) get ideas for some research you would like to do, (b) determine the current state of the art, or (c) discover whether anyone else has carried out your recently conceived study. You should also be trying to determine which journals might be interested in publishing your research when it is completed. After reading a number of articles from different journals, you will begin to have a feel for the level of sophistication required for an article to be published in each journal.

Three primary features of an article are worth attending to once you find one that appears to be related to your topic. First, take a close look at the methodology involved to determine if (a) good experimental control is shown, (b) reliability (interobserver agreement) checks were made in all phases of the study on both dependent and independent variables, and (c) the independent variable was clearly specified so that others could replicate the study. (For a complete specification of methodological requirements, see Steps 3 and 4.) Then check for confounding variables that were not eliminated or controlled for.

Second, consider the subject population that was used. In many instances, the dependent variable studied may not have been appropriate for the participants, in which case you may be able to contribute to the literature by correcting this fault alone. That is, studies are sometimes published where the researcher wishes to show how a certain method can be used to reduce a behavior such as stealing, but the demonstration was made with a population that was not noted for the problem.

Third, give careful attention to the size of the effect that was shown. Did it appear to you to be socially significant? Was any check for social validity carried out? Was there any indication that it produced sizable effects on the clients in other ways (e.g., before the intervention they were hospitalized and now have they been released)? In general, if the results are couched in terms of a statistical analysis instead of a visual display of clear-cut effects, be wary.

Although our field is relatively new, some areas have already been so thoroughly researched that it may be difficult for all but the most experienced researcher to make a contribution. If, as you begin to accumulate note cards on research studies, you notice that there are 20 to 30 articles all concentrated in one small area, you may want to consider a new problem. After all, it is difficult to make a noticeable splash in a crowded swimming pool.

Deciding on the Specific Behavior to Study

Once you have a thorough grasp of the state of the research in your particular area, it is time to begin narrowing down possible choices for the specific aspects of the study. One way to think of potential target behavior changes is in terms of how they will benefit the participant. The notion of a "cusp" (a behavior change that has future positive consequences) captures this approach. As Bosch and Fuqua (2001) suggested, we might look for or give priority to behaviors that will bring the person into contact with new reinforcers, facilitate learning, compete with inappropriate behaviors, or benefit others.

Deciding on the Type of Change to Study

One of the most basic decisions has to do with whether your research will involve *changing the rate of a behavior*, either by increasing it (as in the case of a cusp) or decreasing it (as in the case of self-injurious behaviors); *fostering the acquisition of a behavior* that is not already in the repertoire of the participant; or *changing the stimulus control for a behavior*. You may also wish to include *generalization of the behavior* as part of your study.

Changing the Rate of a Behavior

Changing the rate of a behavior was the goal of many of the early studies in applied behavior analysis in which informal observations and baseline measurement indicated a need either to (a) decrease a high rate of a behavior (e.g., tantrums, aggression, being out of one's seat) or (b) increase a low rate of a behavior (e.g., amount of eye contact, instances of following instructions, or number of math problems completed). It should be noted that a behavior with a zero rate cannot be considered a low-rate behavior; the behavior must already occur with *some* frequency.

If your analysis will involve changing the rate of a behavior, you will need to address several questions. Many features of your research strategy will depend upon the answers, so consider them carefully.

Decreasing the Rate of a Behavior

If an undesired behavior occurs at a high rate, is this due to reinforcement from some source at either a high or an intermittent rate? For example, does a child who throws a tantrum always or occasionally get his or her way? If so, can the source be controlled? Can *you* gain control over the reinforcer, which may be teacher or parent attention? If the schedule is intermittent, about how often does the reinforcement occur? (This has implications for the number of responses that may occur if extinction procedures are used.) Are any "bootleg" reinforcers available if you take away the primary ones? For example, if you get the teacher to stop reinforcing the behavior, will the other students' attention begin to maintain it? Is the high rate due to (a) prompting from some source (e.g., a child has tantrums because other children call him names) or (b) possible medical or dietary complications (as in certain cases of hyperactivity)?

If you successfully decrease the high rate of the behavior, what will fill the void? That is, does the participant have a wide variety of disruptive behaviors that are likely to occur if you greatly reduce tantrums? For instance, if you reduce tantrums, will the participant then start throwing things, assault other students, or run away? Will you have to fill the void by teaching an incompatible behavior at the same time that you begin your reduction procedures?

Are there any naturally occurring reinforcers for a decreased rate of behavior, or is it perhaps the major problem that there are no such reinforcers? Is the high rate supported by negative reinforcers? (E.g., does the child who throws tantrums get his or her way and also escape or avoid being asked to do certain chores?) If there are no naturally occurring reinforcers for the low rate, will you have to provide some temporary or artificial ones? On what schedule must they be delivered?

Is the high-rate behavior occurring because there are no punishment contingencies operating? Is the addition of punishment a feasible and ethical alternative? What is the participant's likely reaction to punishment? Are there any known punishers that are most likely to work? If such contingencies are added artificially to reduce the rate, can they be withdrawn later once the behavior comes under control of the reinforcers? Are the contingencies to be applied to one subject or to several? If the former, what might be the reaction of the other children in the class or the other residents of the ward?

Increasing the Rate of a Behavior

Many of the above questions may be restated for infrequently occurring behaviors; in fact, these two types of behaviors are often impossible to separate. Is the behavior occurring at a low rate because there is no reinforcement programmed? Or, if there are reinforcers programmed, are they simply out of reach because the subject cannot complete the schedule? Is it possible to gain the necessary control over the schedule of existing reinforcement, or will it be necessary to add temporary and artificial reinforcers? If the latter, what will they be? Is the subject actually receiving some reinforcement for a low rate of behavior? Some research has shown that isolate child behavior (low rate of interaction with other children) may be reinforced by the teacher who occasionally comes to the child and gives comfort and attention when the child is not interacting with other children. If this is happening, can you get control over this source of reinforcement?

Is the low rate due to (a) previous or current prompting or instructions ("How many times have I told you to be quiet!") or (b) some dietary or physical condition? There is some evidence, for example, that children who are not alert and participating in school may be suffering from nutritional deficits (e.g., no breakfast) or from a variety of medical conditions including tapeworms, diabetes, or undetected petit mal seizures. Is the low rate of performance due to some physical restriction (e.g., reading slowly or writing poorly because of poor vision)? Ignoring the possibility that a low rate of behavior might be due to nonbehavioral conditions could ruin a study.

Is the behavior unlikely because difficult-to-detect but automatic punishers are in place for the behavior? In behavioral safety, for example, construction workers often do not wear their goggles or hard hats because of the discomfort that they cause. Does the participant have a history of punishment for the behavior in similar settings even though there is none in the present environment? Has the punishment been severe enough to cause "conditioned emotional responses" such as fear or anxiety? If so, the strategy may involve one of the behavior therapy techniques rather than merely programming of reinforcers for the behavior.

One other line of questioning has to do with the opportunity to respond. Is it possible that the participant rarely responds merely because there is only a rare occasion on which to do so? If so, could you change the behavior most easily simply by providing some opportunities?

If your treatment condition involves increased opportunities to respond as well as newly programmed reinforcers for doing so, your study will be confounded. Essentially, you will have to provide the extra opportunities during baseline to have a definitive study.

One final point about high- and low-rate behavior ought to be made. The basic issue to determine, through either observation or a pilot study, is whether the behavior occurs so much or so little because of (a) contingency variables, (b) structural or biological variables, or (c) inadequate repertoire variables (i.e., the subject has the opportunity and the motivation but simply cannot, for example, "get the hang of long division"). The latter case argues for the manipulation of variables that will "teach" the behavior. This is the subject of the next section.

Fostering Acquisition of Behaviors

The acquisition of behaviors that do not occur at all calls for an analysis that is distinct from analysis of behaviors that occur with some (however low) frequency. To a certain extent, information about the participant's past history may prove important because the first fact to establish is whether the behavior has *ever* occurred previously. If it has, then the strategies for reestablishing the behavior may be different from those involved in teaching it for the first time. Having established that the behavior has not occurred in the past will then lead to another series of questions.

We may wish to inquire about how the behavior is *normally* acquired. Is it the type of behavior that one normally learns in childhood (e.g., basic social interaction skills or certain food preferences) or one that is typically learned as an adult (e.g., job-related or problem-solving skills)? Is it a behavior that is normally learned in an informal or unstructured environment, or is it typical to acquire this skill in short but intensive learning experiences over a number of years? An analysis of how the behavior is acquired by most similarly situated participants will give you some estimate of how long you may expect your training to take. As a general rule, behaviors that normally are acquired over a number of years (such as interpersonal skills) may be difficult to teach in a short time. Likewise, certain "culturally conditioned behaviors" (such as saving one's money or being well groomed) may be difficult to teach to adult clients who have a long history of reinforcement for an incompatible behavior.

Instructions Versus Shaping

The determination that a behavior to be examined is of the acquisition variety obviously suggests that the primary form of intervention will be some type of instruction or shaping program. The use of shaping is usually recommended only in those cases where the participant will not or cannot respond to instructions. Pilot or informal work prior to the onset of the study should be used to determine whether shaping or instruction is appropriate. The type and level of instructions that may be used with any given subject population usually cannot be predicted in advance. Thus, pilot work should be carried out to determine how best to teach a particular skill or concept. The language used to teach the rules of safe street crossing to kindergarten children may be much different than that used to teach the same concepts to fourth graders or adolescents with attention deficit hyperactivity disorder.

To show demonstrable experimental control, it is advisable to teach sizable amounts of behavior during any one training session. Having many short sessions over an extended period produces innumerable problems in experimental design that are difficult to overcome (see Step 5).

As with the analysis of low-rate behavior, one must determine if there are any programmed reinforcers in the environment to strengthen the behavior once it is made to occur through instruction. If there are none, you may want to reconsider the decision to work with this behavior. Teaching preschool youngsters to tie their shoes may be inappropriate if they wear only sandals or go barefoot most of the time. Directors of sheltered workshops frequently report difficulty in teaching certain tasks to their clients, but a close analysis may reveal that there are no "real-world" jobs equivalent to sorting clothes or putting washers and nuts on bolts. Rather than trying to develop an effective instruction system for teaching these tasks, behavior analysts may better spend their time working with the workshop director to develop job skills that are more likely to lead to real-world payoffs.

If shaping is to be used, a similar set of questions needs to be raised. What step size is most appropriate for the participant? Is forward or backward chaining more advisable? Can the shaping process be carried out in such a way that it can be described objectively and replicated by others? (Often this is difficult, and videotaping of the process may be necessary to make it replicable.) What reinforcers will be used in the shaping program, and how will you know that they are maximally effective? (One answer, of course, is to pilot-test this aspect separately.)

Whether instructions or shaping procedures are used, some mechanism for ensuring that the training was effective needs to be carefully thought out. For example, if you want to look at the effects of training with children using medical procedures (e.g., self-catheterization; see Neef, Parrish, Hannigan, Page, & Iwata, 1989), it is essential to provide data showing that at the end of *instruction,* all the children can, in fact, operate the catheterization equipment. Any subsequent failure to self-catheterize can then be attributed to some other variables (e.g., lack of motivation).

Generalization of Behavior

One issue of currency in behavior research is the extent to which the acquisition a behavior (a) generalizes over time (i.e., maintenance), (b) begins to occur in settings other than that in which it was taught (stimulus generalization), or (c) may actually cause a nontreated behavior to occur (response generalization). Some research may focus on generalization as the primary question. Witt, Noell, LaFleur, and Mortenson (1997) found, for example, that teachers trained in the use of specific procedures to improve academic performance drifted rapidly to nonuse within a matter of days. In this study, generalization over time was essentially nil. This allowed the researchers to demonstrate the use of a performance feedback system that brought the performance up to near 100% compliance.

In the case of industrial safety, if we train electricians to safely place their tools and use a ladder appropriately while making a repair in one location, will they generalize this behavior to other locations? What about to other tasks? If we can increase a student's participation in math, will it also go up in geography? If we can get the client to manage her drinking, will she stay "dry" for at least a year?

In the process of evaluating a sexual abuse prevention program, Lumley, Miltenberger, Long, Rapp, and Roberts (1998) found that there was essentially no generalization to naturalistic probes with the moderately mentally retarded women who participated. (Naturalistic probes are tests of the behavior in the natural setting after training has been conducted in a laboratory or classroom setting.) Carrying out this sort of applied research is one of the best uses of behavior analysis strategies. Far too often, it is assumed that such treatments *will* change the behavior of those involved and that it *will generalize*. Only by asking pointed questions and carefully designing studies will we really know the answers to such important questions. When behaviors do not generalize, the disappointment that comes with finding out that generalization does not occur often spurs us on to find better treatments.

If, after a careful analysis of the problem, it is determined that generalization is an important question to be answered in your research, several questions must be addressed. How can the opportunity to engage in the behavior be arranged? Will prompts be given? How long do we allow the behavior not to generalize into the new setting before teaching it there? How many settings should we look at for generalization? How much different will they be from the training situation? If generalization over time is important, how will you deal with contingencies not under your control in the intervening period? For example, if parents are taught to effectively manage child tantrums while on shopping trips, how will you handle their "drift" in the use of the procedures? How will you control for possible consequences that they might receive from relatives or other shoppers for using the procedures? Will you train them in advance to deal with possibly derisive comments from others? If you are teaching sharing to preschoolers and want to see if sharing generalizes, how will you control for possible punishment effects of sharing in certain environments? Sharing at school is desirable, but sharing with neighborhood chums may mean that older children take advantage of the child who is kind enough to share toys and snacks. It is a good idea to review the generalization data that other researchers have gathered related to your dependent variable. By doing this, you may be able to pick up some tips on how they dealt with generalization issues. If the available studies related to your topic have not addressed generalization, you may be able to make a contribution to the literature by showing the conditions under which generalization does or does not occur.

Changing Stimulus Controls for a Behavior

Some behavior is problematic not because of the rate of occurrence but rather because of the circumstances under which it occurs. Public masturbation, for example, is a problem because it is public, not because it occurs.

In other cases, certain stimuli may be responsible for problem behavior in idiosyncratic ways. For example, Carr, Yarbrough, and Langdon (1997) discovered that their functional assessments were greatly affected by stimuli in the environment peculiar to each subject being analyzed. For one of their participants, Bart, problem behavior under demand conditions depended entirely on the stimuli that were presented. When Bart was given demands involving puzzles, his rate of throwing materials and self-injurious behavior went up, whereas when the requests involved books, his rate was essentially zero.

Bringing a subject under stimulus control is an important area of inquiry to be pursued by behavioral researchers. Maglieri, DeLeon, Rodriguez-Catter, and Sevin (2000) showed that food stealing in a 14-year-old girl diagnosed with Prader-Willi syndrome could be greatly reduced by bringing the behavior under the control of stickers placed on containers. Stickers were placed on some containers, and a reprimand was paired with taking food from those containers; then stickers were placed on other containers as well. This intervention based on stimulus control showed excellent generalization, with the results eventually extending to the refrigerator when a sticker was placed on the door.

In summary, it is advisable before making specific research plans to have as complete an understanding as possible of the variables that may affect the behavior that you intend to study. By making a distinction between changing the rate of behaviors, enabling acquisition of behaviors, and controlling the stimuli under which behavior occurs, and by determining whether you wish to address generalization in your study, you may begin to determine the research strategies (discussed in Step 7) and resources that will be required.

Doing a Resource Assessment

Once the preliminary decisions have been made about the type of behavior and behavior change to be studied, and once your pilot testing indicates that you are on the right track, it is time to determine what you will need to carry out a successful experiment. In the research world, the other word for *successful* is *publishable*. You must be prepared to modify the scope of your original question (i.e., to reduce the size of it) if it appears that your resources are not adequate for the task. As described earlier, one of the most important requirements for good research is the ability to keep a rational balance between what you want to accomplish and what you can do *well*. Let's review the various elements that are important in this planning stage.

Setting

Clearly, the setting must match the problem that will be addressed, and it must be conducive to research. In addition, it must be relatively accessible (i.e., not too far away or difficult to reach). This is because, in keeping with the nature of the research, you and possibly a team of others will be taking data almost daily. The setting must also be available for your use on a regular basis and possibly for a significant portion of time each day. If you are competing for time or limited space with some other group or ongoing activity, you may have a difficult time completing your project.

If you are engaging in demonstration research, you will want to be sure that the operation of the facility is compatible with your goals. In one study, we were interested in analyzing the leisure-time activities of young women in a halfway house; one plan was to deal with several kinds of creative and recreational activities, including increasing use of crafts material and increased exercise to improve physical fitness. But a closer look at the operation of the setting convinced us that this was too much to tackle at once. There was simply neither the space nor the time each day to fit it all in. We eventually settled on arts and crafts alone as our target. In another study, we wanted to look at street crossing with young children. Before we could successfully identify two schools with the required number of streets in the correct configuration, we found it necessary to make observations of ongoing after-school pedestrian patterns at over 20 elementary schools. In the process of finding schools that met all of our requirements, the original experimental question was reduced considerably in scope. Other issues to consider in reviewing the setting where you plan to work include locations where observers can sit or stand, how many observers can be in the setting at once without disrupting the operation, and the logistics of taking data at the site. In one hospital study (Thurkow, 2001), it was learned that the rooms to be checked included several floors of three different buildings, including one that was several blocks away. After determining how long it took to move from floor to floor and from one building to another, the researchers decided to restrict their data collection to one building. In a study of proper lifting procedures with geriatric patients, researchers determined that it was appropriate to observe only in the common areas of the facility because of privacy issues with the patients. In a study with dogs and their owners, researchers determined that to standardize the experience across families, they had to restrict the observations to a quiet place in the living room, with the TV off and no company present during the treatment phase. This greatly reduced the variability in the baseline data and simplified the instructions to the families involved.

Equipment

A significant number of studies in applied behavior analysis require some sort of equipment either for the actual operation or for the recording of the study. The availability and cost of such equipment will frequently determine the scope of your research.

Experimental Equipment

You will quickly discover that research that requires exotic or specialized equipment is not for the beginner. Most often, you find yourself writing your own computer program and making your own visual display panels, study cubicles, signs, posters, and so on, because of the unavailability or excessive cost of the supplies and equipment. In one study on newspaper recycling, access to a quarter-ton pickup truck was needed. When the truck was unavailable for a short period during the study, an experimenter's car had to be substituted, and the overload almost resulted in the destruction of the shock absorbers and rear axle. Another piece of equipment needed was a portable but reasonably accurate scale for weighing relatively small amounts of paper that individual children would bring in each day. Most of the scales that fit our purposes were of the commercial variety, costing up to $75. We eventually found a baby scale for under $10 that was lightweight, portable, reliable within our needs, and easily calibrated. For a functional assessment study, we needed a device that a client with physical disabilities could operate to turn on and off various electrical appliances (fan, radio, vibrator, light). Unable to find a device that suited our needs, we approached the psychology shop and were told that it would take 2 to 3 months to build the customized device. Six months later, we obtained the device and were able to carry out the study. It is best to have a very realistic view of the equipment that you will be able to acquire and keep repaired throughout the study and to keep your experimental question clearly in line with what you can make readily available.

Recording Equipment

Although the majority of studies published today use live observation, there is clearly a place for audio and video recording devices, depending on the circumstances and the question being asked.

One of the most frequently used pieces of equipment is a tape recorder. Your needs for portability and fidelity will determine the specific recorder that you should purchase. If you need this type of device, you may want to consider one of the miniature models that are currently on the market. Check with one of the consumer testing journals (e.g., *Consumer Reports*) for the best buy. Note that the microphone is a key ingredient to successful audio recording: If you buy a poor-quality microphone, nothing you record will be worthwhile, regardless of the quality of the recorder. Voice recognition software with reported high fidelity of word recognition has recently become affordable. This advance should prove useful to those doing research on protocol analysis or other verbal behavior research projects involving problem solving, interviewing skills, or verification of training.

A second frequently needed device is a camcorder. Currently, a wide variety are available in analog and digital formats. These modern, smaller camcorders are easily carried and are unobtrusive in normal use. The advantage of the more costly digital versions is that editing software (e.g., iMovie2 for Macintosh) is now available so that even amateurs can cut and paste video segments. Video segments can be used for training tapes, outcome tapes, rating by naive consumers for social validation, or training of observers for data collection. In a recent study (Gibbs, 2001), a camcorder with a timestamp feature allowed the recording of canine training sessions and the later decoding of the tapes by trained observers under controlled conditions. Live observation would have been impossible, and reliability for the complicated behavior code would have been very difficult to ensure otherwise.

Stopwatches are a frequently used item and fortunately are much more dependable than most other recording devices. They come in two basic types, 30-second and 60-second sweep (the latter is preferred because it matches the sweep of a standard timepiece so that observers adapt easily to it). In addition, some have color-coded start (green) and stop (red) buttons that make their use more versatile and dependable for observers to operate. Good stopwatches are somewhat expensive, but they will last for years. Be sure to calibrate them regularly and keep them wound tightly (i.e., check calibration once per week and wind daily). Battery-operated digital stopwatches allow very precise stimulus control for observers or trainers.

Personnel Required

In addition to the experimenter, the experimenter's assistant, and the staff present in the setting in which the research is carried out, most behavioral studies will have at least one team of observers. There is a tendency among beginning researchers to try to recruit more people to assist than can be reliably monitored. For example, at some universities, undergraduates may fulfill a research participation requirement or earn course credit for serving as an observer in a research project. The inexperienced researcher will often seek out 10 to 12 of such readily available students to assist in data collection. Only later does he or she realize that it is almost impossible to keep track of this many observers, let alone have them adequately trained so that they will perform well. Three to five such assistants are usually all that can be effectively used. If more are needed, you will probably have to add a second researcher or senior student to monitor them. If this is not feasible, then it is advisable to reduce the scope of the study so that fewer observers are needed.

A note of caution about undergraduate student observers must be stated, particularly regarding their dependability. Often, the time they can spend on an experiment will vary with the demands of their other course work. For example, there is a strikingly high correlation between no-shows and "illness" in observers and the beginning of midterm and final exams. Although an experiment may run continuously for several months, student observers will usually leave for a time between semesters; thus, special arrangements will have to be made to cover for them during quarter or semester breaks. If funds are available to pay observers, many of these problems will be solved. It is customary to pay the current minimum wage for such tasks. This is usually all the beginning researcher can afford and is typically adequate to maintain observers unless the job is especially inconvenient or arduous. Certain kinds of people seem to make better observers than others. Those who are relatively compulsive about being on time, who keep things neat and orderly, and who pay attention to details seem to work out better than those who have a "whatever," somewhat cavalier manner of doing things.

Occasionally, you may require the assistance of a professional person such as a dental hygienist, physical therapist, or speech therapist to assist in some phase of the experiment (e.g., to help you set up criteria for dental hygiene or to judge the adequacy of a therapy you have derived). Generally, such professionals will volunteer to help out if the demand is not too great on their time and if they can see some worthwhile benefit from the research. They should be offered every professional courtesy, and your appreciation should be made clear. Often, you can agree to help other professionals in exchange for their time (e.g., you may help the speech therapist with a particularly difficult client), but in any event, you will want to send a letter of thanks. You may also want to give a professional who has helped you a footnote credit in any publication and perhaps coauthorship if he or she has made a significant contribution.

Time Required to Complete the Study

Time is a factor in resource assessment because how much time you have (and how you spend it) will determine how comprehensive your research project will be. Natural time demarcations will limit some studies, depending upon the setting and the question being asked. Most elementary schools are closed in the summer. Thus, educational research must be run in the August-June period. It is difficult to begin data collection during the first 2 to 3 weeks of school, and the last couple of weeks in the spring are also not to be counted on. In addition, there are numerous holidays, teacher planning days, field trips, assemblies, and so on, that cut into the school year. Conservatively, one may have about 6 actual months to collect data in a normal school year.

The most frequent error that beginning researchers make is to underestimate the amount of time it will take to run their study; the great amount of time required to make preparation for research is also usually not recognized. In fact, start-up time can take from 1 to 3 months, depending on how much pilot work has to be done. You will need time to recruit and train observers, order parts or build equipment, and get your institutional review board (IRB) forms and prospectus prepared, among other things. It is fairly common for behavior analysis studies to run for 4 to 6 months for a master's thesis and sometimes for as long as 9 months to a year for a doctoral dissertation. Obviously, the more complex the study, the longer it will take, so that one has to be constantly balancing the questions to be asked in the research with the time available to answer them.

Perhaps the biggest unknown in behavioral research is how long any one experimental condition will run. In our field, the custom is that conditions are run "to stability" rather than for a fixed time, so it is virtually impossible to know in advance how long a baseline or training condition will take. It is best to overestimate the time just to be safe. Thus, if you are running an experiment with four conditions, you will want to allow a *minimum* of 10 days per condition (or a total of 40 actual "data days"), but to be safe, you will want to allow at least 50 to 65 calendar days to complete the experiment. At 4 days per week (it is not unusual to lose at least 1 day per week due to such unpredictable events as observer or subject absence or illness, equipment breakdown, or bad weather), it could take almost 4 months to run a simple study. Note again that this does not include start-up time and time for pilot testing.

As described earlier, one final factor to be considered in the time assessment has to do with approval from certain agencies to do the research in the first place. To carry out research in most schools, for example, a proposal must be prepared or forms filled out for submission to a research committee of the school board and the IRB. Often, such groups meet *only monthly* (perhaps even less frequently) to consider such proposals, and if you miss the deadline for submission, you will have to wait another 30 days or more before you can begin. Because behavior analysis procedures are almost always benign, you should in some cases be able to obtain approval without the full review process. Observation of people in natural environments, use of positive reinforcement, and training-type interventions usually cause little concern for IRB members. We have had some problems when feedback or other consequences are used. In one study, there was concern that feedback given to supermarket night stock crews might be used by management to change their pay or perhaps fire them. The IRB's position was that if an employee was fired and then challenged the action, he or she might be able to file a related claim against the university. It is a good idea to check with colleagues who have submitted applications and review copies of their packets for tips on wording and how to present certain concepts.

Miscellaneous

A variety of other resources that are often overlooked are required to complete a study successfully. Office supplies, including custom-designed data sheets, clipboards, and notebooks, are essential. Ready access to a digital camera and a copy machine is usually required. Computer software and the skill to use it are essential for creating graphs from spreadsheets. (See

Part 3 for details on graph preparation.) In your expenses, do not forget to include costs of your daily transportation and cell phone fees.

Finally, be sure to take into account the amount of time each day that you can spend on the research. If you are a graduate student taking two or three seminars and you have a 20-hour-per-week departmental assistantship, you may have a hard time squeezing a large research commitment into your schedule. For master's students, budgeting at least 4 hours per day during the time that the thesis is being run is recommended. For doctoral students, it is probably more like 6 hours per day. Plan on spending at least 6 days a week involved in some aspect or other of your study, including supervising the observers; gathering, collating, and graphing data; meeting with your supervisor; continuing to review journal articles; and preparing drafts of manuscripts related to your work. Doing applied behavioral research is about as mentally challenging, exciting, and worthwhile an endeavor as you will find anywhere, but it is time-consuming and taxing on the body.

The purpose of Step 2, then, is to take a general problem or area of interest and to modify and refine it until it begins to take a more definite shape. Many very practical factors must be considered in this narrowing-down process. Not only must you be aware of similar or related research that has already been published, but you must also have a realistic perception of what it takes to run a study that will pay off. Correctly identifying the type of behavior so that you will know what strategy must be employed and understanding the resources required to execute a study are both part of the decision-making process. Bear in mind that the most frequent error made is trying to answer too many questions with too few resources. Having made these deliberations, you should now be prepared to select your dependent and independent variables.

DECIDE ON YOUR DEPENDENT AND INDEPENDENT VARIABLES

MAIN TOPICS

How to Select Your Dependent Variables

Considering Expert Professional Judgment and Authoritative Sources

Common Problems With Dependent Variables

Choosing Independent Variables

Special Considerations When Choosing Independent Variables

LEARNING OBJECTIVES

Step 3 in designing your study involves deciding precisely what your dependent and independent variables will be. In this step, you will make your final decisions on the behavior to measure and manipulate and what your intervention will be. After studying this step, you should be able to

▶ Describe how you will go about selecting your target behavior(s).

▶ Discuss some of the common pitfalls in selecting these behaviors.

▶ Prepare operational definitions of your dependent variables.

▶ Describe how you will construct your intervention.

▶ Discuss some common problems in the selection of independent variables.

▶ Prepare to deal with possible "side effects" of interventions.

Steps 1 and 2 should have prepared you to select subjects and a setting in which to work and should have assisted you in narrowing down the focus of your interest to a manageable scale. You are now ready to make a final determination of the exact behavior you will measure and of the experimental procedures you will implement. Such a discussion could easily become too prescriptive (and thus thwart your creativity) in suggesting the variables to be studied. Thus, Step 3 is written primarily to help you avoid common mistakes rather than to suggest specific dependent and independent variables that you should study.

Dependent Variables

The term *dependent variable* refers to the behavior that you are interested in observing, analyzing, measuring, and changing. The word *dependent* refers to the fact that this variable *depends upon* some experimental manipulations that you will make in the course of the experiment. In behavior analysis research, the dependent variable must be applied; that is, the behavior to be studied must have social significance for the participants. For this reason, among all possible behaviors you could study, a great many are automatically eliminated. Nonetheless, it is important to take clear affirmative steps to show that the behavior you are dealing with does have social significance.

Developing the Rationale for Dependent Variables

It is best to develop the rationale for your dependent variables prior to the research rather than after the fact. This may be done in several ways.

Expert Professional Judgment

Behavior analysts interact with professionals of all types in the course of plying their trade. You might find yourself consulting or collaborating with a physical therapist, management information specialist, special education teacher, safety engineer, or head trauma rehabilitation specialist. The behavior analyst, though an expert in understanding behavior and behavior change, is often seen as a generalist when compared to these professionals. Many of the problems that must be solved in these specialties will have been identified by persons who have expertise in the area. That is, it is the physical therapist or special education teacher who determines that a client or student is not making adequate progress. It is the safety engineer who has pointed out the increase in accidents that is causing an increase in insurance premiums. In establishing a basis for the "applied" dimension, you need to cite the opinion and recommendation of these professionals. Your description of the applied significance may take the form of "The children were brought to our attention by the registered physical therapist of the institution, who indicated that in her opinion, if the children did not receive 'range of motion' exercise of their limbs, the joints would calcify and prevent any future movement" or "The dietician expressed his concern that if this child does not begin to increase his intake of liquids, dehydration and resulting complications will surely occur."

Authoritative Sources

For some kinds of problems, it may be possible to find authoritative sources that will lend credence to a statement that a particular behavior is a problem that should be addressed. You may be able to cite a reference from the National Highway Traffic Safety Administration (NHTSA) on risky driving, a reference from the Surgeon General's Office on dangerous medically related practices, or a report from the American Medical Association on the dangers of high cholesterol and its relationship to consumption of certain foods. Watch for regular reports from such agencies or check their Web pages for updates and archival information. Because there are occasional reversals of opinion on such matters, when you are citing authoritative sources, be sure to use the most up-to-date data you can find (e.g., the NHTSA Web address is <www.nhtsa.gov>).

Descriptive Data for the Reader to Judge

In many instances, the audience you are addressing will be responsive to data you present to convince them that there is a behavior worth modifying. If, for example, you present baseline data showing that the direct care staff in an institution for persons with mental illness spent 75% of their time engaging in "off-task" behavior, or an NHTSA report indicating over 40,000 fatalities and over 3.5 million serious injuries per year from vehicle crashes, you will have made a strong case for any reader sensitive to these issues.

Face Validity and the Absence of Any Effective Research on the Problem

Some of the dependent variables that you may be interested in studying will be of the "obvious social significance" type in that almost any reader would immediately agree that the research was required. If you note in your introduction that aerophagia (chronic and excessive swallowing of air that can cause dizziness, vomiting, anorexia, and possibly death) is a behavioral health problem for which there is no effective long-term treatment (Garcia, Starin, & Churchill, 2001), then you will have made your case for the face validity. The nature of some problems is such that almost any audience will support the need to modify the behavior and carry out good research in the process. If you are working with cocaine-dependent adults (Budney, Higgins, Delaney, Kent, & Bickel, 1991), you need say little more to establish the face validity for your target participants and behavior. Another example of high face validity involves research on children with aphkia (surgically removed lenses), who must learn to wear contact lenses or lose their vision entirely (Mathews, Hodson, Crist, & Laroche, 1992).

Previous Research

A great deal of behavior analysis research stems from previous work. A particular topic may have face validity simply because it has been researched by many prominent people. Risky driving, for example, has been the target of researchers since the early 1990s (Burns & Wilde, 1995; Geller, 1991b; Ludwig & Geller, 1991, 1997, 2000). In the field of traffic safety, it has been shown that risky behavior can be used to predict involvement in fatal car crashes. But because most of the previous work is based on potentially unreliable self-report or archival data, there is a need for research that produces lab-quality data (Boyce & Geller, 2001). Research that lends directly to other research is said to have "heuristic value"; however, one must be careful that it does not become esoteric and of little practical value in the process.

Common Pitfalls in Selecting the Dependent Variable

Uses of Secondary Sources of Data

In one study, the researchers had built a case for the need to investigate methods of reducing disruptive behavior in a residential setting. Unfortunately, the dependent variable consisted of counting the number of instances of disruptive behavior noted by the nurses in their daily log. There was no other definition of the behavior, nor were there any reliability checks on the nurses' observations. In another experiment, the teacher gave tokens to children who had "studied and paid attention" in class. A major problem, however, was that the dependent measure was the number of tokens earned by the students rather than measures of academic output or direct observation of their behavior by an observer. Obviously, the actual behavior *itself* must be measured whenever possible.

Wrong Label for Behavior

Calling a behavior "self-injurious" or "self-destructive" conjures up a child who is battered and bruised, usually restrained, and sometimes heavily medicated. In one study, the definition of self-injurious behavior as "any contact between hand and head" was sufficiently vague that the behavior could have also included noninjurious touching such as scratching one's head. Another study purported to deal with teaching social workers "communication skills." A close examination of the definition, however, revealed that college students (acting in the "role" of social workers) were trained to give one piece of information to a cohort in a "simulated interview setting." Although this form of "gold-bricking" may escape the attention of the unwary, it is not advisable to try to build one's professional status or enhance the field through this means. Any label used must be as precisely descriptive as possible.

Wrong Rate of Behavior

A related issue has to do with a behavior that occurs at a rate that cannot justify its being a significant problem. For example, the rate of behavior is often too low to make an intervention truly worthwhile. A single-subject experiment in which a child had the label *hyperkinetic* is a case in point. Records showed that he had a rate of .42 instances *per day* in his elementary class. This was reduced by half to .20 per day, but the question remains whether this was really a socially significant problem to begin with. Another large-scale project was proposed to show how privileges could be used to increase fifth graders' accuracy on math problems. An examination of the baseline showed that they were roughly 80% to 85% accurate in baseline; no other data substantiating the need for a higher correct rate were presented.

Wrong Subjects

Many behaviors are a problem because they occur in certain subject populations or with subjects of certain ages. Thus, teaching reading to very young children may be less significant than working with elementary school children who cannot read. Likewise, stealing is often a part of the repertoire of "delinquents," yet one study was carried out in an institutionalized situation where the environment was actually arranged in a manner that facilitated theft.

Wrong Behavior

Sometimes studies follow all of the rules for good research, but the wrong behavior is targeted as the independent variable. In a very well-intentioned community-based study, the goal was to enhance child protection in vehicles by encouraging parents to buckle up their children. Unfortunately, the data reported were traffic citations issued. Surprisingly, although the researchers showed that citations actually increased during the intervention, no data were presented on the number of vehicles with children *properly buckled* in their safety seats. A related study on illegal parking in handicapped spaces showed that this common practice could be reduced but had no data on how this affected the appropriate users.

Wrong Setting

It is common practice for laboratory-based approaches to the study of human behavior to "simulate" behavior in an experimental setting. Although this is often appropriate in behavioral research, one must not be misled. Throwing refuse on the ground is generally considered "littering," but does leaving your popcorn box on the floor of a theater constitute littering? Theaters, football and hockey stadiums, and other large indoor and outdoor gathering places have standard procedures and the necessary personnel for dealing with such refuse. Procedures that change the behavior of people who throw their trash along public highways or in national parks would probably come closer to pinpointing a behavior problem in an appropriate setting.

Unproven Problem

The way in which a problem is described will often cause the reader to believe that the problem is significant, but upon closer inspection, the argument for conducting research on this particular topic may not be so convincing. Many teachers will define out-of-seat behavior, talking loudly, or chewing gum as "disruptive," but the researcher needs to proceed with caution. If it is merely disturbing to the teacher but has little noticeable effect on the children's learning, then one might want to consider another dependent variable. Similarly, social skills training needs to be justified by showing that there is some net gain to the child for acquiring the skills. One study involved the reduction of developmentally disabled children's use of an offensive hand gesture. The experiment would have had greater merit if simultaneously, data had been collected on the increased number of sentences written or problems solved once the offensive behavior had been reduced to demonstrate that the problem was of importance academically. If a child is spending his or her time making offensive hand gestures and engaging in the accompanying attention-seeking behaviors, the likelihood is great that he or she is off task and not performing academic tasks some of the time. Reducing the inappropriate behavior should result in an increase in appropriate behavior.

Confounding With the Independent Variable

In most cases, the dependent variable can clearly be discriminated from the independent variable. However, one must be constantly aware that dependent and independent variables can be confounded if proper precautions are not taken. This may happen when, for example, the introduction of the independent variable also involves another event that could change the behavior independently. In one study, a social worker was invited to make regular visits to a group home so that the effects of her visits on the clients' interactions might be assessed. But the person always brought some games, arts and crafts, and other materials, and these materials alone easily could have been responsible for the change independent of the visits. Similarly, systematic feedback to employees on their performance carries with it some implicit specification of the target behavior, attention from a supervisor, and the potential for social pressure from peers. Each of these variables should be controlled and manipulated individually if there is to be no confounding with the independent variable.

Defining the Dependent Variable: Some Rules of Thumb

It may be useful to specify some general rules of thumb that may assist in the definition of any dependent variable. The notion of the behavioral cusp described in Step 2 is always a good place to start. The following are a few more suggestions.

Face Validity

The description of the behavior to be changed should agree with the most standard and common usage. That is, the desired target behavior ought to be a behavior that is routine and appropriate for the subject and setting selected. This is not to say that the problem cannot be unusual, for it is the study of the unique that makes the field grow. But the behavior itself must be readily seen by those external to the setting as socially important.

Using Existing Definitions

The research you are involved with may be part of a series of studies on a common problem that previous authors have examined in some way. To lend the greatest generality to your study, you will want to use the same definition of the dependent variable that others have used if this is at all possible. For example, in a study involved in teaching first-aid skills to students with moderate disabilities (Marchand-Martella et al., 1992), the authors started with definitions provided by the American National Red Cross. It is always good to be cautious and to start by attempting to replicate the usage you find in the literature. If you cannot obtain reliable data with a published definition and protocol, first contact the author and determine if there are details regarding observation that were perhaps left out of the article.

Creating Your Own Definitions

If you are working on a problem that has good face validity but for which there are no existing definitions, you will want to cast your definition in terms that others will readily accept. A perfect example is the recent work of Carolyn Green and Dennis Reid (Green, Gardner, & Reid, 1997; Green & Reid, 1996, 1999) on the measurement of *happiness and unhappiness* in people with profound multiple disabilities. For a study aimed at improving the quality of life of these individuals, it is clear that some dependent measure indicating participants' positive or negative response is of utmost importance. Green and Reid (1996) began with a requirement that the indices had to include observable responses, and they reviewed other research that had referred to similar behaviors. They then constructed their definition: "Happiness was defined as any facial expression or vocalization typically considered to be an indicator of happiness among people without disabilities including smiling, laughing, and yelling while smiling" (p. 69). They then set up a protocol that involved 10 seconds of observation followed by a 5-second recording interval. Participants were observed while they manipulated preferred and nonpreferred stimuli. In addition, taped segments of the participants manipulating the stimuli were shown to two independent groups of practitioners, who were asked to rate the tapes and "observe the degree to which each participant appeared to be happy or unhappy" (p. 71). In the end, there was 95% to 100% agreement on the definitions, and a new dependent variable had been validated.

Pilot Testing of the Dependent Variable

As a final rule of thumb, be sure to pilot-test your dependent variable thoroughly *before the onset* of your baseline. It is best to do all observer training and reliability checks ahead of time so that when the first real data point is plotted, you will have considerable confidence that your data are accurate. Do not be surprised if you go through several iterations of the original definition. You might also find that definitions found in published studies do not meet your needs. Another suggestion is to assess your reliability with the simplest definition. Then add the complexity incrementally and continue to test for reliability. We have found that adding examples of the target behaviors often boosts observer reliability considerably.

Independent Variables

The term *independent variable* describes the variable that you are going to change or manipulate in your study. (The term *independent* seems to have been borrowed from mathematics, where it refers to a value of other variables: e.g., x in the formula $y = 3x^2$.) In an applied science, the field progresses through the development of new, more effective, and more practical independent variables; this is where discovery and creativity seem to be most required to make an impact. Most of the problems that require attention have been established for a long time, but the development of new procedures to deal with them is always needed and welcomed by the research community.

Categories of Independent Variables

From a behavioral perspective, two categories of independent variables can be examined for their effects on human behavior: antecedent environmental events, such as cues, prompts, or instructions, and consequent events, such as reinforcement, extinction procedures, and punishment. Historically, the field has been concerned primarily with the latter, probably because of the early influence of animal operant conditioning, with its heavy emphasis on the study of different schedules of reinforcement. In the early years, applied researchers almost totally ignored the effects that antecedent events might have on behavior and concentrated instead on behaviors for which a lack of "motivation" seemed to be the primary problem. More recently, behavioral researchers have been turning their attention to the study of antecedent stimuli, and it seems clear that this research will make a major contribution to the field in the years to come.

Though many find it surprising, behavior analysts have not restricted themselves to these traditional categories of independent variables. Three other types of individual variables seem to fall within their domain. Structural modification of the environment that will produce behavioral change represents an economical and potentially effective approach to certain types of problems. The establishing operation is also gaining new respect and attention (Iwata, Smith, & Michael, 2000). Establishing operations are events that alter the value of a reinforcer (Michael, 1982). In addition, the study of the effects of biological variables on behavior seems to be of greater and greater interest to behavior analysts. To be maximally effective, of course, we might try to use all of these independent variables simultaneously. This approach has recently led to the development of "package program" research. We will begin with a discussion of consequent stimulus variables.

Consequent Stimulus Variables

The study of the use of consequences to change behavior has dominated the field from its inception. Both Skinner's work (1953) and the animal laboratory research that preceded applied behavior analysis stressed the study of complex ways of arranging reinforcers to change behavior. In addition, the earliest subjects chosen were often functionally nonverbal (e.g., individuals with severe developmental disabilities, individuals with psychoses, and very young children), so that using antecedent stimuli in the form of instructions would have been fruitless. There was also a considerable investment, continuing from Skinner's interest in rate of behavior, in demonstrating that a behavior could be increased or decreased from some already existing rate. Thus, motivational variables were seen to be most relevant. Conceptually, one might say that this research is concerned with the behavior of subjects who already "know" what to do but who don't do it because the existing reinforcement contingencies are not properly arranged. A well-trained behavior analyst might notice that reinforcers currently exist for a behavior but are too delayed or are of the wrong type or amount to sustain a given behavior. The research study might then demonstrate that changing one or more of these dimensions could result in a change of rate.

Behavior analysts have demonstrated almost unparalleled ingenuity in both devising new reinforcers and bringing existing reinforcers into closer proximity to the behavior that requires change. Stimuli ranging from a simple beep from a transmitter consequent on thumb sucking (Stricker, Miltenberger, Garlinghouse, Deaver, & Anderson, 2001) to contingent physical guidance to reduce aerophagia (Garcia et al., 2001) to prizes and money to increase activity usage in people who are elderly (Gallagheer & Keenan, 2000) are only a few of the consequences that have been used recently. There appears to be a substantial market of people who are looking for "positive" solutions rather than punitive solutions to behavior problems. Teachers, parents, school counselors, management consultants, and many others are seeking ways to "motivate" their students, children, or employees. For this reason, behavioral research that explores consequent stimuli and provides an alternative to standard aversive solutions should continue to find acceptance in a wide range of magazines, journals, and other outlets.

Antecedent Stimulus Variables

The analysis of certain types of behavior may suggest that the motivation of the subject is adequate but that some form of cueing or prompting appears necessary. This especially occurs when the response is not complex and may be partly or wholly in the subject's repertoire. In a recent study, two different highly promoted but untested safety signs were placed in a supermarket urging parents to buckle up their children when placing them in the child seat of the grocery cart (Barker, 2001). In the previously described Gallagheer and Keenan (2000) study, the researchers tried two different prompts, one verbal and one visual in the form of a poster, to try to encourage their elderly clients to increase activity usage.

Where the behavior to be changed *is* complex, antecedent stimulus control may take the form of training or instruction. Sarokoff, Taylor, and Poulson (2001) used a unique form of training involving scripts with embedded text to teach conversational skills to autistic children. The researchers then showed that the scripts could be faded, with the natural social contingencies maintaining the conversations. This general strategy seems most applicable where there are reinforcers in the natural environment to support the behavior once it occurs. Our society prefers simple solutions, and prompts or training are often seen as panaceas for difficult problems. There is a great deal of good applied research to be done to determine whether this approach is valid and, if not, what actually is required to change the target behavior.

Structural or Environmental Design Variables

Both antecedent and consequent variables can be costly to implement in terms of personnel; thus, the possibility of being able to change behavior by making a somewhat permanent structural change in the environment seems attractive. If destructive lawn walking can be greatly reduced by rearranging benches, footpaths, and shrubbery, this will clearly be a more cost-effective and feasible alternative than having someone stand in the area giving instructions to stay off the grass or handing out reinforcers for correct walking. To reduce speeding, for example, Ragnarsson and Bjorgvinsson (1991) showed, in a replication of an earlier study, that posting the percentage of drivers who were exceeding the speed limit on a sign at roadside significantly reduced this hazardous driving behavior.

Biological Variables

The relationship between medications, nutritional and biological variables, and behavior has been studied extensively by psychopharmacologists for a number of years, and now behavior analysts are extending that work in applied settings. For example, Pace and Toyer (2000) have shown that a common multiple vitamin can reduce the latency to pica. Gulley and Northup (1997) have developed a model for the accurate behavioral assessment of methylphenidate (Ritalin) in a school setting. Furthermore, comparisons of drugs with behavioral interventions for the same dependent variable appear to be feasible and reliable (Northup et al., 1999; Rapport, Murphy, & Bailey, 1982).

Considerations in the Selection of the Independent Variable

One of the primary contributions of applied behavior analysis is in the development of procedures for use by professionals and paraprofessionals in other fields (e.g., techniques for teachers to use to improve class performance or for foster parents to use in toilet-training young children with developmental disabilities). These people will not necessarily have any sophistication in scientific method or the use of behavioral techniques. Just as an automobile manufacturer must take the needs and resources of his customers into account when designing a new car, so must behavior analysts take the requirements and abilities of their users into account (Bailey, 1991). Essentially, we must fashion our emerging behavioral technology to match the consumers.

Identifying the Consumer

Although it may seem unusual to select the user of the behavioral procedure prior to the onset of the research, this is clearly appropriate. If you are trying to develop a procedure that can be implemented by the average elementary school teacher, you will want to know something about the skills or limitations of the teacher. Most teachers are hard-pressed to find much extra time to carry out a program. In addition, they may have particular difficulty if it requires any complicated bookkeeping techniques. It may be wise to interview potential users about certain aspects of the procedures. Asking a simple question such as "Would you be able to use a procedure that involved your sending a special note home with 10 of your children once per week?" can save the researcher a lot of time by screening out procedures that participants will not use. You can also observe potential consumers in action to make your own decisions about what characteristics an adoptable procedure might have. Is your procedure really designed to be implemented by a teacher aide rather than the teacher? If so, are there a significant number of schools with the extra staff required to make the adoption of the procedures feasible? Does your intervention require that the user be able to read an instruction manual or to operate special equipment? What is the actual cost of the procedure to the user? (Many teachers have given up on token systems once they discovered that *they* had to pay for the backup reinforcers.) Can the costs be borne by the facility? These and other questions need to be raised if the techniques developed for the study are to match the needs and limitations of the consumer.

A Caution About "Side Effects"

Although it may seem premature, it may be a good idea to try to determine if there could be any negative side effects of the implementation of your independent variable. In a study we carried out on stealing among second graders (Switzer, Deal, & Bailey, 1977), using a group contingency, we were concerned that the children would turn against the person who had caused the loss of their privileges. To determine if this could happen, the teacher was alerted to this possibility, and a tape recorder was left running when the teacher had to leave the class. Sociograms were also administered before and after the experiment to measure any possible changes in "social relationships." (Happily our concern was not warranted.) In another study that sought to increase the productivity of roofers (Austin, Kessler, Riccobono, & Bailey, 1996), we determined that their increased work speed at 30 to 40 feet above ground might increase their risk of accidents, so an immediate assessment of safety behaviors was undertaken and a behavioral safety project was added to the productivity package. In other cases, researchers may be involved in increasing the mobility or access to community facilities of participants in some way. Due caution must be exercised in these circumstances to ensure that no injury occurs in the course of the study.

Specifying the Independent Variable Exactly

To meet the *technological* standard for the field, researchers should provide operational definitions of their independent variables. Unfortunately, this is not done the majority of the time (Gresham, 1996). Although the most recent review of treatment integrity (Gresham, Gansle, & Noell, 1993) showed a surprisingly low (16%) percentage of studies that measured the fidelity of the independent variables, this continues to be an important methodological standard for the field. Because it is such a common problem (i.e., it is one of the most frequent reasons for rejection of manuscripts submitted for review), a few suggestions are in order.

First, all relevant aspects of the independent variable should be included in the description. If a token system is employed in a classroom, for example, the number of tokens *given* may not be the only relevant variable. The teacher may begin to *praise* more as a function of having to give tokens for good behavior, or, if the tokens are visible to all students (e.g., as stars on a chart), some peer competition may result.

Second, it may be advisable to guarantee that the independent variable was implemented according to plan by taking data directly on the treatment. Kneringer and Page (1999), for example, trained 13 group home staff on nutritional support behaviors and then took treatment integrity data during unscheduled visits. The data showed that there was very high maintenance of these procedures, and the authors then went on to show that there were positive changes in biological indices (the dependent variable) of the group home residents.

Third, the standards of the field demand more and more that some monitoring or data collection on the implementation of the independent variable be done. Northup et al. (1994) used this strategy with special education teachers who were implementing treatments based on functional assessments. Their data showed considerable variability in treatment integrity, ranging from 52% to 100%; clearly, some teachers were better than others in following the treatment plans. One surprising finding was that even with low integrity there was significant behavior change by the students. In what may represent the beginning of a specialized line of research, Vollmer, Roane, Ringdahl, and Marcus (1999) actually tested the robustness of a common behavioral intervention, differential reinforcement of alternative behavior (DRA). In DRA, the participant is reinforced for engaging in a better alternative to the undesirable behavior. The alternative behavior may not always be incompatible with the undesirable behavior (Burch & Bailey, 1999). With three individuals, the researchers showed that even a partial treatment intervention of DRA can be effective if it has been preceded by the full, correct implementation.

Evaluating "Other" Treatments

In comparative treatment research, some existing or traditional method of modifying a behavior may be compared with a behavioral approach to the same problem. In these cases, we must be careful not to test a "straw man" of the other technique or the comparison will be invalid. In a recent consumer behavior study, for example, Barker (2001) showed that two different industry-developed safety signs had virtually no effect on whether grocery shoppers put their children in the seat and buckled them up. Jordan, Singh, and Repp (1989) compared two treatments for reducing stereotypy: visual screening and "gentle teaching" (GT). Because the latter is not a research-based behavioral treatment, the authors went out of their way to meet all of the specifications established by the originator of GT (McGee, 1986), including viewing videotapes developed by McGee and operationalizing the salient features. In the end, Jordan et al. determined that GT was by far inferior to visual screening in reducing stereotypy and, further, that "bonding," which is supposed to be a by-product, did not occur any more often with GT than with visual screening.

If you want to compare psychotherapy with behavior therapy in the treatment of some form of phobia, the psychotherapy treatment should probably be carried out by someone other than the behavior therapist and preferably by someone who is an *expert* in that form of treatment. If you want to argue that the standard way of dealing with runaways in a detention facility is inadequate, then this "standard way" needs to be replicated so that practitioners will easily recognize it as being correct. This is particularly important if the audience to whom you are addressing your research is made up of traditional researchers as well as behavior analysts.

A Note on "Package Programs"

One strategy in applied behavior analysis is to put several procedures together in a "package" that is then implemented as one procedure. One of the earliest exemplars of this strategy was Azrin and Foxx's *Toilet Training in Less Than a Day* (1974). Their method of training involved modeling, role playing, instructions, practice, reinforcement, and overcorrection, all to be implemented in the same treatment. Most recently this approach appeared in a study (Kahng, Tarbox, & Wilke, 2001) in which a multicomponent treatment was used for food refusal by a 5-year-old mildly mentally retarded boy. Kahng et al.'s package included starting the session with noncontingent preferred items such as books and tapes; these were removed if the boy refused a bite of food and were returned if he accepted. In addition, he was given praise for accepting food and put on extinction for expelling, gagging, or vomiting. Similarly, Asmus et al. (1999) employed a multicomponent treatment probe that included noncontingent free play, specific task instruction, extinction for escape attempts, contingent praise and access to free play, and a choice of free-play items to overcome escape-maintained aberrant behavior in three children aged 3 to 5 years.

This strategy of combining procedures obviously is counter to the traditional scientific approach of breaking the independent variable into its components and determining which part was responsible for the effect. The combining of treatments can be justified, however, on the grounds that there is a need for procedures that work quickly and reliably. In the Kahng et al. study, for example, the 5-year-old was on a gastronomy feeding tube and was refusing 100% of food offered. Such packages (often combining eight or more procedures) may work even if only three or four of them are carried out, thus allowing some imprecision on the part of the implementer. Any "extra baggage" in the package can be justified if it does not appear to require a great deal of additional effort on the part of the person carrying it out. In executing such research, you run the risk that later efforts may reveal that some major components were unnecessary and that some possibly apparently trivial variable was in fact responsible for the majority of the effect. Beginning researchers are cautioned to be judicious in the number of procedures that are to be combined to form the treatment package.

ESTABLISH SOCIAL VALIDITY

MAIN TOPICS

The Main Features of Social Validation

Examples of Research Using Social Validation

Four Operational Steps for Good Social Validation

LEARNING OBJECTIVES

Step 4 in designing your study involves making sure that it is socially valid. You will learn about the three types of social validation, critique research using social validation, and analyze the operational steps. After studying this step, you should be able to

- ▶ Describe the three primary types of social validation.

- ▶ Discuss recent research using social validation.

- ▶ Explain the four operational steps of social validation.

Three Features of Social Validation

As an applied researcher, you must be constantly aware of the need to have a strong rationale for any experimental intervention you propose. The consideration of the social validity (Wolf, 1978) of your study should be seriously undertaken from the outset. You will want to consider three major aspects:

1. Are the goals that I want to achieve shared by the people in the setting and by society?

2. Are the interventions that I am considering likely to be acceptable to the participants and consumers of this research?

3. Will I be able to produce results that will satisfy the consumers? (Wolf, 1978)

The overall goal of social validation is to guarantee that the behavior analyst researcher is working on a "problem of social importance" (Baer, quoted in Wolf, 1978, p. 203). Hopefully, the work will make a contribution that will be appreciated by significant decision makers in the setting where the work is carried out and perhaps by the larger society. When behavioral work is appreciated in the short term, the behavior analyst researcher is welcomed to the setting and given the full cooperation and necessary support to continue research on a day-to-day basis. This is certainly a worthy goal in and of itself. The goal for some research is more long term: namely, to develop procedures that will actually be embraced by the owners and consumers of the setting. If this is your objective, you will need to take two other factors into account. First, though some research shows significant results, the resources involved in producing them (costs, labor, inconvenience, political conflict) may exceed what the owners or consumers can afford. Second, experience has shown that having a setting adopt new research-generated procedures requires not only significant results (e.g., cost savings, increased productivity, more fluent learning) but also a "champion" who will promote the procedures over the long term. Often, the long-term adoption of behavioral procedures is thwarted when the champion leaves the setting through promotion or retirement. Or the champion may become politically ineffective for some reason. Neither of these reasons has anything to do with the significance of the original findings, of course. So, as a new researcher, you will need to determine early on what your goals are and make your preparations accordingly.

Sample Research Using Social Validation

In a recent study (Barker, 2001), for example, the researcher began with a goal of determining the most effective way of reducing child injuries in supermarkets. The general manager of the setting not only was originally quite cooperative but over time became intrigued with the procedures and the findings and became a "champion" of the research. He then promoted the research with his district manager and offered to assist in future research. This fortunate circumstance may lead to the researcher's having some impact with the entire supermarket chain, or it may lead nowhere, depending on the manager's situation down the road. It is uncertain what may be expected 5 years from now. The store may have a new manager who has no idea of what took place in this store a few years ago or a model program where behavior principles are employed enthusiastically by management and an active program of applied behavioral research is evident. New researchers are probably wise to be modest in their initial expectations about adoption and to work diligently to ensure that they have met Wolf's original goals for social validation.

A Brief History of Social Validation

Although there were some early precedents for social validation (Jones & Azrin, 1969; McMichael & Corey, 1969), the first large-scale study to focus on social validation and fully develop a procedure for it was published by Wolf and his colleagues in 1976 (Minkin et al., 1976). The ultimate goal of the research was to develop procedures to improve the social skills of the court-adjudicated young women who were residents of Achievement Place for Girls. Four girls aged 12 to 14 who "were generally deficient in social communication skills with adults" (p. 134) participated. In this study, five female college students and five female junior high students interacted with the participants so that conversational samples could be obtained. Then 13 adults from the local community, who volunteered to serve as "judges," rated the conversational skills of each participant. Minkin et al. ultimately were able to isolate conversational skills that were deemed effective by community judges. They then developed a training program to teach these skills to the Achievement Place participants.

Four Operational Steps of Social Validation

The social validation process has four steps:

1. Gather samples of appropriate and inappropriate behaviors.
2. Submit these to a panel of judges for subjective evaluation.
3. Develop reliable, quantifiable definitions and measurements of these behaviors, correlate them with the "subjective" evaluations, and train the target participants in the measurable behaviors.
4. Have the panel of judges (possibly new) rate the behaviors and correlate with the objective measures.

The implications of this process, according to Wolf (1978), were that behavioral researchers "can establish the social importance or validity of complex classes of behavior that have subjective labels" (p. 209). This essentially opened up the field of behavior analysis to a wide range of subjective behaviors, including "happiness, creativity, affection, trust, beauty, concern, satisfaction, fairness, joy, love, freedom and dignity" (p. 206). And "if those things described by subjective labels were the things that were most important to people, then those were the things, even though they might be complex, that we should become more concerned with. After all, as an applied science of human behavior, we supposedly were dedicated to helping people become better able to achieve their reinforcers" (p. 206).

Examples of Research Using Social Validation

Since social validation was originally described, many studies have included it as a part of their methodology, and, in 1991, a special issue of the

Journal of Applied Behavioral Analysis (JABA) was devoted largely to the topic (Geller, 1991a). In that issue, Fawcett (1991) expanded on the original four-step process and suggested 10 steps that he had found useful in his community research. Winett, Moore, and Anderson (1991) demonstrated how social validity could be extended to the study of disease prevention and health promotion.

As discussed in Step 3, Dennis Reid and Carolyn Green (Green, Gardner, & Reid, 1997; Green & Reid, 1996, 1999) took Wolf's model and applied it to the development of a definition of "happiness" for individuals with severe and profound developmental disabilities. This is an important step with this population, for these participants are nonverbal, and determining their preferences and reactions to certain conditions is essential to improving their quality of life.

In a demonstration of how simple it can be to establish social validation in some instances, Allen, Loiben, Allen, and Stanley (1992) used social validation in a study designed to reduce the disruptive behavior of children undergoing restorative dental treatment. To determine if their objective measures of disruptive behavior were valid, two pediatric dentists independently rated videotapes of the children during baseline and treatment conditions. The data showed that on a 6-point Likert scale, the children rated 5.4 ("very disruptive") during baseline and 2.6 ("cooperative") during the treatment.

Dunlap and his colleagues (Dunlap, Kern-Dunlap, Clarke, & Robbins, 1991) went to greater lengths to provide a measure of social validity with their curricular revision interventions. Basically, their strategy was to attempt to reduce severe behavior problems by determining through functional analysis what elements of a curriculum were causing the behavior problems and then making the necessary modifications in academic demands to ameliorate them. Their quantitative data showed dramatic reductions in disruptive behavior and increases in on-task behavior when the tasks were made more functional, when the tasks were shortened, and when the 12-year-old severely emotionally disturbed student was given some choice of activities and assignments. Dunlap et al. (1991) then surveyed over 20 individuals connected with the student's program, including her teachers, the school principal, the secretary, the bus driver, and other instructional and support personnel. On an eight-item questionnaire, the results indicated that the student's progress was "much more positive following the introduction of the revised curriculum" (p. 394).

One final study has built on previous work in social validity and set a new standard for thoroughness in the identification of critical conversational skills for students with disabilities (Hughes et al., 1998). The authors observed 320 general education students and 39 special education students over a 2-month period. From this they identified 97 behaviors and 33 conversational topics that occurred during lunch periods. These topics were then reduced to nine conversational categories and 10 topic codes for which the investigators could attain greater than 80% reliability category by category. The researchers then determined that four behaviors were significantly different between the general education and special education students, and they proceeded to manipulate them experimentally using amateur actors in four videotaped scenes. Following this, 60 individuals served as judges of the conversational skills they viewed on a 5-point scale. Using an elaborate set of statistical measures, Hughes et al. were able to determine with great precision that three skills were critical: rate and percentage of time initiating and responding to conversations, percentage of time attending to the other person, and not engaging in distracting motor behavior. Future research on social validation will have to take into account the advances made in this particular study. For serious students of the topic, it is a "must-read."

Habilitative Validity

A question has been raised (Hawkins, 1991) about the value of social validity as it is often carried out. Hawkins is concerned that asking consumers about the success of a treatment intervention and finding that they support it is measuring only their verbal behavior. What we actually want to know, as Kazdin (2001) has indicated, is whether they will seek, cooperate with, and persistently implement behavioral programming. Hawkins (1991) questioned the value of some consumers' opinions, calling them "merely a second opinion from a different viewpoint" (p. 208). He suggested that more research was needed to determine the actual "habilitative validity" of consumers' answers to certain questions about treatments to which they are exposed. Actual habilitative validity is important because this is the measure of the actual treatment outcome rather than simply the verbal report of the participant. A person with heart disease could report that he or she "feels healthier" after several weeks of an exercise program. An appropriate habilitative validity measure in this case would be cholesterol measures, blood pressure readings, and cardiac tests.

For the new researcher, it is advised that considerable thought be given to the issue of social validity. If you want to have an impact with your research, you will want to make sure that the target behaviors you select are not just convenient or easy to measure but important to those involved (Allen & Warzak, 2000). From this brief review of a few studies, you can get a glimpse of the methodology involved and pursue it further once you choose your final target behaviors. By closely reviewing articles that are similar to the study you plan to carry out and examining their measurement approach to social validity, you should be able to devise some acceptable measure of the social significance for the participants. Your next step is to flesh out the details of your data collection system.

5

CREATE YOUR DATA
COLLECTION SYSTEMS

MAIN TOPICS

The Four Primary Dimensions of Behavior

Three Principal Types of Measurement

How to Set Up a Data Collection System

Selecting and Training Observers

Conducting Interobserver Checks

Calculating Interobserver Reliability

LEARNING OBJECTIVES

In Step 5, we consider all of the issues related to setting up your data collection system and making sure it is reliable. You will learn how to select and train observers, calculate reliability, and deal with your observers. After reading this step, you should be able to

▶ Describe and give examples of each of the four dimensions of behavior.

- Discuss the three primary forms of data collection.

- Explain the four methods of direct observation.

- State how you would set up a data collection system.

- Describe how you would deal with observer drift, bias, and influence.

- Calculate occurrence, nonoccurrence, and total reliability.

Any conclusion to be drawn from your study will be a direct result of the data you collect. If you define a behavior incorrectly or measure a dimension of behavior that is irrelevant, then all of the rest of your work will be for naught. You can lay the groundwork for avoiding these and other errors in measurement by briefly reviewing the dimensions that any given target behavior may have.

Dimensions of Behavior

Frequency/Rate

Frequency simply refers to the number of times that a *discrete* behavior occurs in a standardized observation period. In most applied research, the session *length* is deliberately kept constant so that the data will usually be reported strictly as the total number of responses that occurred per session. The term *rate* is used whenever the frequency is expressed per unit of time—as when, for example, sessions are of different lengths, thus preventing any direct comparison of the total frequencies of the behavior. (In this case, the frequency would be divided by, say, the number of minutes in each session to give a *rate per minute* measure.)

Skinner (1950, 1966, 1969) argued that *rate of emission* of a response ought to be the basic datum of a science of behavior. The argument is based upon a presumed desire on the part of the behavioral scientist to predict (and perhaps control) behavior and an assumption that prediction is dependent upon knowing the *probability* that a given response will occur. Though rate will not directly yield a probability value, it is seen as superior to latency or magnitude of behavior and is considered a "step in the right direction" by Skinner (1966, p. 16).

Reporting the total number of responses per session seems preferred for some dependent variables, perhaps because only whole numbers are involved in describing the results (e.g., it seems easier to envision a child completing, say, an average of 38 correct problems per 45-minute period than .84 per minute).

In the animal laboratory, responses were *functionally* (actually, operationally) defined; that is, *any* response that would activate the lever was counted. The rat could press it with its nose or hit it with his body or tail, and the microswitch attached to the lever would automatically count the response. But in applied research, it has been difficult to find such convenient ways to handle complex human behavior, and more often than not, the topography of the response *is* important. *Topography* refers to the physical characteristics of a behavior such as biting or aggression. An observer uses a definition of a response, such as hitting, that describes the *way* in which the act is usually carried out and records a tally *each time* it is observed.

For many target behaviors, the *repetition of one topography* is the salient dimension, so it should be the primary dependent variable. Two requirements for a response to be measured using frequency are that it is (a) *discrete* (i.e., has a clear onset and offset) and (b) *uniform* (i.e., occurs for about the same magnitude and duration).

Frequency counts can be used with behavior products (e.g., words written, problems solved, kilowatts consumed) or behavior itself (e.g., disruptive acts, words spoken fluently, independent walking steps taken). In some instances, a count may be made of the *number of people* who make a similar response (e.g., the number of parents who take their children to a dental clinic, adults who attend a meeting, or college students who recycle paper).

Duration

The length of time that it takes to complete a response or the total amount of time that a response occurs is often an important dimension of study. How long a child plays with certain other children or toys or carries on a conversation may be precisely the concern of the therapist or teacher. The teacher may not care how many toys are played with or the number of children contacted as long as the contact is prolonged. Any behavior where speed at a task is concerned is obviously appropriate for a duration measure, as in the case of time spent solving a problem or putting a puzzle together. The length of fluent speech is another behavior where duration might be the important dimension. It might be the goal of an ambulation program to teach a child to stand without support (i.e., balance) for greater and greater durations. A recent example of the advantage of a duration measure was given by DeLeon, Iwata, Conners, and Wallace (1999), who used duration of item engagement as a measure of preference during a reinforcer assessment with individuals diagnosed with mental retardation. The primary requirement for duration is that the behavior have a discrete onset and offset (usually the duration is *not* uniform; if it were, a frequency count would be made).

Latency

In some instances, the key variable is how long (from some specified cue) it takes for response onset to occur. This measure is often used when the response is to an instruction, request, or command. One may want to have workers show up on time or developmentally disabled children respond to a question within some reasonably short period. The primary requirement is that the response have a discrete onset; it is presumed that once onset occurs, the rest of the response chain (if there is one) will follow automatically without interruption. If there is interruption, the definition of the response needs to be revisited and perhaps reconsidered as a frequency. A unique application of latency was seen recently a study by Harding et al. (2001) analyzing response class hierarchies. The authors needed a sensitive measure to determine whether certain early responses in a sequence were related to subsequent topographies. Using their response latency analysis, they suggested that treatment of a mild behavior that typically precedes a more severe behavior can be used to reduce the probability of the severe behavior. Pace and Toyer (2000) used *latency to first response* as their dependent measure of pica.

Magnitude

When the topography of a response is more or less uniform but the amount or intensity of the behavior changes in some way, a measurement of magnitude may be in order. Apparently, this dimension is not often studied, but examples may include such events as changes in blood pressure in patients with hypertension, noise level in a classroom, or penile circumference in sex research. Changes in the magnitude of a response almost always involve measurement by use of some instrument. Where this is not the case, magnitude is estimated by an observer and perhaps given a rating. The only requirement is that the range over which the change is to take place must be of measurable proportions. One excellent example of an instrument that measures magnitude is the Self-Injury Trauma Scale (SIT; Iwata, Pace, Kissel, Nau, & Farber, 1990); it includes a severity scale for abrasions, lacerations, and contusions that exceeds 85% reliability.

The determination of the dimension of a behavior that is to be observed (and presumably changed) should be made in conjunction with the staff of the setting where the participant is located. In most cases, the correct dimension will be obvious, but in others, there may be some question. If a child has a high rate of head banging, for example, would it be more desirable to lower the rate or the magnitude? If you have an isolate child, do you want to measure duration of contacts with others or count the number of contacts made? If you have a worker on an assembly line who is slow and clumsy, do you want to measure time on task or number of items produced? In each case, the answer may be *both*, and to measure several dimensions of a response simultaneously is certainly desirable if you can muster the equipment and resources to do so. What you need to measure each dimension and how to do it are the topics for our next section.

Types of Measurement

For any given behavior that you wish to study, you may have a wide or restricted set of measurement options from which to choose. Some behaviors have concrete results that literally represent "hard data." But in many cases, the behavior under study is ephemeral and leaves no permanent trace in the environment. Knowing which type of behavior you are dealing with will determine the measurement system you set up.

Product Measurement

Behavior that results in something permanent (problems worked, parts assembled, pages written) left in the environment can serve as incontrovertible evidence of the type and amount of behavior as well as behavior change. It is desirable wherever possible to determine if there is some way either to select the dependent variable so that a permanent effect will be left or to modify customary practices to yield a product.

In one rather unusual example, Dahlquist and Gil (1986) designed a multicomponent intervention to increase flossing by 7- to 11-year-old children. Their permanent product measure was the "used floss," which was examined (presumably using latex gloves) to determine if it was "flattened, shredded, and discolored" (p. 257). In a more standard application, Noell et al. (2000) used student-produced workbook pages that could be scored at a later time to show the effects of a teacher-implemented peer tutoring program. In almost all cases, the permanent product measure is not the only measure. It is common to take two or three other forms of data to confirm that the product was produced by the participants being studied. In the flossing study, for example, Dahlquist and Gil (1986) also completed regular plaque assessments. They used a standard Personal Hygiene Performance Index and had the children keep simultaneous self-monitoring charts of flossing.

In some projects involving the manipulation of materials, such as blocks or paints with preschool children, the "product" is either torn down or sent home with the participant at the end of the day. Because the definition of the artistic or creative behavior involved may be quite complex, it is desirable to preserve the product for later reexamination in light of unexpected behavior changes. Thus, the use of a photograph becomes a method of preserving the product. Digital cameras are preferred because you can examine the photo instantly to determine if it is adequate before disassembling the project.

A large proportion of the behavior analyst's target behaviors involve complex movements or interactions between persons. Such dependent variables almost always require the use of observers to make a "track" of the performance. The possibility of recording the behavior using either audio or video recording devices for later review should not be overlooked.

Ellingson et al. (2000) videotaped in their homes two "typically developing" children aged 7 and 10 who engaged in chronic finger sucking. These 10- and 20-minute segments were then scored later using a "real-time" recording method (Miltenberger, Rapp, & Long, 1999). It would have been difficult to take live data under these circumstances without disturbing the household.

There is another good reason to make video recordings. The participant may begin to engage in a substantially different behavior that was not included in your original observation code late in baseline or during a treatment condition. By having this permanent record of early sessions, you have the flexibility to go back and rescore the early sessions to make the necessary adjustments.

Automated Data Collection

Perhaps the next most solid and reliable type of data collection is direct measurement by a machine, computer, or instrument. Historically, all of the behavior of interest to the animal operant conditioner was measured by microswitch operations. Such devices still provide many advantages over the use of observers. For this reason, they are highly desirable as tools for the behavioral researcher. The key problem, of course, is to find some characteristic of a behavior that lends itself to automated measurement. At the same time, the behavior must have face validity. In addition, as pointed out by Azrin, Rubin, O'Brien, Ayllon, and Roll (1968), the device used must be designed in such a way that *all* instances of the target behavior are recorded. There should be no false negatives, and no instances of nontarget behavior (false positives) should be recorded.

One exciting new example of this type of methodology is the "smart car" (Boyce & Geller, 2001). The "smart car" was a 1995 Oldsmobile Aurora outfitted with four hidden cameras the size of a pinhead. Sensors transmitted data about steering wheel position, brake position, and acceleration readings in the lateral and longitudinal planes to an in-vehicle data collection computer. The computer provided real-time measures of driving behavior. Of course, all of the input in a system such as this has to be integrated to make sense of the data, and this is done with trained observers.

Azrin and his colleagues were the researchers most involved in the early years in the development of mechanical measurement of behavior. They devised apparatuses for measuring slouching (Azrin et al., 1968; O'Brien & Azrin, 1970), smoking (Azrin & Powell, 1968; Powell & Azrin, 1968), and toilet training (Azrin, Bugle, & O'Brien, 1971; Azrin & Foxx, 1971). Other researchers have used devices in sheltered workshops to automatically record work completed (Schroeder, 1972; Tate, 1968).

Finally, in classrooms where noise level can be a considerable problem, the use of a decibel meter has been shown to be efficient, accurate, and reliable (Jackson & Wallace, 1974; Schmidt & Ulrich, 1969; Wilson & Hopkins, 1973). A device that not only measures noise level but also delivers reinforcers for extended periods of quiet behavior has also been reported (Strang & George, 1975). In a fairly recent study, France and Hudson (1990) used a voice-activated relay and a microphone calibrated at 80 decibels to record incidents of waking up during the night.

Although the advantages of an apparatus or computer definition of behavior are obvious, some disadvantages must be recognized. First, many complicated behaviors (e.g., social interaction) simply are not suited to automated definitions; the topography is often complex, and only a trained observer can determine if all of the criteria for a response have been met. Second, in a case where a computer or other device is used, it may be possible for the clever participant to circumvent the device in some way.

In actual practice, the vast majority of behavior analysis studies deal with complex behavior necessitating the use of observers. It is to this topic that we now turn.

Direct Observation

The use of specially trained persons to observe and record the behavior of target participants clearly predates their use in behavioral analysis research; it is not our purpose to review the history of such procedures here. Rather, the goal is to describe and illustrate the various strategies for employing observers under a variety of circumstances.

The beginning researcher will have to determine what type of equipment to use in data collection. The simplest, cheapest, and most readily available involves nothing more than a recording sheet, a timer (watch,

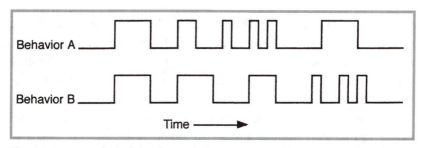

Figure 2.5-1. Hypothetical data for two behaviors generated by an observer operating a two-channel event recorder. The event record displays both frequency and duration of behaviors recorded.

stopwatch, or audible signal from a recorder), and a pen. One step up is a low-tech method that produces "real-time" data (Miltenberger et al., 1999). It involves videotaping the participant and then later using special data sheets and setting the VCR timer to zero at the start of the session. A fairly recent and possibly pricier option is the use of hand-held computers for data collection (Kahng & Iwata, 1998). These computerized data collection systems range in cost from "free" to nearly $5,000. The more sophisticated ones will allow you to record up to 999 different responses and to collect frequency, duration, interval, time sample, latency, and interresponse time. Computerized data collection systems can also be used for calculating various forms of interobserver agreement and can produce a graph of observational data (Kahng & Iwata, 1998). Before investing in one of these computerized systems, however, you should understand the basics of data collection itself.

Event Recording

Event recording originally involved the deflection of a pen, activated by an observer, on a roll of paper moving at a constant speed. When a pushbutton was held down and then released, a record was made of the onset, duration, and termination of the response being measured. A record like that shown in Figure 2.5-1 was generated.

One advantage of this type of recording was that both frequency and duration of responses could be graphically represented. Retrieving *frequency data* from an event record involved counting the number of pen deflections (regardless of duration). Deriving a *duration* involved using a ruler and summing the distance of each deflection. The figure obtained was then compared with the rate of movement of the paper to yield a total duration measure for all responses per session. This was a cumbersome and inexact exercise at best.

This figure was then compared with the rate of movement of the paper to yield a total duration measure for all responses per session.

Sometimes a record may show similar responses with differing durations. This raises a question about what exactly is being measured, and perhaps missed, as the next section, on frequency counts, will explore further.

Frequency Count

The simplest and most straightforward use of observers occurs when the unit of behavior under study has been defined so that a simple tally is made each time the behavior occurs. As shown in Figure 2.5-2, a frequency count eliminates the duration dimension of behavior and is appropriate where the responses are fairly uniform in duration.

The least expensive way to record frequency is with a hand counter (office supply) or wrist counter (found in golf shops). If more than one participant or behavior is involved, then a counter with multiple channels is required. It is always desirable to collect data in a way that allows for as fine-grained an analysis as possible. For example, if you are counting the number of responses in a 45-minute period, it may be advisable to keep track of the data in 3- or 5-minute blocks. Not only will you be able to de-

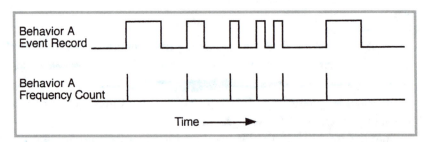

Figure 2.5-2. Hypothetical data for two behaviors generated by an observer operating a two-channel event recorder. The event record (upper) displays both frequency and duration of behaviors recorded; the lower record shows only frequency.

Date: 9/15/99   Start: 3:00   End: 3:05   P: Mike

	1	2	3	4	5	6	7	8	9	10	Total
Min 1 Aggression				X		X					2
Manding	X		X							X	3
Min 2 Aggression		X									1
Manding				X		X					2

Figure 2.5-3. Portion of a standard observation form for recording a frequency count for two behaviors in 6-second intervals
NOTE: A behavior-analytic term for asking for things (demanding/commanding)

termine any changes in rate within a session, but you will also have multiple opportunities for reliability checks with an independent observer. If you use 5-minute intervals, for example, you will be able to check observer agreement nine times during the 45-minute period rather than simply once for the entire 45-minute interval.

The task of observing and recording human behavior is such that more than one behavior can usually be measured at once. It is not uncommon for an observer to be able to score up to six categories of behavior simultaneously and reliably as long as the rate of occurrence is not exceptionally high.

With multiple behaviors to be counted, it is a good idea to have a standard data sheet prepared and supplied to your observers at the beginning of each session. Your score sheet should be adapted to your own needs, but an example of a standard form may help you in designing your own. Be sure to allow plenty of room for the tallies in each box. As shown in the example in Figure 2.5-3 (after Richman, Wacker, & Winborn, 2001), there are two categories of behavior, and frequency is scored in 6-second intervals.

Duration

If the goal of your research is to modify the duration of a given response, then you will have to follow a different measurement strategy to collect the data. The true measurement of duration requires that a timing instrument (e.g., stopwatch) be turned on and off congruently with the occurrence and nonoccurrence of the behavior. This is probably more easily done with a computerized system. DeLeon et al. (1999), for example, used duration as a very sensitive measure of behavior that enabled them to determine preference where standard approach-based preference assessments were ambiguous. In their study, they dedicated one observer to focusing exclusively on the duration of engagement and were able to show 88.7% reliability using a ±1-second agreement standard. One way to evaluate the *quality* of interactions is through a measure of their durations. Kamps et al. (1992), for example, employed duration as one measure of social interaction for students with autism, using an NEC 8300 laptop computer that took 5-minute samples of the three students randomly. France and Hudson (1990) used duration as a primary measure of waking up at night in a study to reduce and manage infant sleep disturbance. In this case, the primary data were collected by parents on a sleep record sheet and were later verified in daily telephone checks and voice-activated relay.

If the percentage of time that a behavior occurs (rather than actual duration itself) is the dependent variable of interest, then this may be more easily derived from an *interval* recording observation system.

Interval

The use of time intervals in recording behavior is probably the most frequently employed measurement system. This procedure involves taking some standard experimental session (e.g., 30 to 45 minutes) and dividing it into short intervals (e.g., 5 to 20 seconds). Each short interval is then used to record the occurrence of the behavior. The use of a time interval recording system depends upon some definition of when a response will be scored as occurring. A decision as to whether the entire interval is to be observed (continuous observation) or only some part of it (momentary or time-sampling observation) must also be made. There are many variations in the use of interval recording, and some confusion surrounds the process. Research has shown that different methods of recording the *same* behavior can produce different outcomes (Powell, Martindale, & Kulp, 1975).

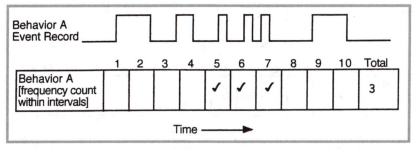

Figure 2.5-4. Continuous interval observation, with a tally made of the frequency of the behavior per 6-second interval. A comparison with an event record of the same behavior is also shown.

Continuous Observation With Interval Recording. In continuous observation, the observer is instructed to observe the behavior for the *full length of the interval*. For example, a 6-second interval could be used to record some feature of the behavior either *during* or *at the end* of the interval.

Three continuous observation methods are used. The first of these is *frequency count*. With this method, one records the frequency of the behavior in *each* interval. For example, a tally may be made (per 10- or 20-second block) each time a child looks up from his or her schoolwork. Figure 2.5-4 shows how an observation sheet for this might look. Obviously, the behavior in question must be of short duration (note that three responses that are longer than the intervals are not counted in this example). Also, it cannot occur too rapidly, or the observer will not be able to keep an accurate count. It can be difficult to obtain high reliability with this type of system.

The second method is *whole-interval response.* In this more frequently used system, someone observes the whole interval and makes *one* tally mark if the behavior occurs *during the whole interval*. Figure 2.5-5 shows a sample of this method. In this system, if the behavior deviates from the definition even once during the interval, no tally is made; thus, this method is inclined to produce a conservative estimate of the actual amount of time that a behavior occurs. This may be desirable in some instances but may produce very unrepresentative data in other cases.

A third method of continuous observation using intervals is *partial-interval response.* In this system, the target response does not have to occur

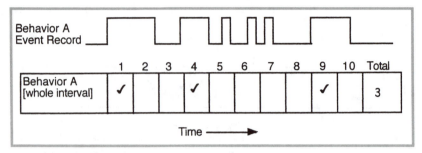

Figure 2.5-5. A sample observation form using a *whole-interval* response definition compared with an event record

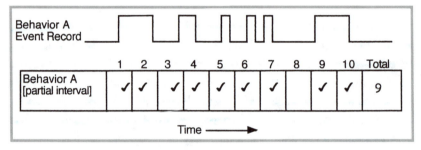

Figure 2.5-6. Example of whole-interval observation where the *first occurrence only* of the behavior is recorded in each interval

for the full length of the interval in order to be scored. There are two major variations on this method.

In one of these, a very common strategy, the observer watches for the full interval but simply scores the *first occurrence* of the target behavior. Thus, as shown in Figure 2.5-6, *one* tally is marked regardless of whether the behavior occurs once only briefly or whether it happens several times. Such a system is employed when the duration or frequency of behavior is of little consequence. This method is typically used with rapidly occurring (i.e., short-duration) responses. One might use this method to score whether an autistic child interacted with another student or glanced up from schoolwork. This measure can obviously yield unrepresentative data if the target response regularly occurs several times per interval; one improvement would naturally be to shorten the interval from, for example, 20 seconds to 6 seconds so that it would be rare for more than one response to occur per 6-second interval. When the data from this system are summarized, they will typically be presented as the *percentage of intervals during which at least one response occurred*. If you had 50 out of 100 such intervals scored, it would be erroneous to report either that the behavior occurred 50% of the time or that it occurred 50 times.

The other partial-interval response method involves a definition of the behavior that specifies a partial *minimal duration*. That is, it specifies that *the behavior must occur for some proportion of the interval* (see Figure 2.5-7). If you are using 10-second intervals, for instance, your definition of behavior may specify that "the response must occur for at least 5 seconds in order for an interval to be scored." To obtain the data, you may instruct observers to "judge whether the behavior occurred at least half of the interval" (though it may be difficult to obtain reliability on this) or ask them to turn a stopwatch on and off to keep a duration measure. Either system is difficult for observers because they must keep track of two different short time periods as well as watching for the response and scoring it on the observation sheet. A much simpler alternative, in fact, is just to shorten the interval (in this case, to 5 seconds) and require a full-interval response before a tally is made.

Momentary Observation (Time Sampling). Having observers continuously watch a participant for some length of time (e.g., 30 to 45 minutes) may not be feasible under many circumstances, and gathering data on large numbers of people over an extended period of time is virtually impossible. However, it may be practicable to occasionally check on the participants to

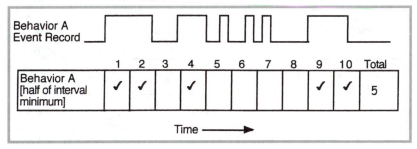

Figure 2.5-7. Example of whole-interval observation where the response must occur for part of the interval (in this case, half of the interval) in order to be scored

see if the behavior is occurring or not. Such a system involves the momentary observation of behavior and is usually referred to as time sampling. Three variables in time sampling must be specified: (a) how often a sample is taken, (b) the scheduling of the samples (i.e., either fixed or random), and (c) the length of the sample (i.e., a "moment" or a few seconds). A study of quality of care in nursing homes (Shore, Lerman, Smith, Iwata, & DeLeon, 1995) provided an excellent demonstration of the value of time sampling. It used a "semirandom" schedule of observations over a 13-hour period each day for 5 weeks. Observers proceeded to each predesignated area and made their recordings at the "moment" of observation. Shore et al. used this method to great advantage to record the behavior of staff, the condition of the nursing home, and resident condition as well as resident activity.

An example of time sampling is shown in Figure 2.5-8. This example makes clear that some data are lost by the "moment" requirement of time sampling. Behavior A occurred over most of the second 15-minute interval but stopped just prior to the sample being taken, so it is not recorded. Also, in the second hour, three responses occurred but were not recorded because they were not ongoing at the end of the intervals in which the observations were taken. Mudford, Beale, and Singh (1990) quantified this phenomenon and pointed out that behaviors of short duration are often missed in long-interval (e.g., once per hour) time sampling. At short intervals (15 seconds), momentary time sampling is quite accurate (Saudargas & Zanolli, 1990), but for longer intervals, expect increased error for low-frequency, low-duration behaviors.

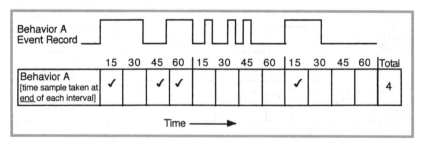

Figure 2.5-8. Example of the time-sampling method, with checks made at the end of each 15-minute interval, to determine occurrence versus nonoccurrence of behavior over a 3-hour time period

The general strategy in time sampling is to take as many samples as possible (the more the better). After it has been determined how much data is to be collected (e.g., data collection four times per hour or eight times per day), the researcher can develop the schedule for making the observations.

The decision about whether to conduct *fixed or random sampling* needs to be made in light of the relationship between the observation system and any contingencies that may be in place later on. If the observation system is uncorrelated with the contingencies (e.g., the observer takes the data on out-of-seat behavior, but the teacher makes his or her own independent judgments of the response), then a fixed time sample is acceptable. If, on the other hand, the data that are taken then *determine* whether a reinforcer or punisher is to be delivered, the observations must out of necessity be random. Otherwise, the participants would soon learn to be in their seat for a few seconds only once every 15 minutes.

Randomizing the sample can be achieved in a number of ways. The observer may set a timer according to a randomly generated set of numbers, throw a die, draw a number from a container, or use a random number generator. It is probably an error to leave the determination of when to observe up to the observer because bias may be introduced. If the instructions were simply to "observe four times per hour" with no further specification, the observer could easily bias a sample by taking all of the data in a short period (e.g., at the beginning or end of the session) on the basis of convenience.

The final decision that must be made in time sampling is *the length of the sample.* Because time sampling can be used only in determining whether a behavior was occurring or not occurring, the length of the observation, presumably, does not need to be very long. To employ a photographic metaphor, it should be a "snapshot." In many instances, there is no description given of the length of the sample (e.g., "The teacher 'glanced' at the students on the average of every 10 minutes"). The lack of specification can lead to potential biasing in the observation, however, particularly when the target behavior has a short duration. Consider the situation in which the observer seeks out the participant (e.g., on the playground) and observes whether he or she is engaging in cooperative play. The child may be engaging in solitary play, but if the observer continues watching for a few seconds, the hoped-for cooperation may occur and be recorded. Thus, it is advisable to keep the length of the sample to the absolute minimum and to have some standardization of the procedure (e.g., "Find the child and observe for no longer than 3 seconds; record whatever behavior was occurring at the end of that time"). Keeping the observers blind to the purpose of the study also helps to reduce bias.

Mixed Periodic and Continuous Observation.   In some studies, a data collection system is employed that involves occasionally observing the participant(s) and then having the observation run for several intervals. In classroom studies, it is fairly common to observe all the children in one row for, say, 30 seconds (i.e., five 6-second intervals) and then to move to the next row and repeat the observation. In this way, each row is "time-sampled" about every 3 or 4 minutes, but the observations are actually *continuous* because the students will be observed for the *full* 30-second duration.

Research on Observation Methods

Research on various observation systems has been carried out since the earliest days of behavioral research. In one study (Kubany & Sloggett, 1973), it was found that relatively infrequent time sampling in a classroom (on the average of every 4 minutes) yielded a very high reliability (89%) with a system that used a very frequent recording of behavior (time sample every 15 seconds). The authors suggested that many researchers have spent more time than was necessary to collect sufficient data to make reliable inferences. When data collection systems use a relatively simple categorization of behavior ("on task," "passive," or "disruptive"), the findings may not generalize to more complex behavior.

A second study involving four participants (Thomson, Holmberg, & Baer, 1974) compared various parameters of a mixed observation system with the continuous recording of behavior. Using a 64-minute session as their base, the researchers observed for 4-minute periods (i.e., continuously for twenty-four 10-second intervals). They then sequentially observed the next three participants for the same length of time. This resulted in a much smaller discrepancy than simply observing one of the four participants for the first quarter of the period (i.e., for 16 contiguous minutes). This sequential method was also superior to alternating between one teacher-child pair for the remainder of the period. Thus, continuous 4-minute observations (per participant) made every 16 minutes appear to produce a sufficient quantity of data to be reliable.

A study by Powell et al. (1975) compared a continuous measure of duration of in-seat behavior with three other methods of recording the same behavior: (a) momentary (i.e., time sampling), (b) whole-interval, and (c) partial-interval response methods. Using the continuous measure as the reference point, the researchers found that time sampling produced quite accurate agreement compared with the continuous method (i.e., within 8%). Overall, the whole-interval response definition did give a conservative measure of behavior, and the partial-interval definition gave increased scores. Both whole-interval and partial-interval methods were accurate compared to the continuous measure (i.e., within 5% or less) when the length of the observation interval was in the 10- to 20-second range. Error increased greatly with intervals of more than 40 seconds.

The target behavior that was measured in the study was of low frequency and long duration (i.e., the participant would leave her chair only a couple of times per 20-minute session), and it is not clear how these results would be affected by a high-frequency, short-duration behavior. Nonetheless, it appears that as long as the intervals are short (i.e., 10 to 20 seconds), either time sampling or whole- or partial-interval recording will be fairly accurate measures. When the definition of the target behavior indicates that it must occur for the whole interval to be marked, it is clear that a conservative estimate will be made; in contrast, the partial-interval method produces a more liberal and inflated (although still not inaccurate) score.

Finally, Harrop and Daniels (1986) attempted to compare the accuracy of momentary time sampling and partial-interval recording using a computer simulation of different lengths of emitted behaviors ranging from 1 to 20 seconds. For these parameters, they found that partial-interval recording is more sensitive than momentary time sampling in detecting relative changes in behavior. Partial-interval recording, of course, underestimates change with high-rate behaviors (because only one response per interval is recorded) and will always provide a more conservative estimate of behavior change for this reason. In choosing your observation system, you should be guided by two recommendations: (a) Try to use the same observation system that has been used in previous studies in your area of research, and (b) make sure that your data collection system accurately represents the phenomenon that you are trying to study.

Setting Up the Data Collection System

The mechanics of setting up your data collection system obviously depend upon many factors involving the nature of the setting (i.e., how often and under what circumstances you *can* collect the data), the target behavior(s), and your resources (e.g., funds for computer-based equipment or the availability of observers).

Frequent Collection of Data

As a general rule, you will want to set up your experiment in such a way that you can collect the most data in the shortest time possible. It is standard practice to establish some time period during the day that is designated as the *observation session*. It would be a rare study in which data were taken continuously throughout the day. To have validity for your audience as a meaningful sample of behavior, this session should be a fairly substantial period of time. In some settings, there are natural time periods (e.g., 45-minute class periods in public schools or the customary length of a meeting or dinner meal), but in others, you will have to establish these periods. Lengths of time from 30 minutes to 1 hour are fairly standard in behavior analysis. Anything shorter than 30 minutes will probably require some justification.

In an attempt to gather as much data as possible in as short a time as possible, several strategies may be employed. The first involves simply trying to *avoid* losing data. As described earlier, it is not uncommon to lose one day's data out of five; but the cautious experimenter will be able to improve on this average considerably. By constantly keeping in touch with the key person in the setting and anticipating problems, you may be able to prevent the loss.

Data loss can also occur if either participants or observers fail to show up or if there is an equipment malfunction. If you prompt participants and have backup observers, you may be able to save some data. Thoroughly checking and testing any equipment *every day*, with time allowed for replacement or repair should it prove faulty, is a habit that all aspiring researchers should adopt. Another way of putting this is that the experimenter should be vigilant in anticipating *any* potential losses of data and aggressive in taking steps to correct the situation. Just throwing your hands up and saying, "Well, we didn't get any data today because . . ." is frowned upon by major professors and colleagues as well.

Another strategy to stretch your time is to run your experiment more than just 5 days per week. Although it may be inconvenient to the experimenter or others (observers), it is possible in many settings to take data on weekends or other days off. By doing so, you may secure as much as 20% more data over the same calendar period. A similar "stretching" device is to have more than one session per day where possible. If the nature of your research is such that it is seen as highly desirable by the key people, they may be more than willing to have their subjects participate more often. Each session must have validity as to its being a substantial period of time. It is inappropriate simply to take a 30-minute session and divide it into two 15-minute sessions. If two sessions per day are possible, they need to be separated by sufficient time to allow for any experimental changes and perhaps provide a rest period for the participants. Having one in the morning and another in the late afternoon will usually give enough separation so that the sessions can be considered independent. An interesting finding from one study (Wallace & Iwata, 1999) with regard to functional assessment session length was that when 5-minute, 10-minute, and 15-minute sessions were compared, essentially no difference was seen between the 10- and 15-minute sessions, suggesting that assessment efficiency could be increased by using shorter sessions.

Choosing or Developing
Your Measurement Instrument

As a general rule, your measurement instrument should be one with which other researchers are familiar. If it is one that you have constructed yourself, it should have sufficient face validity to be persuasive. If at all possible, any apparatus used should be standardized and readily available to others. If you are using observers and do not have access to a computerized data collection system, you will have to develop an observation form, behavioral definitions, and a scoring system for the behaviors that are to be observed.

The Observation Form

Studies in applied behavior analysis are unique enough so that no standard observation forms are in existence, and it is common practice for experimenters to devise forms to suit their own purposes. Actual data sheets rarely appear in print. An exception is Shore et al.'s (1995) study of geriatric patients in a nursing home, which provides the form that the observers used. Another example of data sheets in print is Boyce and Geller's (2001) data sheets for measuring driving behavior.

Every form should have at least three sections. Figure 2.5-9 shows a sample form reduced in size with the major sections. Somewhere on the sheet (the top seems preferred), you will want a place to record certain descriptive information regarding each session. If there is more than one session per day or if sessions can be of different length, you will want to record the start and stop time of each one. If different participants are observed on different days, it will be important to have a place to preserve this information. Unusual events will happen from time to time that need to be noted for future reference, and these comments go at the bottom. Comments may be written on the back of the sheet, but unless there is at least a place on the front of the sheet to note that these observations have been made, they can easily be lost.

The heart of the form is in the observation boxes that are provided. The goal is to make it as easy and foolproof as possible for the observers to collect accurate data. By having a separate line of boxes for each behavior category, you can greatly reduce scoring errors; having the length of the interval printed above the boxes helps keep track of intervals.

Having a space between the rows of observation boxes helps prevent scoring a given behavior in a wrong row; a total-per-minute box is placed on the right side. The sample sheet in Figure 2.5-9 is set up for two behaviors and could easily be modified to accommodate four or five behaviors. With that many behaviors, it might be advisable to leave space on the top of the form for the definition of each behavior to be observed. This might reduce the number of minutes that could be recorded on each sheet, how-

Observation and Session Information

Observer: ____________ Location: ____________

Date: ________ Start: ______ End: ______ P: ____________

		1	2	3	4	5	6	7	8	9	10	Total
Min 1	Behavior 1											
	Behavior 2											
Min 2	Behavior 1											
	Behavior 2											
Min 3	Behavior 1											
	Behavior 2											
Min 4	Behavior 1											
	Behavior 2											
Min 5	Behavior 1											
	Behavior 2											
Min 6	Behavior 1											
	Behavior 2											
Min 7	Behavior 1											
	Behavior 2											
Min 8	Behavior 1											
	Behavior 2											
Min 9	Behavior 1											
	Behavior 2											
Min 10	Behavior 1											
	Behavior 2											

Data Collection Boxes

Miscellaneous Information

Reliability Observer: ____________

Comments: ____________

Figure 2.5-9. Sample observation form

ever. The sample sheet is made up for 10 minutes of 6-second observations, so you will need to use more than one sheet if your sessions are longer. Under normal circumstances, it is probably best to design the sheet so that all the data for one whole session can be put on one piece of paper. This can be accomplished by making the boxes smaller. Legal-size paper can be used if necessary.

The third major section is for recording the name of the reliability checker, if there is one, and any comments that the observer feels might help later to understand any unusual circumstances that might have occurred that day.

Reliability data will ordinarily be calculated on a separate sheet.

The Observation Protocol

Transforming ongoing behavior into quantifiable data requires an observation protocol that specifies (a) the behavioral definitions to be employed and (b) the actual method to be used by observers in recording the behavior.

Behavioral Definitions.   The extensiveness of detail of the definitions obviously depends upon the complexity of the behavior under study. Thus, some definitions may be relatively short, such as these from Harding et al. (2001): "*Mild behavior* was defined as tantrums and task refusal. *Severe behavior* was defined as any attempt to engage in self injury, aggression, or property destruction" (p. 62).

A good example of multiple-response definitions can be seen in Oliver, Oxener, Hearn, and Hall's (2001) study on the effects of social proximity on aggressive behaviors (Table 2.5-1). An even more complex set of definitions is shown in Table 2.5-2. These were used in measuring the environment, resident condition, resident activity, and staff activity in the Shore et al. (1995) study in a nursing home.

In some research, you will find it appropriate to use a standard code for the behavior under study. Kamps et al. (1992) used the "Social Interaction Code" developed by previous researchers (Niemeyer & McEvoy, 1989). McKenzie et al. (1991) used a comprehensive direct observation system known as BEACHES (Behaviors of Eating and Activity for Children's Health Evaluation System) in conjunction with a laptop computer to study children's dietary and physical activity.

Two criteria for acceptable definitions must be kept in mind. First, the description *must* have face validity and be congruent with the label used. If your label is "problem solving," for example, but the task really involves putting washers on bolts, then you can expect criticism from reviewers. If participants are taught "public speaking," they should engage in the behavior in front of a legitimate audience, not merely three or four people pulled

Table 2.5-1   Example of Multiple Definitions

Topography	Definitions
Hair flicking	Movement of the head from side to side so as to direct hair into the therapist's face
Biting	Actual or attempted closure of upper and lower teeth on any part of the therapist's body
Kicking	Actual or attempted forceful contact of the foot against the therapist's body
Scratching	Actual or attempted contact with the fingernails against the therapist's skin
Vocalizations	Swearing or forceful verbal directions toward the therapist
Inappropriate touching	Actual or attempted contact with the therapist's breasts or genital area
Pushing	Forceful movement of the therapist using the hands or shoulders
Hitting	Actual or attempted forceful contact of the hands against the therapist's body
Spitting	Actual or attempted expulsion of saliva in the direction of the therapist
Grabbing	Actual or attempted grasping of the hands on the upper part of the therapist's clothing
Hair pulling	Closure of fingers on the therapist's hair with a tugging motion

SOURCE: From "Effects of Social Proximity on Multiple Aggressive Behaviors," by C. Oliver, G. Oxener, M. Hearn, and S. Hall, 2001, *Journal of Applied Behavior Analysis, 34,* pp. 85-88. Copyright 2001 by the Society for the Experimental Analysis of Behavior. Reprinted with permission.

in from a hallway. Second, an acceptable definition of behavior is defined in part by whether two independent observers can agree that the behavior occurred. Thus, to be acceptable, a definition *must* be reliable. This will be covered in more detail later in this step.

Recording Method.   The second part of the observation code consists of instructions to observers on how to actually score a behavior. It is at this point that one of the previously described observation systems must be specified. That is, you must instruct the observer to count each response

---

Table 2.5-2   Example of Extensive Definitions

Environment

a. Cleanliness: Score (–) if presence of urine or feces, three or more items of trash, food, or containers on the floor or furniture, unstored linen or clothing. Score (+) otherwise.

b. Safety: Score (–) if broken furniture, toxins (including unattended medication carts), glass, or other dangerous items within reach; presence of structural hazards. Score (+) otherwise.

c. Supplies and materials: Score (+) if materials relevant to ongoing activities are available. Score (–) otherwise.

d. Supervision: Score (+) if at least one staff member is present. Score (–) otherwise.

Resident condition (indicate number present and number meeting the following criteria)

a. Grooming: Resident's clothing is untorn, and body and hair are free from visible dirt, food particles, or other soil.

b. Clothing: Resident is wearing shirt and pants (or dress) that are properly zipped, buttoned, or otherwise closed, and shoes (if outside bedroom)

c. Free from restraint: Resident is not wearing restraints or protective equipment (exclude geri-chairs and seat belts in wheelchairs)

d. Free from injury: Resident does not have a visible current injury (open wound or scab, bruise, bandage, cast, etc.)

(frequency), glance at the participant at the end of the interval (time sampling), observe the whole interval and score the first occurrence only, or use some other such method. The recording method will also ordinarily describe the place that the observer is to sit or stand ("Go to the back of the classroom and take a seat behind the last row of children") and whether there are any other conventions to follow ("Observers are not to talk to participants. If you are asked what you are doing, simply tell them you are working and are busy and cannot talk to them now").

In addition, there may be rules for making certain decisions regarding the use of the definitions: For example, "If two different responses occur in the same interval, score the first one only." Finally, the ordinary procedural

**Resident activity (indicate number present
and number engaged in the following)**

a. Appropriate social: Resident is interactive with staff or another resident. Also indicate which of the following behaviors have occurred:

  1. Conversation: Resident is interacting with staff
  2. Receiving instructions or care: Resident is receiving assistance or instruction from another
  3. Sharing materials: Resident is engaged in a game with another or is receiving materials

b. Appropriate nonsocial: Resident is exhibiting appropriate behavior but not interacting with another. If resident is moving wheelchair or walking, mark "A" for ambulation. Also indicate which of the following behaviors occurred:

  1. Self-care: Resident is dressing, combing hair, or engaged in other self-care activity
  2. Interact with leisure materials: Resident is engaged in solitary activity (e.g., reading, sewing)
  3. Attend to TV: Resident's eyes are oriented toward the TV while the TV is on
  4. Eating: Resident is placing food or drink in mouth, chewing, or manipulating utensils in the presence of food

c. Inappropriate: Resident is engaged in one of the following behaviors (indicate which one):

  1. Self-injury: Resident is engaged in self-directed behavior that produces physical harm

SOURCE: From "Direct Assessment of Quality of Care in a Geriatric Nursing Home," by B. Shore, D. Lerman, R. Smith, B. Iwata, and I. DeLeon, 1995, *Journal of Applied Behavior Analysis, 28,* pp. 435-448. Copyright 1995 by the Society for the Experimental Analysis of Behavior. Reprinted with permission.

steps may be specified. For example, if more than one participant is being observed, observations can be on an alternating system (e.g., "Observe the student sitting in Seat 1 for 30 seconds, then move to Seat 2, Seat 3, and so on, through all 10 seats. If any seat is unoccupied, go immediately to the next occupied seat in the correct order"). Typically, these instructions will be attached to the definitions and the observation form and will be used extensively while the observers are being trained.

Once you have made a preliminary determination of how your observation system will work, try it out yourself. That is, before you attempt to train observers on the definition and recording method, go to the setting and determine if it is feasible to carry out the system the way you describe.

Often, you will quickly discover that adjustments have to be made. You should continue to note any problems that will require explanations to your observers. Only when you have made all modifications in the definitions and recording method should you attempt to train your observers.

Using Observers

The use of observers in behavioral research can prove to be anxiety producing if the whole endeavor is not approached cautiously. One of the first problems to be dealt with involves the selection of those persons who will serve as observers. One common source of observers is the college or university. Undergraduate students can often earn academic credit for participating as research assistants in a project.

Selection

Once you have an approximate idea of how many observers you will require and how many you can effectively supervise, you can begin the recruitment process. Basically, you will want people who are available at certain times, who can provide their own transportation, and who have some interest in the problem at hand. With announcements posted in classrooms or brief presentations in behavior analysis classes, you may locate more people (potential observers) than you need. You can then make your selection. You may want to determine how reliable and resourceful candidates are by asking them to attend a series of training sessions; ask them to be at a certain place at a set time with notebook paper, clipboard, black pen, and a watch with a sweep second hand. You will discover after a few meetings that some potential observers who initially profess great interest will always be late or will fail to show without warning. The ingenuity of the excuse should not be allowed to throw you off as to the actual reliability of the person. You will also hit upon a few "superobservers" who come early, with three or four pens and pencils, a clipboard with a stopwatch attached, and perhaps an observation sheet that "seemed to be an improvement over the one we used last night." Years of experience suggest that the latter type ultimately make much better observers. It is best not to try and rehabilitate the poorly prepared people just so they can help you out.

Training

The way in which observers are trained varies as much as the types of problems that are studied, and there are no established rules. Generally, one must have a series of meetings where *all* of the potential observers can meet at one time to learn and discuss the system. If you have access to a VCR, you may speed up the training process considerably by playing tapes showing the behavior to be observed and scored.

The first step is to tell them a little about the study they will be participating in and to give them a "pep talk" about how important it is to the participant, to you, and the to "welfare of humanity" that the study be carried out. Avoid any statements that would lead them to have any bias or that would affect their objectivity toward the behavior they are about to observe. "We want to evaluate the effects of various treatments on children's social interactions" is better than "I want to show that teacher attention is a more powerful reinforcer than . . ."

If your code includes several behaviors, you may want to start with one behavior and have observers observe the behavior for a minute or two. Then stop the tape and go over their scoring. It is a good idea to iron out differences in interpretation of the observation code by calling their attention to details of the code and by making additions to the code itself if necessary: "That's a good point, Bob, I hadn't considered the problem of the student who puts his head down while he has his hand up. Why don't we add an extra rule that says 'hand up' is scored as on task as long as . . . " The notion that some definitions are arbitrary is hard for some inexperienced observers to comprehend. "But he just looked up from his work for a second, I don't see why the whole interval is marked as off task." Your own personal experience in using the protocol will be invaluable at this point. If you have done a proper job of testing out the system, there should be very few changes. Be prepared to defend your scoring system and to make modifications as necessary (provided they are in keeping with experimental rigor) as you proceed.

Some simple observation codes can be taught in 3 to 4 hours of training over as many days. Other, more complex codes may require up to 10 hours of training. Be sure to keep track of your training time, as this will have to be reported in your Method section. As soon as the observers are ready to go to the setting to use their new skills, you should begin taking reliability measures with each of them. It is generally a good idea for the *experimenter* to complete at least two successful reliability checks with each observer. In addition, at this time you may designate someone to be a "primary observer" for certain categories of behavior or participants. For example, in a classroom-based study, you could have one person serve as the primary observer for the teacher and another for two or three students. If you were observing multiple categories of behavior, such as disruption, out-of-seat behavior, and on-task behavior, an observer could be assigned to each category. One of your observers could make several checks with each of the other observers as well. In the final analysis, to make sure that you go into the first real day of data collection with a thoroughly reliable system, you will want to have all observers functioning at the 90% or more level of reliability. For calculating reliability, you should use one of the more conservative methods (described later in this chapter) on at least four occasions.

Keeping Observers Happy

Observers are people too. They will have good days and bad, they can get tired or bored, and they can develop their own private definitions of behavior. When observers begin to drift away from your original definitions and seemingly start to respond to their own definitions, we call this observer "drift." To keep observers happy, it is a good idea to have excellent rapport and a good communication system with them. Try to get to know each observer personally. Use first names and have them call you by your first name. Ask for their comments and suggestions regularly. Give them articles to read that they may find of interest (but that do not give away the purpose of your study). You can also consider taking observers out for lunch. Of course, it is important to give liberal praise and approval on a *regular basis* for their participation. However, make sure in your attempts to be nice that you avoid reinforcing observers for turning in certain types of data. This could cause a bias in your study. Let observers know you are thoroughly appreciative of their assistance and that you know it sometimes gets boring. Bring up often the importance of the findings, and if you are a graduate student, have your major professor sit in on a meeting and praise their work. If you can be empathetic and let the observers know that you care about them, you usually will be able to keep morale high. For those who make a particular effort, you may want to tell them that they will get credit for their good work in the form of a footnote. Some observers would like to go on to graduate school, and your offer of a letter of reference may mean a lot to them. Managing the observation team to keep it functioning properly is a great deal of work, and numerous complications must be anticipated if the product (data collected) is to have reliability and validity.

Complications in the Use of Observers

Whenever observers are used to score behavior, certain questions seem naturally to crop up. Would two people, observing independently, agree on the score? Can observers become less accurate over time? Do observers influence the behavior of the participants they are observing? These and other questions will be discussed as we consider the methodological complications of using observers.

Conducting Interobserver Reliability Checks

The possibility that, even given a precise definition of behavior, an observer might not be scoring accurately was anticipated early in the development of the field. Some initial steps were taken to show that the observer and the observations system could be relied upon (Allen et al., 1964). Conceptually, the solution is straightforward: interobserver reliability checks. These involve having two people who are trained in the same way observe the same behavior simultaneously. These "reliability" observers use the same definitions and scoring system. The problem is much more complex than this, however, and a detailed explanation needs to be provided. Before discussing the research on problems of observer reliability, some summary recommendations will be made. These are based on current empirically based publication standards with the flagship journal, the *Journal of Applied Behavior Analysis*.

Frequency of Reliability Checks

Simply doing reliability checks among observers *prior* to the experiment to show that they agree is not an adequate test of the trustworthiness of the observation system, nor is taking only one or two checks during some portion of the study. As will be explained later, changes in the frequency of the target behavior can affect the reliability, and observers may "drift" in the use of the definitions over time. Standards for frequency of reliability in recently published articles show that the majority of authors are reporting that 30% and higher of opportunities (i.e., sessions, trials, problems, etc.) are being checked by an independent observer. In some instances, 100% reliability checks can be seen. To be safe, the 30% guideline should be followed at a minimum.

Recommended Reliability Procedures

There are a number of standard procedures for carrying out reliability checks. First, reliability observers should have the same vantage point for their observations as the primary observer. They should be roughly the same distance away and have approximately the same angle of vision of the target participant as the primary observer. The two observers must not be able to respond visually or auditorily to one another's scoring. This involves several correction factors. If observers are seated side by side, one may be able to tell when the other is making a mark. Thus, the observation code should require *a mark in every interval,* not just when a target behavior occurs. Some convention such as a plus (+) sign if the behavior occurs and a zero (0) if it does not occur is fairly standard. Some experimenters will use an observation sheet with preprinted symbols in the boxes; the observer then simply checks or circles the appropriate symbol in each box. If the observers are using counters instead of tally sheets, steps must be taken to ensure that one observer cannot *hear* the other's clicks; the same rule applies to the use of stopwatches in duration measures.

To ensure that both observers are using the *exact same interval* for scoring, special procedures are often instituted. If stopwatches are used, they must be synchronized prior to use to ensure that they are accurate. The best method is to start them and let them run for the length of the full session (e.g., 45 minutes) and then stop them and check the position on the second hand. If they are off more than a second or two, have the stopwatches adjusted. In practice, the primary observer will usually start both watches (one in each hand) and then give one watch to the second observer. In this way, the different reaction times of the observers are eliminated as a source of error. To ensure that the observers remain in synchrony, some signal at the beginning of each minute period may be used. The reliability checker may quietly whisper "Two" to designate the beginning of the first interval of observation of the second minute, for example. If the second observer finds herself out of synchrony, she is instructed to mark the spot and go immediately to the correct interval.

Another method to improve observer agreement is to have observers responding to the same cue. Thus, a large electric sweep-second or digital clock may be mounted on a wall in line of sight of both observers. Another system is more elaborate and involves the observers' getting their cues for observation from an audible signal. This may be either a "beeper" that puts out a signal, say, every 10 seconds, or a tape-recorded message that the observers receive through earphones. The latter system can greatly reduce scoring in the wrong interval by actually naming each interval as it is observed. Thus, the tape may indicate, "Minute one . . . second interval . . . third interval . . . fourth interval . . . minute two . . .," and so on. In some systems, the observer will watch for 10 seconds and then score for 5 seconds. A tape for this system may then indicate, "Observe one, . . . record one, . . . observe two, . . . record two . . .," and so on.

If possible, reliability checks should be supervised by the experimenter to ensure that the observers did not in fact communicate with one another. Because either observer could be influenced by the experimenter's expectations, by knowledge of the experimental conditions, or by the experimenter's presence, steps should be taken to prevent these sources of bias (Kent, Kanowitz, O'Leary, & Cheiken, 1977). In studies where primary observers may develop hypotheses about effects because they are aware of changes from condition to condition, an outside "naive" observer should be brought in. This person may be used only occasionally in the experiment so that he or she will be unaware that there are any changes in conditions and can be more easily shielded from expected outcomes. The same procedure can be used to correct for "consensual observer drift." The latter occurs when the primary observer and reliability checker both begin gradually deviating from the original definition in a systematic way as the study proceeds. When this occurs, reliability is high but the validity of the resulting data is questionable.

Once the reliability check has been completed, the sheet should be handed to the experimenter, who will then carry out the actual comparison of scores. This will prevent the observers from discussing differences they had in coding and agreeing upon their own possibly idiosyncratic conventions for defining a behavior. If you notice systematic differences in observer data, you should discuss it with observers separately. If a change in definition is made, it must be added to the written definition so that others can replicate the observation system.

If possible, reliability checks should be carried out with the observers unaware. If only one observer is used, this is almost impossible. If two are regularly used, then their observation sheet may be designed in such a way as to direct them to actually take data on the same person simultaneously during various portions of the sessions. These portions can then be compared to derive a reliability score.

Research on Factors Affecting Observer Reliability

Many of the recommendations made above are based upon research specifically aimed at studying the factors that can affect an observer's score. For the researcher interested in pursuing the topic further, each factor is briefly discussed.

Knowledge of the Reliability Check.   It appears that simply knowing when a reliability check is being made can influence the observer involved. Discrepancies ranging from 10% (O'Leary & Kent, 1973) to 25% (Kent et al., 1977; Romanczyk, Kent, Diament, & O'Leary, 1973) have been reported between observers when covert reliability assessments have been compared with overt assessments. O'Leary and Kent (1973) also reported that having the observer present can increase reliability by 10%. Surprisingly, they also reported that errors in calculating reliability scores are frequently made by observers and that this can increase their scores by up to 10% as well.

Observer "Drift."   That observers can gradually begin to modify the original code, although still remaining reliable among themselves, has been documented by Johnson and Bolstad (1973) and O'Leary and Kent (1973). The problem is probably a serious one, especially in studies that run for sev-

eral months and measure relatively small differences in behavior from condition to condition.

Observer Bias.   Having observers respond systematically to some variable
other than the behavior at hand is a ubiquitous and long-standing problem.
Rosenthal (1966) reported that observers can be biased not only in their
judgments of complex behavior but also in their scoring of events as objective as the number of right and left turns in a runway maze. The extreme
case where observers actually fake the data is rare, but the results can be
devastating (Azrin, Holz, Ulrich, & Goldiamond, 1961). In a systematic
study of the effects of instructions and feedback to observers, O'Leary,
Kent, and Kanowitz (1975) found that these two scores of bias together
could result in 6% to 34% differences in observer ratings.

Observer Influence.   The possibility that the presence of an observer can
affect the normal performance of the participants must always be of concern to the experimenter. You will probably need to take steps to make your
observers as inconspicuous as possible.

Calculating Interobserver Reliability

   The purpose of the reliability check is to provide you with some measure
of the extent of the agreement of two persons independently observing under the same conditions. By frequently demonstrating that the observer
and the observation system (behavioral definitions, observation code, and
data collection method) are dependable, you assure your audience that any
reported differences in behavior are not due to changing definitions, observer bias, or measurement error. High reliability is especially important if
the changes in behavior are relatively small (e.g., if your results showed a
difference of 15% between two treatments but your reliability was only
70%, then most of the effect might be accounted for by the inaccurate measurement system rather than the "treatments").
   The most common and currently accepted way of presenting reliability
data is in terms of a *percent agreement* (also known in some circles as "exact
agreement coefficients"): that is, a number that shows the percentage of instances in which two independent observers agreed. Methods of calculat-

ing reliability vary depending upon whether the data represent actual frequencies (also magnitude or duration) or result from some form of interval measurement. A second method of calculating reliability uses a correlation coefficient and will also be discussed.

Before calculating reliability, you must choose which categories of observation will be subjected to the analysis. You might have run a study, for example, in which "teacher approvals" was a target behavior and consisted of "verbal praise," "approval gestures" (e.g., a pat on the back), and "approval symbols" (e.g., happy faces drawn on the student's papers), each of which was scored individually. Does each behavior need to have a reliability check run on it? The answer depends upon what data are to be presented to the audience. If the three categories are to be collapsed and the graph will show only "teacher approvals," then the unit of analysis need only be this larger category. If, on the other hand, the individual components are to be presented, then each must be shown to have acceptable reliability.

Frequency, Magnitude, and Duration Measures

Whenever the dependent variable is measured in such a way as to yield a number that represents how *often,* in what *strength,* or for how *long* a behavior occurs, then a percentage of agreement may be calculated by using the following formula:

Percent Agreement = (Smaller Score/Larger Score) × 100%

The following are some examples:

$$32/35 = 91\%$$
$$71/73 = 97\%$$
$$214/297 = 72\%$$

In the case of frequency and duration measures, one must be cautious in the use made of the resulting percentage figure because even if the reliability is high, this does not necessarily mean that the two observers were observing the same behavior at the same time. Let's return to Example 1. Suppose that the two observers' data were actually collected in 5-minute

Minutes										
	5	10	15	20	25	30	35	40	45	Total
Observer A	6	10	8	7	0	0	2	2	2	35
Observer B	1	3	2	6	0	5	8	7	0	32

$$\frac{32}{35} = 91\% \text{ Agreement}$$

Figure 2.5-10. Total reliability issues

Minutes										
	5	10	15	20	25	30	35	40	45	Mean
Observer A	6	10	8	7	0	0	2	2	2	
Observer B	1	3	2	6	0	5	8	7	0	
Quotient	.17	.30	.25	.86	--	.00	.25	.29	.00	.26

Figure 2.5-11. Block-by-block reliability for the same data

intervals over the 45-minute period and that the distribution of their scores was shown in Figure 2.5-10.

By comparing the scores in each pair of boxes, you can see that it is possible to have a high agreement for the total number of responses (91%) even though the observers were obviously not responding to the same behaviors. One obvious and rather stringent correction is to calculate a block-by-block agreement percentage for each of the 5-minute intervals and then to average them (see Figure 2.5-11). (Note: Agreement that a behavior did *not* occur is not included in the calculation.)

Recommendations for Frequency Reliability

There are two primary recommendations for frequency reliability. First, where possible, the collection of frequency data should be made in some way so as to allow for the comparison of smaller samples. Percent agreement on these samples should then be used as a more rigorous test of your observation system than simply the total frequency agreement. Second, if this is not possible, the credibility for the total frequency measure can be improved *only* by taking a large number of reliability checks (e.g., every other day). That is, one may argue that for any given comparison, two observers may have been observing completely different behaviors. However, this seems less and less probable the more comparisons that are made.

Interval Measures

When the data for an experiment are collected in small intervals and the results are presented as the percentage of intervals in which a behavior occurred, the calculation of reliability becomes much more complex than with frequency. Basically, the procedure involves comparing the two observers' records interval by interval and noting whether they agreed or disagreed. Thus, the standard formula is

$$\text{Interval Agreement} = (\text{Agreements/Disagreements}) \times 100\%$$

There are two major problems, however. The first has to do with the definition of *agreement* that is used, and the second involves the interaction between the rate of occurrence of the behavior (base rate) and random or "chance" agreement, which we will discuss shortly.

Consider the 2-minute record shown in Figure 2.5-12 for two observers using a 6-second-interval recording system. The continuous versus time-sampling or whole- versus partial-interval distinction is not critical at this point.

If you simply compared the total number of intervals checked by both observers—that is, *total frequency reliability*—you might think that they had reached perfect agreement:

$$\text{Percent Total Frequency} = (\text{Total of Observer With Low Score/Total of Observer With High Score}) \times 100$$

$$3/3 \times 100 = 100\% \text{ reliability}$$

Another way of determining reliability is to compare each interval to determine if they agree on the occurrences *and* nonoccurrences of their

	1	2	3	4	5	6	7	8	9	10	Total
Observer A	✓	0	0	0	✓	0	0	0	✓	0	3
Observer B	0	0	0	0	✓	0	0	0	✓	✓	3
Occurrence-Nonoccurrence	D	A	A	A	A	A	A	A	A	D	$\frac{8}{10}$
Occurrence Only	D				A				A	D	$\frac{2}{4}$
Nonoccurrence Only	D	A	A	A		A	A	A		D	$\frac{6}{8}$

Figure 2.5-12. Data for two observers using 6-second intervals over 2 minutes. A = agreement for each type of definition, and D = disagreement for each one. A check mark indicates that the observer scored the behavior as occurring; a zero (0) means that the behavior did not occur.

scoring—that is, *occurrence-nonoccurrence reliability*. As can be seen, they agreed on 10 of the 12 intervals, which would fit into the following formula:

$$(\text{Percent Occurrence/Nonoccurrence}) = [A^*/(A^* + D)] \times 100$$

where A* includes those intervals in which both observers said the behavior occurred or both said it did not occur.

$$8/10 \times 100 = 80\% \text{ reliability}$$

This figure of 80% is at the lower edge of the range of acceptability. However, it may be noted that many of the agreements involved intervals where it was agreed that the behavior did *not* occur. Such agreement could easily occur with a low-rate behavior if both observers were simply not paying attention.

A method of correcting for this is to compute two alternate reliability percentages (Bijou, Peterson, & Ault, 1968; Hawkins & Dotson, 1975). The first of these is used to determine the reliability only of the scoring of the *occurrence* of the behavior that was observed:

$$\text{Percent Occurrence} = [A_O/(A_O + D)] \times 100\%$$

where A_O includes *only* those intervals where both observers said a behavior *occurred*.

$$2/4 \times 100 = 50\% \text{ reliability}$$

In contrast to the previous method, occurrence reliability suggests that the reliability of measurement was extremely poor and would be unacceptable.

The next method of computing reliability takes into account the possibility that two observers could agree by chance alone if the base rate of the behavior was extremely high. In this case, you would want to know if the observers agreed when the behavior did *not* occur. This method is called *nonoccurrence* reliability.

$$\text{Percent Nonoccurrence} = [A_N/(A_N + D)] \times 100\%$$

where A_N includes *only* those intervals where both observers indicated that the behavior did *not* occur.

$$6/8 \times 100 = 75\% \text{ reliability}$$

It is clear that there is a relationship between the rate at which a response naturally occurs and the percent agreement that two observers might obtain by chance (Johnson & Bolstad, 1973). As the frequency increases, so does the number of agreements. There have been calls for researchers to provide "chance agreement" scores in their submitted manuscripts (Birkimer & Brown, 1979) or to adopt "exact probability" (Yelton, Wildman, & Erickson, 1977) as the standard for reliability. Neither of these suggestions has caught on, however, and it would seem rather that the vast majority of contemporary studies published today follow the original recommendation of Bijou et al. (1968), which was to report occurrence reliability for very low-rate behaviors and nonoccurrence reliability for high-rate behaviors. It should be noted that reviewers and editors seem to require very high reliabilities (i.e., 90% for both standard types) to convince them of the robustness of the observation system.

The social contribution of a science of behavior depends upon its ability to develop a technology that effectively solves pressing social problems.

This requires the researcher to focus upon the development of powerful procedures that produce durable effects. When the differences in observed behavior between experimental conditions are large and have little or no overlap with data points in contrasting conditions, the importance of great precision in observer measurement is less than when differences are small and inconsistent. However, during the analysis of variables, small or transient effects may be observed. When this occurs, the discussion of these effects will require that greater attention be paid to the precision of observer measurement. Here are a few suggestions that may assist you in dealing with observer and reliability-of-measurement issues.

1. Evaluation of observer performance should concentrate upon *observer stimulus control* as reflected in the percentage of interobserver agreement. Observer records should *not* be pooled in an effort to estimate the performance of some hypothetical population of observers. Instead, differences between the records of observers should be examined to determine what the contributing causes are.

2. Try to reduce the complexity of the observer's task to a minimum. Requiring the observer to code a large variety of behaviors or to record during very complex experimental situations may contribute to reduced accuracy.

3. Observers should be selected with extreme care. Ideally, they should have no vested interest in the results of an experiment. They should be differentially reinforced only on the basis of the extent of their accuracy as assessed by interobserver agreement measures.

4. Train your observers *extensively* prior to the commencement of your study. Inadequate training will slow you down later on and perhaps require you to abandon the project entirely.

5. Make sure your observers are not aware of changing experimental phases or the extent to which the data being gathered adhere to the expectations of the researcher. Obtaining and keeping observers naive is frequently an insurmountable problem, and the researcher may institute procedures to disguise or obscure cues that identify experimental conditions. Some researchers will rotate observers or

hold back observers for reliability checks so that they do not pick up cues from the changes in experimental conditions themselves. When standardized training conditions are employed, they should *not* prepare the observer to expect particular sequences of behavior. Training stimuli to which the observer is exposed should ideally involve the *random* presentation of behavioral episodes that might occur in any potential experimental situation. All of this would be a precaution against establishing a particular observer expectation.

6. The actual computation of data points used in analysis should *not* be left solely in the hands of the observers, nor should the calculation of interobserver percent agreements. Observers who are not ultimately responsible for the statements to be made about data may be inclined to carry to the researcher what he or she would be pleased to see. Mathematical computation, due to its potential for error, must therefore be closely supervised.

7. Ideally, an observer should be led to assume that the evaluation of the accuracy of his or her performance is occurring continuously. Because the presence of a second observer and the characteristics of this person have been shown to influence accuracy, stimuli that correlate with intermittent observer evaluation should be minimized.

8. As a precaution to reduce the possibility of observer "drift," observers should be periodically retrained using standardized stimuli (e.g., videotape). Possibly, new observers may be trained and employed for comparison at various points in the experiment. Do reliability checks in about 30% of the sessions or days of observations. Make sure that you collect reliability data in each and every condition.

9. You might try plotting the data of your primary and secondary observers on your daily working graphs. This will allow for a visual inspection of the variation between observers. It will also permit you to evaluate whether the choice of reliability evaluation sessions was appropriate if they were less frequent than every session.

10. With regard to the assessment of interval observation systems, the researcher should present a breakdown of the total interobserver agreement figure (i.e., percent occurrence agreement and percent

nonoccurrence agreement). Both occurrence and nonoccurrence agreement percentages may be important depending upon the focus of the study. Averaged interobserver comparison figures are *not* recommended. The presentation of individual comparison scores allows for inspection of variation throughout the experimental program.

The acceptability of single reliability formulas such as phi and kappa (see Harris & Lehey, 1978; Hartmann, 1977) is not apparent in recently published studies in applied behavior analysis. These methods as well as the probability formula recommended by Yelton et al. (1977) are more abstract numbers that are not equivalent to straightforward percent agreements. Interpretation of these numbers is not a simple task because they incorporate several variables beyond simple percent agreement, and some require considerable statistical sophistication. At this point, it is not recommended that these more abstract summary figures be presented *in lieu of* the well-known and rather "homely" occurrence and nonoccurrence percent agreement figures. If you present total, occurrence, and nonoccurrence percentages accompanied by a representation of obtained secondary observer measures, you can be reasonably confident that you have presented a fair picture of the quality of your data collection system. This is especially true if changes in data resulting from experimental manipulation are substantial and consistent. As we have noted previously, these functional relationships are of paramount importance in the development of a powerful technology of behavior.

In this step, we have reviewed a considerable number of issues and procedures related to the development of your data collection system. If you are working on a research project at this time, you will have determined the dimensions of behavior you are going to measure, matched your recording procedure to the behavior, and devised an observation code and data sheet. You may also have begun recruiting or selecting observers, although this should not be done prematurely. You will probably want to come back to Step 4 after you have completed Steps 5 and 6 to determine how you will calculate your interobserver reliabilities.

With most of the difficult decisions made, you have only to determine which research design is most appropriate to the behavior you are studying. This is the topic of the next step.

6

PILOT TEST YOUR
KEY VARIABLES

MAIN TOPICS

The Role and Importance of Pilot Testing
Pilot Testing Your Measurement System
Pilot Testing Your Independent Variables

LEARNING OBJECTIVES

In Step 6, we discuss the importance of pilot testing the variables that will play an important role in your study. Here you will learn how to test out your observation system and to check out your independent variables. After examining this step, you should be able to

- Discuss the importance of pilot testing in behavioral research.

- Describe how the pilot testing of a measurement system is carried out.

- Use the checklists to pilot test your measurement system and independent variables.

One feature of research that is rarely discussed in print is *pilot testing*. This is an informal, loosely structured set of procedures where the researcher explores, probes, and tests many of the parameters of the study being planned. Once a target behavior is selected, for example, it is necessary to work out the exact definitions that will be used to capture the data and the protocols to be used by observers. Having reviewed the literature, you may discover that standard definitions and observation protocols already exist, and you will begin by using those. You may discover, somewhat to your surprise, that the definitions and protocols that are in print do not actually work when you attempt to use them. Do not be discouraged; this could actually be the source of some research in and of itself.

Pilot Testing Your Measurement System

Let's assume for now that you are doing research on a behavior that hasn't been studied before. Pilot testing, in this case, usually starts with your informally and unobtrusively observing the participants and taking notes, but usually not data per se, on several occasions. At this point, you are trying to determine the approximate frequency, duration, and perhaps intensity of the behavior, optimal times and locations for observations, and any barriers to reliable observation that must be overcome. Over the course of half a dozen such informal sessions, you will usually be able to determine unobtrusive places to locate the observers where they can view the participants, not be in the way, and not draw attention to themselves. In addition, the handwritten notes should gradually yield details for response definitions and promising observation methods (e.g., frequency, whole interval, partial interval). A first draft of a data sheet may also be developed in this time frame. Pilot testing continues as you train potential observers and have them try out the definitions, protocols, and data sheets. At this point, you will have committed to a specific type of measurement and a specific protocol. The protocol is a detailed set of instructions on how the observation is to be carried out. Your informal work during this pilot-testing phase will probably tell you whether you will have to change, for example, from 10-second to 6-second observation intervals or from 30-minute to 1-hour time sampling. You may have initially thought that you would be able to observe for 30 minutes at a time, but now you discover that something has come up and you will have to settle for 20-minute sessions. All of these decisions obviously have to come *before* the first real data point is collected because once you start the study, the data collection cannot change.

After another five or six practice sessions, you may be ready to do some reliability checking. This will initially be carried out between the researcher and one or two observers who have proven in the earlier pilot sessions to be alert, attentive, reliable, and highly motivated. Typically, initial reliability checks show problems with definitions and protocols. Don't get discouraged. It is at this point that you will make changes in how the behavior is defined and in the observation procedures themselves. For example, you may discover that more detail is needed in the definition than you first thought would be necessary. Or you may decide to add examples to the definition sheet to give added clarity.

One possible way to short-cut the time to develop your observational methodology is to videotape the participants. The tapes can then be played in the lab under controlled conditions. With the use of videotape, definitions and protocols can be worked out more quickly and with less effort. Basically, you will be pilot testing various behavior definitions to see if they can produce reliable agreements. If not, you can fairly quickly change the definitions or the data collection method and try again. Note that you will still have to determine if observers trained in the lab to high reliability will be able to generalize their accuracy to the setting itself. Experience has shown that there is usually a period of adaptation to the live environment. After all, there are many distractions in the live environment that your observers will not have to contend with in the lab.

Another possibility is to simply have all the data recorded on tape in the experimental setting and all data collected in the lab. That is, the only persons visiting the setting are you and your cameraperson. This experimentally desirable situation is sometimes difficult to accomplish because permission to video is not always obtainable. However, it is worth attempting to do this given the savings in wear and tear on your observers and the logistics of making trips to and from the setting. One final note: Videotaping of sessions brings with it the vagaries of equipment malfunctions, camera operator reliability, marking, storage, and retrieval of tapes.

Table 2.6-1 is a checklist of 10 steps for pilot testing your measurement system.

Table 2.6-1   Ten Steps for Pilot Testing Your Measurement System

1. Conduct informal observations/note taking.
2. Determine the approximate frequency, duration, or intensity of the behavior.
3. Select the pilot observers and identify barriers to reliable observation.
4. Identify location and details for observers.
5. Develop response definitions and observation methods.
6. Develop first draft of data sheet.
7. Train observers.
8. Try out data sheet and protocols.
9. Revise as needed.
10. Retest data collection with reliability and modify as needed.

Pilot Testing Your Independent Variable(s)

Being a successful researcher means knowing that your independent variables are likely to have a certain impact on your participants. In some cases, you have this confidence because you have seen the treatment in action informally or you have personal experience with it. However, it is still necessary to work out the details of exactly how the intervention will be deployed. Doing so in the middle of a study is not the right time. Training methods, for example, need to be pilot tested to see how long the training needs to go on, how intensive it needs to be, and how the participants react to it. Teaching the proper way to lift and move geriatric patients may need to involve not just modeling but also role playing, feedback, and practice. The training sessions may need to be stretched out over several days rather than presented in one session.

If cues or discriminative stimuli are used, you will have to determine their optimal placement for maximal effect. Signs used to prompt safe behavior, for example, may need to be moved from one location to another to determine proper positioning for optimal viewing. The size of the signs, the nature of the message, and the use of color all must be pilot tested to determine if they will attract attention.

Ordinarily, some data will be collected with pilot participants who are not a part of your soon-to-be-run study. These data can be somewhat informal but should give a reliable semblance of the way the study will be run when it is ready to begin. In some studies, if you cannot directly expose the pilot participants to the intervention, you may discover that you can obtain a good deal of insight into how they might react just by showing them samples.

In a recent study, we were concerned about how we might provide feedback to electricians and painters about their safe behaviors in climbing ladders and handling certain equipment (Barnette, 1999). Our pilot informants looked at various formats for graphs, discussed with us the pros and cons of getting feedback directly from their supervisor versus having it in graphic form, and so on. It was these extensive interviews that ultimately shaped our final decision on the safety feedback intervention.

In an after-school study, we were concerned with two problems: (a) how to get the teachers to produce lesson plans that were functional and interesting and (b) how to get them to actually implement the plans. Various options were presented to two teachers who were not going to be a part of the study but who worked in the after-school program. They helped us understand that these part-time teachers had never really been trained in writing lesson plans, did not have any resources for this, and would probably not respond to simple written materials. As a result, we developed a hands-on lesson plan workshop, trained the supervisor how to run it, and then took independent variable integrity measures to make sure all of the elements were covered. Having shown that teachers were trained to a certain criterion, we could then move on to the next phase. This phase was feedback on performance, where once again the pilot participants helped us design an effective system for our after-school teachers (Lucker, 1998).

Any and all procedures that you anticipate using should be pilot-tested to the point that you feel confident that they will work in the actual study. This includes, as previously mentioned, all observation procedures; all methods of training observers; all instructions to teachers, parents, assistant managers, or others who will be involved; and all interventions from prompts to feedback to reinforcers. Particularly with regard to consequences, make sure that you are using known, effective reinforcers. These should be discovered and refined prior to the onset of the study. Something as simple as a point system clearly needs to be thought through carefully. Will the system be tangible or symbolic? What exactly will you tell the participants about the points? If these are tangible (i.e., tokens), is there any way that they can be counterfeited? Can they be pilfered? Can they be bartered? How many points will you give? How often can they be exchanged? What will they be exchanged for? In many cases, you can take your cue as to the parameters of the treatment interventions from published studies. In other cases, you are on your own to develop effective protocols.

Whether you will need institutional review board (IRB) approval to do your pilot work is a gray area and depends upon local conventions; check with colleagues in your lab to make this determination. In most cases, it is understood that a certain amount of pilot testing is acceptable to work out the parameters of the study.

Table 2.6-2 is a checklist of 10 steps for pilot testing your independent variables.

Table 2.6-2   Ten Steps for Pilot Testing Your Independent Variable(s)

1. Select participants who will not be involved in the study.

2. Test all antecedent stimuli (cues, prompts, signs, instructions) to determine optimal parameters for effectiveness with these participants.

3. Test-run any training that will be conducted on pilot participants to determine optimal duration, acceptability, and effectiveness.

4. Revise and test again if not satisfactory.

5. Pilot test any feedback that will be used. This may range from interviews and focus groups to actual small-scale implementation.

6. Pilot test any consequences that you will be using. If you are using reinforcers, make sure you have done a reinforcer assessment.

7. Debrief pilot subjects to determine their subjective reaction to feedback and consequence manipulations.

8. Review your data on the effects of your intervention on your dependent variables to determine if the size of effect is sufficient.

9. If not, modify the independent variable and try again.

10. Check to make sure that the use of feedback and consequences in the environment is not disruptive and does not cause any form of inappropriate behavior (e.g., unnecessary competition among participants or bootlegging, theft, or forgery of reinforcers)

Some say that the pilot-testing phase is the most exciting part of doing any applied research. This is possibly where you will learn the most about your subject matter, under the least stressful conditions, with the greatest payoff. It is during this time that you will be able to mold and form your study to suit your objectives. In the pilot-testing phase, you will be able to determine if your plan is grandiose or manageable, whether your great new technique has promise, or whether it was just a fluke. Pilot testing should give you confidence that you know how to conduct your study so that there are no great disappointments and no surprises.

IDENTIFY THE APPROPRIATE RESEARCH DESIGN

MAIN TOPICS _____

The Purpose of Research Design—Demonstrating Experimental Control

A Review of Single-Subject Design Logic

The Role of Exploratory Designs

Using Powerful Reversal Designs

Applying Multiple Baseline Designs Where Appropriate

When to Use Multielement Designs

Using Changing-Criterion Designs

Considering the Limiting Conditions of Single-Subject Designs

When to Use Group Designs

LEARNING OBJECTIVES _____

In Step 7, we stress the importance of matching the experimental design to the problem you have chosen. Here you will review the exploratory de-

141

signs and fully explore the more powerful ones, including their limiting conditions. After studying this step, you should be able to

- Describe the purpose and logic of single-subject design.

- Explain the role of visual analysis in using single-subject designs.

- Distinguish between the weak or exploratory designs and the more powerful behavior-analytic research designs.

- Draw examples of reversal, multiple-baseline, multielement, and changing-criterion designs.

- Give examples of the combined use of several research designs and tell when they would be employed.

- Discuss the limiting conditions of behavior analysis research designs.

The Purpose of Research Design

A great many people, including artists, historians, economists, and sociologists, are interested in understanding behavior, which is to say that behavior analysts are not alone in our fascination with this elusive subject matter. However, the type of knowledge sought by the behaviorist *is* unique. The economist may be interested in the relationship between income and lifestyle, the anthropologist may seek out the correlation between family membership and social status, the novelist may be seeking some driving force behind a particularly bizarre behavior. The *understanding* that results from such an analysis may be highly provocative or entertaining, but at the same time, it is simply static, descriptive, and correlational. The behavior analyst, on the other hand, is interested in understanding human behavior in the sense that we know what the demonstrated *cause-effect relationships* are between some environmental event and the resulting behavior. To *really* understand behavior is to be able to say that A *causes* B, not merely that B *follows* A. This type of knowledge can result only from the *experimental manipulation* of events, for only through this mechanism can one rule out all other alternative explanations.

The behavior analyst is not interested in studying just any behavior or manipulating random variables for curiosity's sake alone. Rather, the whole purpose is to develop and manipulate those variables that will result in therapeutic change for the participant and, in the process, to demonstrate that these variables, and not some outside variable, were the ones responsible for the behavior change (Campbell & Stanley, 1970).

The standard method for demonstrating experimental control in psychological research is, of course, the group statistical design in which participants are randomly assigned to groups and different groups receive different treatments. The data are then analyzed using statistical procedures to show that an effect of the size seen could occur *by chance* only some proportion of the time (e.g., 5 times out of 100, or $p < .05$, which is a commonly used level of significance test). Such research that involves the short-term study of many participants is clearly antithetical to the goals of a behavior analysis approach in which we wish to understand the behavior of individual participants. Indeed, the use of larger numbers of participants virtually wipes out any hope of this type of understanding because individual differences are obscured by the averaging process that is required by the statistical design (Sidman, 1960). Skinner's legacy (1969) to our field has been that "the data from an individual participant behaving under well-specified conditions should provide unequivocal evidence of an independent variable's effect and that such an effect should be visible to the naked eye" (quoted in Morgan & Morgan, 2001, p. 121; see also Burch, 2000).

The need for research designs by which to understand the behavior of single subjects has been largely met by the adaptation of existing designs (developed in animal operant conditioning) to applied problems. The goal of these designs is to demonstrate the *functional relationship* between an event and a target behavior. The term *functional* is used in a cause-effect sense and refers to an experimental arrangement where a contingency is "turned on and off" repeatedly. If the behavior occurs each time the contingency is "turned on" and ceases each time it is "turned off," then a functional relationship has been demonstrated. Operant conditioners cannot take credit for inventing this experimental control technique, as it was originally devised by Claude Bernard in his research in experimental physiology, circa 1850 (Olmsted & Olmsted, 1952).

Although this goal of unequivocal experimental control is desirable, it is not always easily achieved. But the relatively short history of the field suggests that such control is attainable if the necessary preparations and precautions are taken. Many of the factors that do allow for the systematic study of behavior have been described in Steps 1, 2, and 3. It now remains to find an experimental design that is most appropriate to the behavior that you are interested in studying. Before that discussion is presented, however, let us briefly review some of the nondefinitive, exploratory "designs." As we do so, it will become obvious that the demonstration of experimental control is most often shown through a *visual* presentation of the data in graphic form rather than through a statistical analysis.

Characteristics and Logic of Single-Subject Design Research

Single-subject/participant design research is distinctively different from group statistical hypothesis-testing designs found throughout the rest of psychology and is superior in many ways, particularly for those who are interested in evaluating the effects of therapeutic interventions with individuals (Morgan & Morgan, 2001).

Baseline Logic

The first feature that distinguishes behavioral research designs is the repeated measurement of the target behavior. We assume that there will be variability from session to session or day to day, and rather than trying to eliminate it statistically, we are interested in seeing what it looks like. We assume that without any intervention, the behavior will reach some steady state and that we will be able both to determine the bandwidth of the variability and to detect any trends in the data that will help us understand the need for interventions (see Figure 2.7-1, top). Behavior that is trending in the direction of a possible treatment effect presents a serious problem for the behavior analysis researcher. The only recourse when this happens is to have a longer baseline or to start over with a different definition of behavior or a different recording method. The goal of baseline logic is predictability; that is, at some point after 8 or 10 data points, you should be able to predict with some accuracy where the next data point will fall. In fact, this is a good exercise for budding researchers. In your study, using working graphs (i.e., rough graphs done on graph paper with penciled-in data

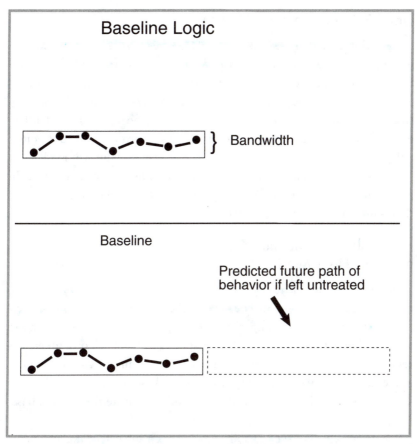

Figure 2.7-1. The graph at the top shows a baseline and the schematic representation of the bandwidth of the variability of the data. The graph at the bottom shows the predicted future path of the data if no changes are made in the environment.

points), put a small box showing where you think the next data point will be. Do this each day, and see if you get closer and closer to predicting the next day's data point. When you are predicting with great accuracy, you are following baseline logic and are ready to stop taking baseline data and to implement your first intervention. An extension of baseline logic is to assume that if no changes were made, the behavior would continue on indefinitely, as shown in Figure 2.7-1, bottom.

Graphic Representation of Data

Behavior analysts love looking at data and analyzing it closely. We like having continuous contact with the data on a daily or "real-time" basis. Showing the data to colleagues and getting their reactions as a study proceeds is one of the true joys of doing behavior analysis research. In the early stages of a study, you may find yourself graphing the data in several different ways to determine which makes the most sense to you and your potential "consumers." Your consumers will be colleagues who will read about your work in a journal article at some point in the not-too-distant future. In almost all cases, you will be graphing the data of individual subjects rather than summarized or aggregate data.

Each Subject/Participant Serves as His or Her Own Control

As discussed earlier, you may only have a few participants in your study, and for the most part you will be making each serve as his or her own control rather than making comparisons across participants. You will be more interested in determining how Betty responds to feedback or a token system than in comparing Betty with Patricia, for example. And to demonstrate experimental control, you may return to baseline, at which point you will be interested in seeing if Betty's new data replicate the original baseline.

We fully expect to see variability within each subject's data, and as behavior analysts, we are quite interested in the environmental or other factors that might produce it. We are not interested in "neutralizing" the variability through sophisticated statistical procedures. Variability is not a nuisance to be eliminated; rather, it is the heart of human behavior. Variability is highlighted in our graphic representations of real-time phenomena as it unfolds in each experiment.

Replication

Another hallmark of behavior analysis research is the emphasis on repeated demonstrations of the effects of an intervention with each participant. A "one-time" effect is not impressive to behavior analysts. We want to see robust treatments that can be counted on to produce a certain effect each time they are applied. And we would like to see this replicated with several subjects just to make sure that it is not some idiosyncratic effect for one person.

Visual Analysis of Data

The final and perhaps most signature and somewhat controversial feature of behavior analysis research is that decisions about changing conditions and conclusions about the findings are reached by visual analysis of the data. There has been much debate over this feature, but in the final analysis, the consensus of the field seems clear: Behavior analysts feel confident that they can adequately compare baselines with interventions (taking variability and trending into account) and determine which were effective and which were not. Because the interventions are replicated both within and across studies, it is not just a personal judgment call; the ultimate determination of validity is made by colleagues through the journal review process and through replication in other labs across the country. The determination of the applied worth of a study (effect size) is often determined not by some statistical measure but rather by whether the findings are adopted by users such as parents, teachers, or therapists. In applied settings, other factors such as cost-effectiveness, acceptability, and side effects also come into play. This will become very apparent as we begin looking at the research designs most often used in behavior analysis research.

Exploratory Methods/Weak "Designs"

There are many occasions when tight experimental control is not necessary or even possible for making a contribution in behavior analysis. The early stages of any field are marked by fascinating anecdotes, unusual case studies, or even systematic (but not experimental) observations. Even though they are later surpassed by more sophisticated methods, such case studies can make an important heuristic contribution to the field.

Case Studies

Some of the first applications of operant techniques took the form of case studies: descriptions (not necessarily quantitative) of methods used to change behavior. One of the earliest (Fuller, 1949) reported the use of a sugar-milk solution to reinforce arm raising in a profoundly mentally retarded person. Other cases typical of the time reported the use of gum to reinforce verbal behavior in psychotics (Issacs, Thomas, & Goldiamond, 1960) and the treatment of anorexia nervosa (Bachrach, Erwin, & Mohr, 1965). Ullmann and Krasner's book *Case Studies in Behavior Modification* (1965) has an impressive collection of these early studies. Applications and descriptions of this sort represent a source of stimulation for other researchers, but in and of themselves, case studies cannot be used as a basis for drawing conclusions about cause-effect relations. There are just too many potential confounding variables operating that could account for the effect. Examples of these potential confounding variables include other coincidental events, maturation, and possible observer bias.

B-Only (Treatment) and AB (Baseline-Treatment) "Designs"

One step closer to a definitive study is one in which some quantification of the dependent variable is carried out and changes in the behavior are plotted over time to show improvement. Because this type of study has only a treatment condition, it is referred to as a B-only design. The term *design* is used somewhat advisedly because no experimental control is actually shown. Williams's (1959) description of extinction as a treatment for eliminating bedtime crying is a good example of this approach. Figure 2.7-2 shows that during the first extinction period, crying dropped off rapidly after 45 minutes of crying the first night. Following the accidental reinforcement of crying by the aunt after the 10th session, the extinction process was repeated, yielding essentially the same results.

The AB design improves on the B-only design by providing a measure of the behavior prior to treatment. This added information can tell the reader whether the behavior seen during the baseline would *predict* the effect seen in the treatment condition. There are many variations of the AB design, and some are more persuasive than others. Consider the hypothetical data shown in Figure 2.7-3. As you can see, having only *one* data point for the baseline leaves some doubt as to the actual level of the behavior prior to the treatment. As shown in Figure 2.7-4, it is possible that if more baseline data

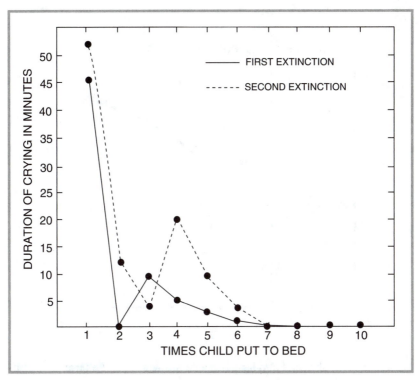

Figure 2.7-2. Length of crying in two extinction series as a function of successive occasions of being put to bed
SOURCE: From "The Elimination of Tantrum Behavior by Extinction Procedures," by C. Williams, 1959, *Journal of Abnormal and Social Psychology*, 59, 269. Copyright 1959 by the *Journal of Abnormal and Social Psychology*. Reprinted with permission.

had been collected, the behavior during "treatment" would be shown to be merely a continuation of a trend (although undetected) in baseline.

Another way that the AB design can be weakened is by a failure to allow the data to stabilize prior to the introduction of a treatment. As shown in Figure 2.7-5, the last few data points of the baseline condition are critical in determining the trend of the data.

Similarly, as shown in Figure 2.7-6, if there is too much variability in the baseline data (and if the baseline is not long enough to predict the level of the behavior if no change were introduced), it is difficult for a believable experimental effect to be shown. The dashed lines show possible trends in the baseline if more data points had been collected.

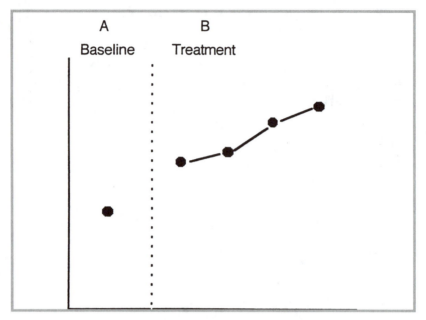

Figure 2.7-3. Hypothetical data for an AB design

Figure 2.7-7 shows that a long baseline alone does not guarantee a convincing demonstration of experimental control; if the effect of the treatment is slow in coming, then questions are raised as to whether it was in fact the treatment that was responsible for the change.

Thus, for an AB design to be convincing, it would appear that several conditions must be met: (a) the baseline must be fairly long, (b) the data must be quite stable, (c) the effect must be rapid, and (d) there must be little or no overlap between the baseline and treatment points. So if you had data like those shown in Figure 2.7-8, you might be tempted to give credit to the treatment for the change. However, even in this most persuasive visual effect, the question still remains, Was the treatment really responsible for the behavior change? In the case of a long-standing problem where a prebaseline measure would show it extending back for several months (e.g., self-injurious behavior), an explanation to this effect might add some believability. Nonetheless, if one is to rule out other coincidental variables, some demonstration of experimental control (e.g., a reversal or multiple baseline design) must be shown.

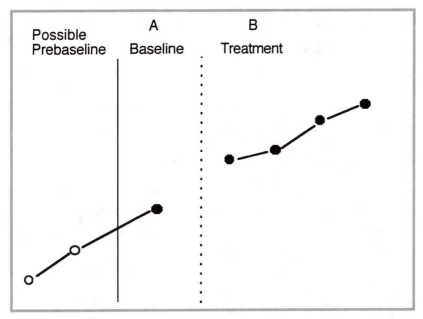

Figure 2.7-4. Hypothetical data for an AB design, with the added information provided by possible prebaseline data

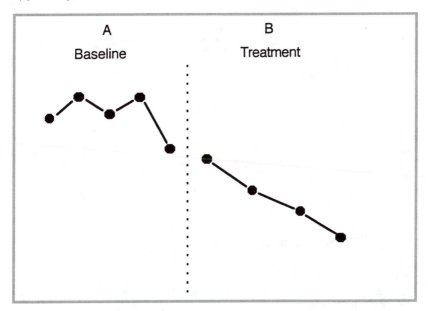

Figure 2.7-5. Hypothetical data for an AB design where trending occurs just prior to treatment onset

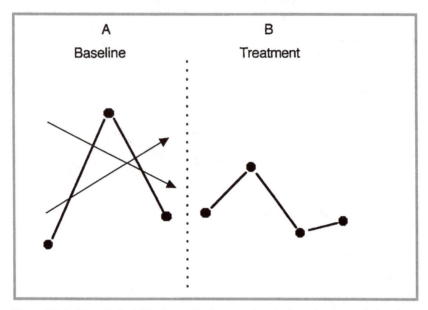

Figure 2.7-6. Hypothetical data for an AB design with only three data points in baseline. Dashed lines indicate possible trends in baseline.

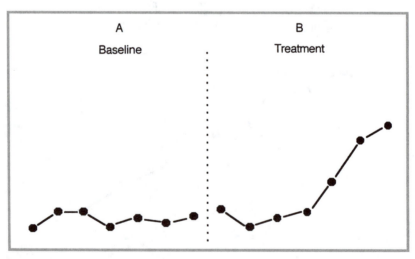

Figure 2.7-7. Hypothetical data for an AB design where the "effect" is delayed from the onset of the treatment

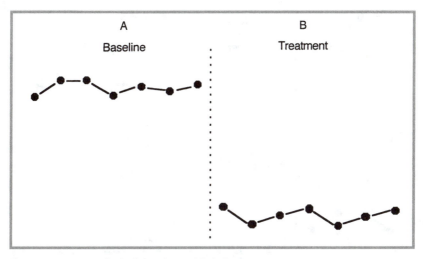

Figure 2.7-8. Hypothetical data for an AB design

ABC (Additive) Design

One variation on the AB is to add a second or third (or more) treatment to the sequence, as shown in Figure 2.7-9. But there are several problems with conducting a study in this way that prevent it from being a solid research design. First, in the AB part of the study, because there is no replication of the B condition, we cannot be certain that the change in B was due to that treatment or to some outside variable. The problem continues and is confounded with the addition of the C condition. With it, we cannot be sure whether, if C had followed A, the same effects would have been seen as shown in Figure 2.5-10. Is the change in C merely a slow-acting effect of B, or could B possibly have "sensitized" the participant so that C now has an effect?

The ABC design can obviously be extended (and has been in many published studies) to an ABCD, ABCDE, and so on. But each succeeding condition only adds confounding to an already weak design, so this method is categorized as an exploratory design. That is, it may be used in pilot work to discover a treatment that may then be used in a more definitive design later that employs the necessary controls.

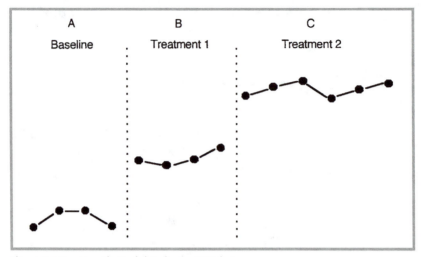

Figure 2.7-9. Hypothetical data for an ABC design

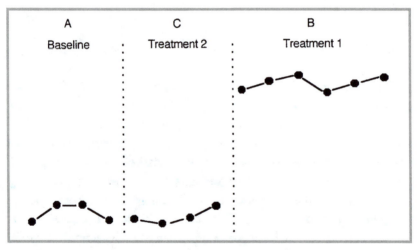

Figure 2.7-10. Hypothetical data showing possible effects if the C condition had come first (top) or if the B condition had simply been continued (bottom)

Behavioral Analysis Research Designs

Currently, a number of experimental designs are widely used in behavior analysis research to demonstrate the functional relationship between a behavior and a treatment or intervention. Although often called "single-subject" or "N = 1" designs, their usage is not restricted to single participants but can be applied equally effectively to groups (e.g., a classroom of subjects). Furthermore, there are circumstances when the more traditional group comparison (i.e., experimental and control group) designs may be useful in analyzing certain treatment effects. In all, there are five research designs that provide a wide range of possible choices to the experimenter. As will become clear, each has its own strengths and limitations, and the purpose of this presentation is to guide the researcher to select the design most appropriately suited to the behavior being studied or the question being asked. That is, the researcher should start with a problem or a question and seek a design to solve it, rather than starting with a research design and forcing the design on a problem.

Reversal Designs: ABA, BAB, ABAB

Experimental control may be demonstrated most directly by repeatedly turning the behavior "on and off," which is exactly what the reversal (also known as the withdrawal) design does. When properly employed, this design can present convincing evidence that a treatment is responsible for a behavior change because the onset of the intervention is followed by the onset of the behavior, and when the procedure is removed, the behavior also returns to its previous level.

When to Use the Reversal Design

The design may be used with any behavior (a) that *is* reversible and (b) where the return of the behavior to baseline levels will cause no ill effects to the participant.

The requirement of reversibility is significant and may require some pilot testing and preplanning on your part to determine if it can be met. If your study involves an acquisition behavior, for example, this design will be inappropriate. That is, if the nature of the behavior is such that once it begins to occur, it will come in contact with existing reinforcers, then it clearly will not be reversible. This particularly holds for any functional skill or academic task that might be taught to a participant. If you reinforce a child for reading or swimming, it is entirely likely that the natural conse-

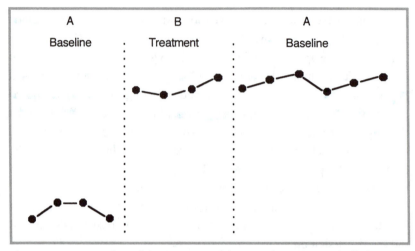

Figure 2.7-11. Hypothetical data in a reversal design with a nonreversal of behavior

quences will maintain the behavior once you withdraw the contingency. It is often difficult to determine if a behavior, once reinforced, will reverse or not, and to that extent, the use of the design involves a certain amount of risk, as shown in Figure 2.7-11. If the behavior does not return to baseline levels, one *cannot* be sure whether the intervention or some outside variable (which may be still operating) actually caused the behavior to change.

The reversal design should be used only in those cases where no harm to the participant or others could possibly result. Thus, if the behavior during baseline consisted of face scratching, fire setting, or stealing, the use of a reversal design would not be appropriate. The reversal design is used most often when the independent variable is either some extrinsic reinforcement condition (e.g., the participant receives tokens, money, or praise) or consequence that has temporary effects (time-out or extinction). It can also, of course, be used in the study of biological variables such as vitamins, medications, or assistive devices as long as proper medical controls are used.

ABA

The ABA design represents the minimal requirement for demonstrating experimental control and does so by showing that when the procedure is

applied, the behavior changes and when it is withdrawn, the behavior returns to pretreatment levels. Figure 2.7-12 shows an example of the use of
the ABA design where the goal was to persuade police officers to enforce
existing safety seat laws (Lavelle, Hovell, West, & Wahlgren, 1992). Citations for failure to use safety seats increased from 10 per month to over 50
and then fell back to the 10- to 20-range in the return to baseline (follow-up). The conclusions are somewhat weakened by the up-trend just
prior to the onset of the intervention and by the 2-month delay in the onset
of the treatment.

The ABA design is not used very often, perhaps because (a) it lacks the
key element of a replication of the intervention and (b) there are negative
implications to returning a participant to the baseline merely for experimental reasons, with no attempt made to have the presumably desirable
procedure reintroduced later.

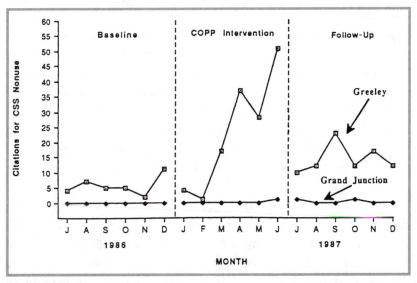

Figure 2.7-12.   Frequency of ticketing for nonuse of safety seats by Greeley
(intervention site) and Grand Junction (control site) officers for the 6-month baseline,
intervention, and follow-up periods (July 1986-December 1987). Officer training began
in January 1987 and was completed within 8 weeks.
SOURCE: From "Promoting Law Enforcement for Child Protection: A Community Analysis," by
J. Lavelle, M. Hovell, M. West, and D. Wahlgren, 1992, *Journal of Applied Behavior Analysis, 25,*
pp. 885-892. Copyright 1992 by the Society for the Experimental Analysis of Behavior. Reprinted with
permission.

BAB

The BAB design is somewhat unusual in that it begins with a treatment rather than a baseline. Typically, the justification is that the behavior of interest was already being treated and perhaps anecdotal evidence indicated that the treatment was effective. To make the point that this was the case, it is necessary to withdraw the intervention and show that the behavior will return to the previous untreated state. You will need to be certain that this reversal will not cause undue stress or harm to the individual and take active steps to ensure this safety (see Step 6 for more details on this situation). Figure 2.7-13 shows just such a case (Pace & Toyer, 2000), where a 9-year-old girl with chronic pica was studied. The "baseline" consisted of the conditions in place when the researchers entered the scene. Here Dana (the participant) was taking iron supplements and the multivitamin that was suspected of being effective in reducing the pica. The parents reported that there had been "no instances of pica in the previous 3 weeks" and that this was coincidental with the administration of the multivitamin. Pace and Toyer proceeded to take data on "latency to pica" under controlled conditions for 11 observations over 3 days. The vitamin was then withdrawn, and 11 more sessions were run. As Figure 2.7-13 shows, Dana's latencies were near zero on six of eight sessions when she was alone, showing a very high probability of the maladaptive behavior when the vitamin was removed. Further demonstration of experimental control was shown when the multivitamin was readministered and the latencies increased to the maximum levels (i.e., she did not engage in pica at all) over a 5-day "B" period.

Another example of the circumstances under which a BAB design might be appropriate can be seen in Robinson, Newby, and Ganzell's (1981) study using a token economy with underachieving hyperactive children. The authors were called in under near-emergency circumstances because the children were all but out of control and the teacher was on the verge of quitting. They quickly established a token economy (the B condition) and began taking data on the number of assignments completed. They then withheld the tokens for 5 days (the A condition); output immediately dropped. The authors then reinstituted the token economy and demonstrated a replication of the original results.

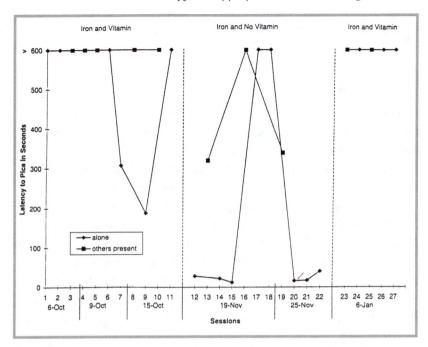

Figure 2.7-13. Latency to pica during alone and others-present conditions. This is a good example of the use of the BAB design.

SOURCE: From "The Effects of a Vitamin Supplement on the Pica of a Child With Severe Mental Retardation," by G. Pace and E. Toyer, 2000, *Journal of Applied Behavior Analysis, 33,* pp. 619-622. Copyright 2000 by the Society for the Experimental Analysis of Behavior. Reprinted with permission.

A unique and very appropriate use of a variation of the BAB design was employed by Northup et al. (1994). They used a BABABA design (see their Figure 4, p. 43, middle panel) to demonstrate treatment integrity for their technical assistance model. Basically, the treatments (B conditions) were in effect almost continually throughout this phase with the A (reversal conditions) serving more like brief probes for no treatment.

The prime weakness of this design is the lack of a baseline where the original level of the behavior documents the need for some intervention. In the Robinson et al. (1981) study, for example, the authors could have taken a few days' baseline data prior to the onset of the token economy and strengthened their research design. Without this information, no comparison for the level of the A condition is possible, and thus the cause-effect relationship is weakened. Believability (Baer et al., 1968; Johnston &

Pennypacker, 1993) in this case rests on the anecdotal information provided in the introduction of the article.

ABAB Design

The ABAB design improves upon the ABA by taking the logical step of reinstituting the B condition (which was presumably shown to be effective). When this is done, the "on-off" effect is most evident, and when used properly, the design is one of the most powerful in demonstrating experimental control. The key to the persuasiveness is the *replication* of both the baseline and the treatment condition. Figure 2.7-14 shows the use of ABAB in demonstrating the effectiveness of a personal safety prompt delivered by grocery carriers to patrons returning to their cars (Engerman, Austin, & Bailey, 1997). One slight weakness in these data is that the second baseline did not exactly replicate the first, although this was in the direction of an even lower level of seat belt usage. The reapplication of the personal prompt thus appears to have had an even slightly stronger effect with the second replication.

The ABAB design is the workhorse of single-subject designs and constitutes the backbone of the fundamental demonstration of experimental control in behavior analysis. In recent years, creative researchers have developed a wide range of variations on the ABAB, thereby further demonstrating the power of this most basic of designs.

Variations on the Reversal Design

One simple permutation of the reversal design is to add a follow-up condition, making the design an ABABC. In one recent example, shown in Figure 2.7-15, Garcia et al. (2001) added a stimulus control assessment condition following their basic demonstration of experimental control of aerophagia.

A second variation on the reversal design involves adding a second intervention (a C condition) that is compared with the first (i.e., a B condition). Stricker, Miltenberger, Garlinghouse, Deaver, and Anderson (2001) wanted to show that their tone-producing awareness enhancement device (AED) was responsible for a reduction in thumb sucking and to control for the possibility that the effect was one of simply wearing the device alone. In

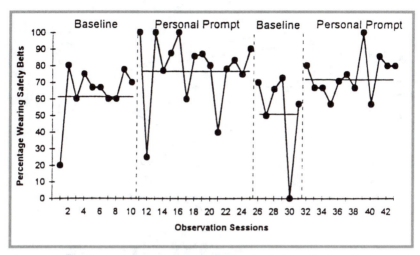

Figure 2.7-14. The percentage of patrons wearing safety belts across four phases: baseline (A), personal prompt (B), baseline (A), and personal prompt (B)
SOURCE: From "Prompting Patron Safety Belt Use at a Supermarket," by J. Engerman, J. Austin, and J. Bailey, 1997, *Journal of Applied Behavior Analysis, 30*, pp. 577-579. Copyright 1997 by the Society for the Experimental Analysis of Behavior. Reprinted with permission.

their ABCBAC design, shown in Figure 2.7-16, they clearly demonstrated that it was the *active* nature of the device that made it effective.

Other obvious variations on the basic ABAB design include combining treatments in the B condition (Wilder, Masuda, O'Connor, & Baham, 2001) and adding second or even third elements for comparison, producing ABACAD or ABCBCACADAD (Ringdahl, Vollmer, Borrero, & Connell, 2001) designs. Keeney, Fisher, Adelinis, and Wilder (2000) cleverly used an ABCAC design to compare noncontingent reinforcers with a response cost procedure.

Limiting Conditions of the Reversal Design

An examination of many studies (some successful, some not) suggests certain conditions under which the ABAB design loses its persuasiveness. Figure 2.5-17 is a close facsimile of data once seriously submitted for journal review. On close examination, it suggests several of these conditions.

Stability. Because a visual inspection of the data is the primary basis for drawing conclusions, each condition must be run until stability (i.e., you

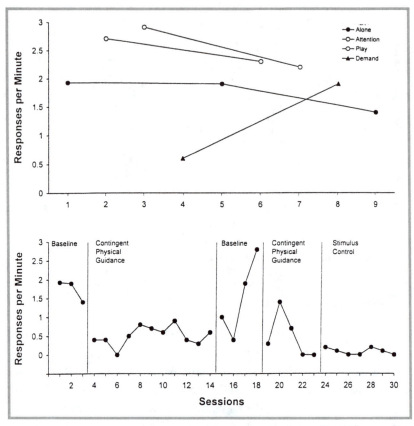

Figure 2.7-15. Number of aerophagia responses per minute during baseline, contingent physical guidance, and stimulus control assessment sessions
SOURCE: From "Treating Aerophagia With Contingent Physical Guidance," by D. Garcia, S. Starin, and R. Churchill, 2001, *Journal of Applied Behavior Analysis, 34,* pp. 89-92. Copyright 2001 by the Society for the Experimental Analysis of Behavior. Reprinted with permission.

can begin to predict where the next data point will be) is achieved. The data can be trending, but it must be in a direction opposite that of the expected treatment effects. In Figure 2.7-17, the data in the first A condition are clearly trending down. The data from B are predictable from A, so that no conclusion about the punishment effects of B may be drawn at all. The criticism holds for every condition in Figure 2.7-17, where too few data points per condition prevent *any* prediction of the next point (i.e., there are up and down trends in almost every treatment phase).

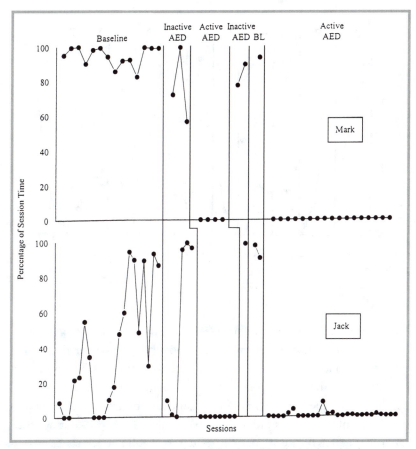

Figure 2.7-16. Percentage of session time of thumb sucking for Mark and Jack across baseline (BL), inactive AED, and active AED conditions
SOURCE: From "Evaluation of an Awareness Enhancement Device for the Treatment of Thumb Sucking in Children," by J. Stricker, R. Miltenberger, M. Garlinghouse, C. Deaver, and C. Anderson, 2001, *Journal of Applied Behavior Analysis, 34,* pp. 77-80. Copyright 2001 by the Society for the Experimental Analysis of Behavior. Reprinted with permission.

Replicability of Procedure and Effect.   For a convincing demonstration of experimental control to be shown, each procedure instituted should be later reinstituted; each time the procedure occurs, approximately the same effects must be seen. In Figure 2.7-17, the D condition, for example, produced a different effect the second time it was applied than it did the first. Different effects were also seen almost every time the baseline (A) was run, and the B condition was not replicated at all. Simply running a condition twice is not sufficient if different results are seen each time.

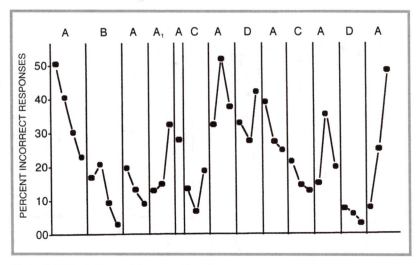

Figure 2.7-17. A 13-condition reversal design

Sequence Effects. If more than one treatment condition is introduced (and if each is replicated at least once), the possibility for sequence effects is great. In the data shown in Figure 2.7-17, we do not know whether the second effect of D (if there was one) was due to having been preceded by two C conditions or whether the first D was ineffective because it has been preceded by only one C condition, and so on. Also, simply separating treatments with a baseline does not eliminate the possible sequence effects, as was apparently the plan in the design used here. Generally speaking, the reversal design is *not* a good one for comparing an assortment of treatments unless you have a good deal of time, a very stable environment, and a very accessible and cooperative participant; to compare several treatments, some method of correcting for sequence must be incorporated, such as having different participants receive the treatments in different order or arranging the treatments in different orders and showing that regardless of the order, the same effect can be achieved.

Producing the "Reversal" Effect

The baseline condition of the reversal is almost always just that: an assessment of the frequency of occurrence of the behavior *prior* to any intervention. This presumes that during baseline, no systematic use of any contingencies is operating; thus, the reversal phase usually represents a return to *baseline* (any reinforcers that were given are withdrawn). Technically, however, the onset of a reinforcement condition actually represents two changes: (a) introduction of the reinforcer and (b) the establishment of the *contingency* of reinforcement. Recent research on noncontingent reinforcement (NCR) has suggested, contrary to earlier thinking, that NCR may in fact change behavior rather dramatically by affecting the establishing operation in place at the time of the experimental session.

So rather than returning to baseline following a reinforcement condition, it may be more prudent to run an NCR condition to make this determination. If the behavior returns to baseline levels, then experimental control (perhaps superior to a return to baseline control) has been shown. That is, you have also demonstrated that it *was* the contingency and not just the reinforcer that was responsible for the behavior change.

The second method also demonstrates that the critical change was the contingency by arranging for the reinforcers in the reversal to be made contingent upon any response other than the target behavior (differential reinforcement of other behaviors [DRO]). This DRO procedure essentially reinforces the participant for *not* responding. One applied study carried out to evaluate these two alternatives (Goetz, Holmberg, & LeBlanc, 1975) suggested that the DRO is superior. That is, the reversal of behavior occurs much more rapidly with the DRO than with the NCR procedure. One decision you will have to make if you choose the DRO route is whether you will use an *interval* or *momentary* DRO (Lindberg, Iwata, Kahng, & DeLeon, 1999).

There do not appear to be any strong arguments against the DRO as a reversal control procedure except that the original baseline condition is not exactly replicated. But because the primary goal is to demonstrate that the behavior changes with the introduction of the independent variable, how you return to baseline may not be important. What is important is the time it takes to reverse the behavior and whether there are side effects connected with the reversal. Extinction may produce side effects that are undesirable, thus tipping the scale in favor of a DRO arrangement.

Multiple-Baseline Designs

The multiple-baseline design is one in which some treatment condition is applied successively across two or more baselines that have been established. As just described, the reversal design is not applicable in cases where (a) the target behavior is nonreversible or (b) where though the target behavior is reversible, reversing it would be unethical. The multiple baseline, in contrast, is perfectly suited to handle such cases because it has two variations, one appropriate for each of these situations. In addition, the design is most versatile in that it can be used across behaviors, participants, or settings. These dimensions of the design will be discussed under the headings of *Treatment Arrangement* and *Types of Applications*.

Treatment Arrangement

Moving Treatment.   When the target behavior is of the nonreversible type, the treatment condition is applied to one "leg" of the baseline until a stable effect is seen. As shown in Figure 2.7-18, in the "moving treatment," the contingency is then *removed* from the first behavior and applied on the second, again, until stability is reached. This process is repeated for as many baselines as have been taken.

If the experimenter has erred and one or more baselines reverse when the contingency is removed, no harm is done; the contingency can simply be reapplied to that particular baseline. In fact, a reversal design within a multiple baseline will then have been shown.

Cumulative Treatment.   In those cases where the behavior is reversible, but reversing it would be unethical or harmful or both, the strategy is to apply the treatment to each behavior in succession, keeping the treatment in effect after the baseline is treated. As shown by the arrows in Figure 2.7-18, the contingency is applied cumulatively across three baselines.

Types of Applications

The versatility of the multiple baseline is extended further by the types of situations to which it is applicable. Next we shall review these and look at two examples of multiple baseline studies.

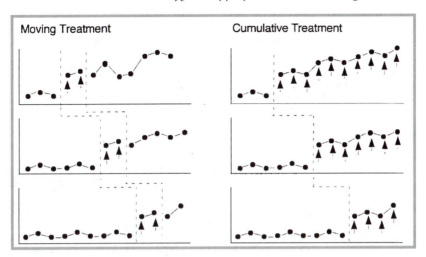

Figure 2.7-18. Stylized graphs of two types of multiple baselines. Arrows indicate when the treatment is applied to the behavior.

Applications Across Different Behaviors of the Same Participant. In many instances, the behavior analyst will be interested in changing several behaviors of the target participant. Because it is usually not feasible to begin working with all of them at once, applying the treatment across several target behaviors in succession is not only appropriate for the experimental design but also convenient for the experimenter and puts less stress on the participant. An example is shown in Figure 2.7-19, where Wood, Frank, and Wacker (1998) used this design to clearly show that an instructional package for multiplication facts was effective in producing near 100% accuracy across six types of strategies (behaviors). Note: This is an example of the "moving" treatment multiple baseline where the instructional package was applied for three sessions to each strategy and then moved to the next one.

A dramatic example of the use of the multiple baseline across behaviors can be seen in a study by Gena, Krantz, McClannahan, and Poulson (1996). They showed that a treatment package consisting of modeling, prompting, and reinforcement could be used to increase the rates of *affective behaviors* from 0% to 100% in a matter of a few sessions. Studies like this best demonstrate the power of the multiple-baseline design in showing causal relationships between independent and dependent variables as well as size of effect.

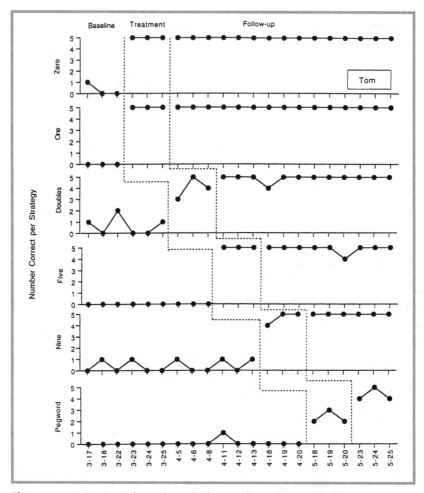

Figure 2.7-19. Tom's results on the multiplication facts tests
SOURCE: From "Teaching Multiplication Facts to Students With Learning Disabilities," by D. Wood, A. Frank, and D. Wacker, 1998, *Journal of Applied Behavior Analysis, 31,* pp. 323-338. Copyright 1998 by the Society for the Experimental Analysis of Behavior. Reprinted with permission.

Applications Across Participants.   For some types of studies, the nature of the independent variable is such that the most convincing demonstration of experimental control will be across participants. Each participant is used as his or her own control, and the robustness of the treatment is shown by the fact that it is equally effective with different individuals. Figure 2.7-20 shows a good example of this design in which Roscoe, Iwata, and Goh (1998) used a treatment that consisted of either NCR or EXT to reduce self-injurious behavior. (In this study, the EXT condition was extinction. Extinction occurs when a behavior that has been previously reinforced is no longer reinforced. The result is that the behavior no longer occurs.) Note that this is a nice example of a "nested" design where a multielement design is embedded within a multiple-baseline design.

One question that often comes up in designing a study involves the number of demonstrations of experimental control that are necessary to "prove" that the intervention was responsible for the behavior change. Although the Roscoe et al. (1998) study used three subjects, it is possible to use two (see Schepis, Reid, Behrmann, & Sutton, 1998, Figure 4) if conditions are ideal. That is, if the baselines are very stable with little variability in bandwidth, there is virtually no trending, and the intervention produces large (i.e. nonoverlapping) effects.

Applications Across Settings. The third variation in the multiple baseline involves a demonstration of experimental control where the treatment is applied successively (usually with the same participant and behavior) across different settings or times. A timely and interesting example may be seen in Figure 2.7-21, where prompts and praise were used to increase the appropriate engagement of older adults in activities of daily living (Engelman, Altus, & Mathews, 1999). The intervention was applied across morning and afternoon shifts of certified nursing assistants (CNAs). This is a series of three multiple baselines (replications) across two shifts with each participant.

Another timely study of a contemporary problem in the culture used a similar design. Allen (1998) demonstrated the use of a simplified habit reversal procedure to reduce angry outbursts during tournament and non-tournament tennis matches. Although the data are clear for this one participant (outbursts were reduced from 6 to 10 per match to near zero), further replications with other subjects will strengthen the findings. Note that the *Journal of Applied Behavior Analysis* encourages researchers to submit replications of studies; this is a good way for new researchers to get started in the field.

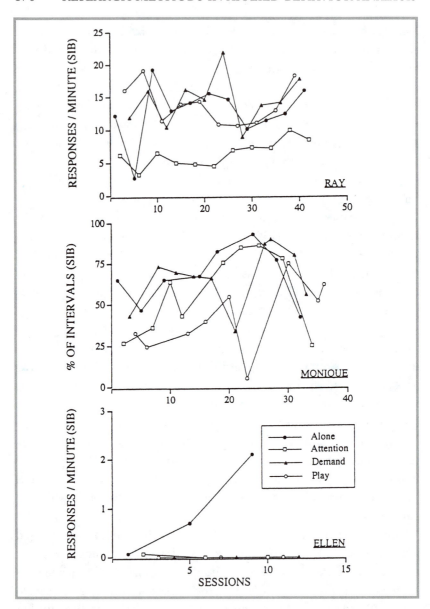

Figure 2.7-20. Self-injurious behavior observed during baseline and treatment (NCR vs. EXT) conditions for Ray (top panel), Monique (middle panel), and Ellen (bottom panel)

SOURCE: From "A Comparison of Noncontingent Reinforcement and Sensory Extinction as Treatments for Self-injurious Behavior," by E. Roscoe, B. Iwata, and H. Goh, 1998, *Journal of Applied Behavior Analysis, 31,* pp. 635-646. Copyright 1998 by the Society for the Experimental Analysis of Behavior. Reprinted with permission.

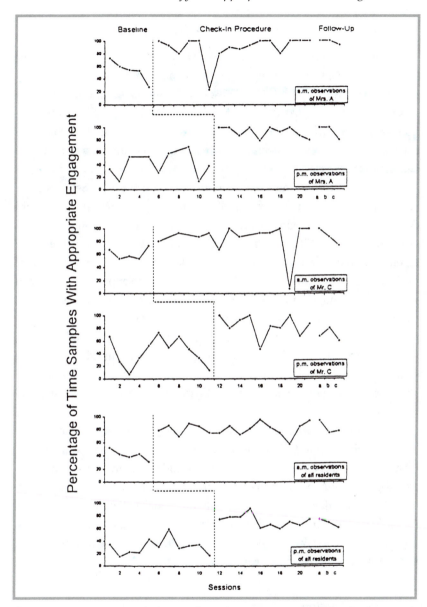

Figure 2.7-21. Percentage of time samples with appropriate engagement for Mrs. A and Mr. C and mean aggregate data for all five residents. The dotted lines indicate when each CNA was trained to conduct the check-in procedure.
SOURCE: From "Increasing Engagement in Daily Activities by Older Adults With Dementia," by K. Engelman, D. Altus, and R. Mathews, 1999, *Journal of Applied Behavior Analysis, 32,* pp. 107-110. Copyright 1999 by the Society for the Experimental Analysis of Behavior. Reprinted with permission.

Variations on the Multiple-Baseline Design

One variation on the multiple-baseline design was suggested by Horner and Baer (1978). Called the multiple-probe technique, this design is an alternative to continuous baseline measurement and saves time and possibly reduces reactivity by taking "probes" (data samples) just prior to interventions in the several baselines that are in place. The design appears to be primarily useful for training interventions where continuous measurement alone might actually cause the participant to acquire some new skill.

A good example of this design can be seen in a study by Schepis et al. (1998) that evaluated the effects of a voice output communication aid (VOCA) along with naturalistic teaching strategies on communication skills with autistic children. As can be seen in Figure 2.7-22, baselines were taken on two children and two routines. Note that the observations were taken at fairly close intervals in the early stages of the experiment and then were thinned out to prevent accidental skill acquisition. "Probes" were taken just before the onset of training plus VOCA for Ben and Cory in snack routines and nearly immediately before the onset of the independent variable for the play routines. This constitutes a four-leg multiple probe design and provides convincing evidence that the naturalistic teaching plus VOCA was effective in increasing the autistic children's communication interactions.

Many other researchers have found the multiple-probe technique to be of value, including Marchand-Martella et al. (1992), who used it to demonstrate the effects of a peer-delivered first-aid program. Werts, Caldwell, and Wolery (1996) used a variation of the design to have peer models without disabilities demonstrate chains of functional behaviors for disabled classmates. This "multiple-probe design across response chains" was ideally suited to the task of demonstrating experimental control and saved a great deal of time for the researchers in the process.

Limiting Conditions of the
Multiple-Baseline Design

Functional Equivalence of Baselines.   The demonstration of experimental control in the multiple baseline *depends* upon approximately equal effects

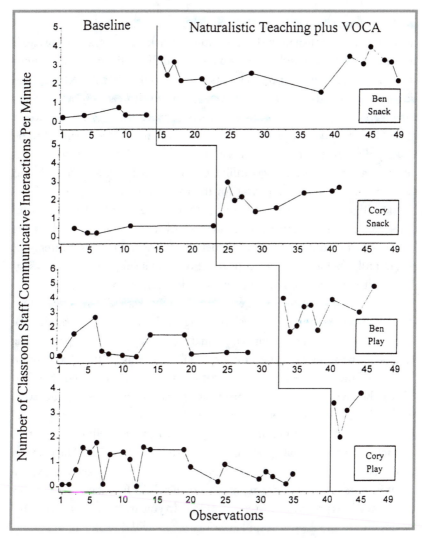

Figure 2.7-22. The number of staff communicative interactions per minute with Ben and Cory during both experimental conditions during the snack and play routines
SOURCE: From "Increasing Communicative Interactions of Young Children With Autism Using a Voice Output Communication Aid and Naturalistic Teaching," by M. Schepis, D. Reid, M. Behrmann, and K. Sutton, 1998, *Journal of Applied Behavior Analysis, 31*, pp. 561-578. Copyright 1998 by the Society for the Experimental Analysis of Behavior. Reprinted with permission.

of the treatment being observed with *each* baseline. If a large effect is seen with one and a small effect is seen with another, the overall outcome can be less than convincing. Thus, it is the task of the experimenter to ensure that the baselines are as functionally equivalent as possible. This is usually not difficult to accomplish in the case of a multiple baseline across settings with the same participants and behavior but can be quite difficult when baselines for different behaviors or participants are involved. When a multiple baseline across a behavior is used, the most common strategy is to arrange for the responses to be as similar (and yet distinctive) as possible. In the Wood et al. (1998) study, for example, the math facts tests were designed to be equally difficult but required different problem-solving strategies so that generalization across tests was unlikely. Similarly, Schepis et al. (1998) used comparable snack and play tasks for their two subjects.

Viewed abstractly, it would appear that in these and other successful studies where the baselines are "similar but different behaviors," there are certain commonalities. Usually, the behaviors are "natural" subcategories of the molar behavior under consideration, and a subjective analysis suggests that they require approximately equal "effort" or skill to perform. Finally, their operant or baseline levels should indicate that they are about equally likely to occur (i.e., they have roughly the same rate or frequency). If the behaviors do not occur with equal frequency, then interpreting the results of a treatment may be tenuous. Magee and Ellis (2000) cleverly conducted a functional analysis prior to their study and predicted that out-of-seat behavior, yelling, inappropriate gestures, and destruction were likely all members of the same response class. Later, when out-of-seat behavior was put on extinction, yelling increased; when yelling was put on extinction, inappropriate gestures and destruction increased. The true test of the equivalence of the behaviors in the design comes once the experiment is under way and approximately equal results have been seen. Using the suggestions provided in Step 2 should help you arrive at appropriate behaviors for your study. Compulsive researchers will do some pilot testing, perhaps using functional analysis, to determine if a calculated guess was in fact correct. If not, a new selection will have to be made and further pilot testing carried out.

Trending.   Just as with the reversal design, the researcher must keep careful watch on the daily fluctuation in data because any trend in the direction of an expected increase can destroy the power of the design, as illustrated in Figure 2.7-23.

Generalization.   Perhaps the most serious concern in the use of the multiple baseline is that a treatment will affect not only the target behavior but also one of the other baselines. As shown in Figure 2.7-24, such an effect utterly destroys the usability of the multiple baseline because it is impossible to determine if the change in behavior was due to your intervention or to some outside variable.

   The only way to "save" such data is to withdraw or reverse the treatment, but this option is usually not feasible in light of the original rationale for the use of the multiple baseline (i.e., the behavior was irreversible or it was undesirable to let it reverse). In practice, the only alternative is to drop the experiment and select another set of behaviors, participants, or settings for baselines and begin again.

Multiple Treatments.   The multiple-baseline design is most appropriate for demonstrating the effects of a *single* independent variable (Baer et al., 1968). When you wish to compare the effects of two or more interventions, complications arising out of sequence and order effects plague the design, as can be seen in a clinical study with children's motor tics. Woods, Miltenberger, and Lumley (1996) wanted to evaluate the components of a habit-reversal treatment (Azrin & Nunn, 1973) for motor tics. First, they analyzed the components and ranked them according to least-to-most effort to implement. As shown in Figure 2.7-25, the "awareness training" component had little effect on Keith's mouth tics but a major impact on Jack's neck tics and questionable effects on Brandi's hand tic. Two additional components were added to Keith's treatment and had some effect, but for him it was the "competing response training" that appeared to be responsible for the final major reduction in mouth tics. (Response generalization appeared to set in on about Day 22 for Keith's eye tic, adding one more complication.) This same multicomponent package was used with Keith's eye tic and with Chip's leg tic. (Note the apparent generalization to Chip's arm tic in the fourth panel from the top.) Finally, for Brandi, it was the self-monitoring added to the awareness training that was effective in helping her reduce her hand tic.

   The problem with possible sequence effects can clearly be seen in this example. We do not know, for example, whether the "competing response training" would have worked if it had been used as the first intervention

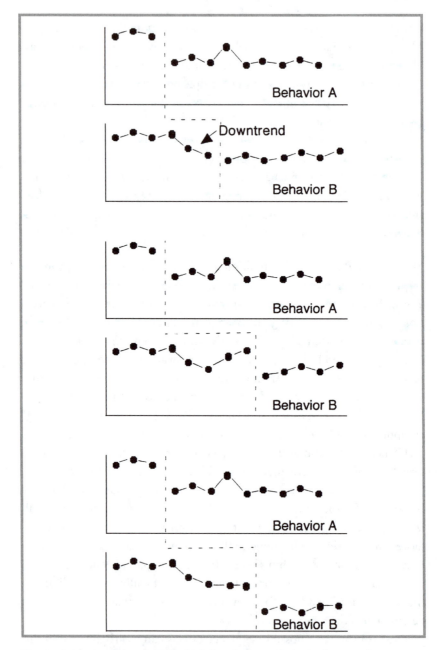

Figure 2.7-23. Loss of power of multiple baseline as a result of a downtrend in Behavior B just prior to treatment, top panel. The middle and bottom panels indicate that allowing Behavior B to return to stability at either the original or the new level restores the power of the design.

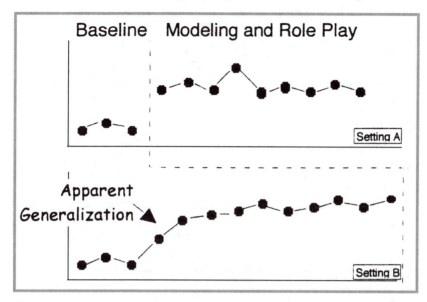

Figure 2.7-24. Impact of generalization of a treatment effect on the interpretability of the results in a multiple baseline design

with Keith's mouth tic. Likewise with Chip's leg tic, it simply cannot be concluded that the whole package was necessary for him, especially in light of the data just preceding this condition. Finally, we do not know whether the awareness training would have been necessary with Brandi if self-monitoring had been used first.

Human behavior is exceedingly complicated, as the data from this study show. Some children responded to some components and other children to completely different ones, and in the final analysis, it is not clear how you would proceed with a new child entering for treatment. Studies like this clearly illustrate the complications involved in making treatment comparisons within a multiple-baseline design. But under special circumstances, the integrity of the multiple baseline can be maintained with multiple treatments. These involve the addition of conditions or phases after an initial intervention.

One way to deal with the sequence effects is to add and subtract the components. Shirley, Iwata, Kahng, Mazaleski, and Lerman (1997) had a good model for this design in their study of functional communication

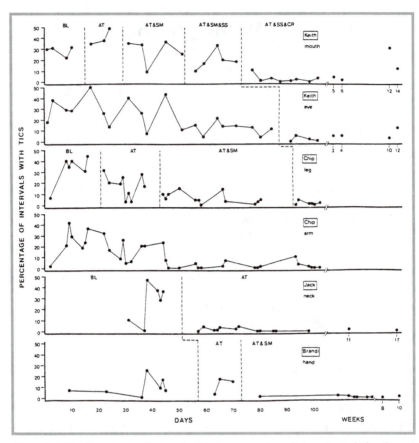

Figure 2.7-25. Percentage of intervals with tics across days. Data collected after the break in the graph indicate follow-up data across weeks after implementation of the final treatment phase for each child. BL, baseline; AT, awareness training; AT & SM, awareness training plus self-monitoring; AT & SM & SS, awareness training plus self-monitoring and social support; AT & CR & SS, awareness training, competing response training, and social support.

SOURCE: From "Sequential Application of Major Habit-Reversal Components to Treat Motor Tics in Children," by D. Woods, R. Miltenberger, and V. Lumley, 1996, *Journal of Applied Behavior Analysis, 29*, pp. 483-493. Copyright 1996 by the Society for the Experimental Analysis of Behavior. Reprinted with permission.

training (FCT). As shown in Figure 2.7-26, when FCT alone was implemented, there was no change in self-injurious behavior for three participants with profound mental retardation. When extinction was added, the self-injurious behavior initially increased and then dropped to near zero; with one participant, Sue, when the extinction condition was dropped, the self-injurious behavior increased. For the other two participants, self-injurious behavior remained at low levels when the FCT-alone condition was reinstituted.

This use of a reversal design within a multiple baseline would appear to contradict one of the primary assumptions of employing the multiple-baseline design, namely, that either the behavior would not reverse or that it would not be in the participant's best interest. In this case, the self-injurious was clearly reversible, but with very short sessions of 10 to 15 minutes and with close supervision, safety could be assured.

One clearly acceptable use of multiple treatments involves the use of follow-up, maintenance, or generalization training following an initial treatment. Ducharme and Holburn (1997), for example, used two treatments in their multiple-baseline-across-subjects design to study the generalization of social skills in children with hearing impairments. Their Treatment 1 was a social skills training package, and their Treatment 2 added generalization programming. As shown in Figure 2.7-27, it is clear from an examination of the top panel that no generalization occurred with Treatment 1 alone. Furthermore, when generalization programming was added, social skills began to generalize noticeably.

This is an excellent example of an embedded multiple baseline where there are two dependent variables for each subject (i.e., one for the training setting and another for the generalization setting). Thus, the design could be described as a multiple-baseline-across-behaviors design embedded within a multiple-baseline-across-subjects design.

Multielement Baseline Designs

A third experimental design that may have wide applicability is known as the multielement baseline design (or simply the multielement design) (Thompson, Iwata, Conners, & Roscoe, 1999). The design is based upon the multiple schedule (Ferster & Skinner, 1957) and was discussed at length by Sidman (1960, pp. 323-340), although its advantages for applied research were not elucidated until the mid-1970s (Ulman & Sulzer-Azaroff, 1975). The multielement design (also called the alternating treatments design) got its biggest boost in 1982 when Brian Iwata and his colleagues (Iwata, Dorsey, Slifer, Bauman, & Richman, 1982, 1994) chose this

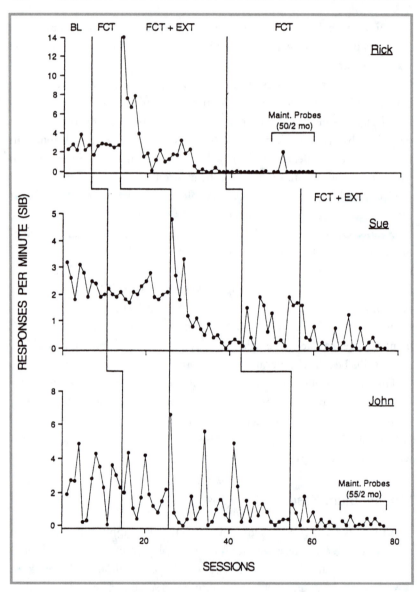

Figure 2.7-26. Rate of self-injurious behavior (SIB) for each participant during baseline and across treatment conditions (FCT alone and FCT plus extinction)

SOURCE: From "Does Functional Communication Training Compete With Ongoing Contingencies of Reinforcement? An Analysis During Response Acquisition and Maintenance," by M. Shirley, B. Iwata, S. Kahng, J. Mazaleski, and D. Lerman, 1997, *Journal of Applied Behavior Analysis, 30,* pp. 93-104. Copyright 1997 by the Society for the Experimental Analysis of Behavior. Reprinted with permission.

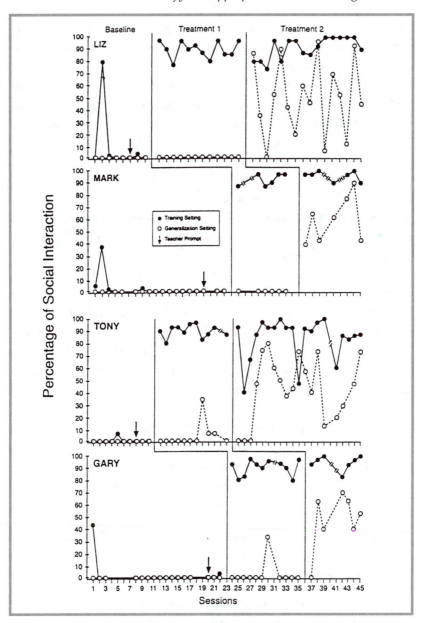

Figure 2.7-27. Percentage of social interactions in training and generalization settings for Liz, Mark, Tony, and Gary across experimental conditions

SOURCE: From "Programming Generalization of Social Skills in Preschool Children With Hearing Impairments," by D. Ducharme and S. Holborn, 1997, *Journal of Applied Behavior Analysis, 30,* pp. 639-651. Copyright 1997 by the Society for the Experimental Analysis of Behavior. Reprinted with permission.

methodology to demonstrate functional analysis in the treatment of self-injury. In the past few years, it has become perhaps the most frequently used design in behavior analysis.

The design logic operates by bringing the same behavior (of one or more participants) under the control of several different experimental procedures, each of which is associated with a different discriminative stimulus. When shown graphically, the data points for each of the separate conditions are connected, and any systematic deviation from the baseline or a control condition demonstrates experimental control or allows for an evaluation of the independent variable. Typically, the order of the conditions will vary randomly so that no predictable pattern is presented to the participants, so at the same time, order and sequence effects are eliminated (Higgins-Hains & Baer, 1989).

A recent example of this design is seen in a study by Worsdell, Iwata, Conners, Kahng, and Thompson (2000), as shown in Figure 2.7-28. Here the authors were examining the relative influences of establishing operations (EOs) and reinforcement contingencies on problem behaviors. Overlapping data points for the various conditions often make it difficult to determine which were the controlling variables; stable data such as Rich's data are relatively easy to interpret.

Embedding a multielement design within a multiple baseline, as shown in Figure 2.7-29, is a way of gathering a great deal of information in one experiment. In this case, this was the ideal design to ask the question that the authors (Conners et al., 2000) were interested in: Does adding discriminative stimuli facilitate differential responding during functional analyses?

When to Use the Multielement Design

The multielement design is ideally suited to circumstances where several different contingency arrangements or biological variables need to be compared simultaneously. From the Conners et al. (2000) study just discussed, and from Sidman's advice (1960), adding discriminative stimuli for each contingency seems like a good recommendation. You need to be able to al-

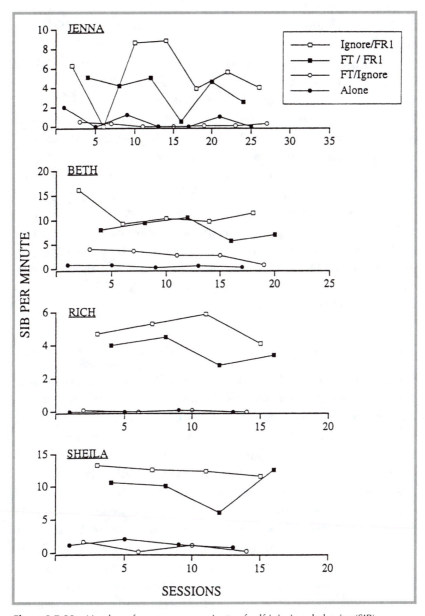

Figure 2.7-28. Number of responses per minute of self-injurious behavior (SIB) exhibited by Jenna, Beth, Rich, and Sheila across functional analysis conditions

SOURCE: From "Relative Influences of Establishing Operations and Reinforcement Contingencies on Self-Injurious Behavior During Functional Analyses," by A. Worsdell, B. Iwata, J. Conners, S. Kahng, and R. Thompson, 2000, *Journal of Applied Behavior Analysis, 33,* pp. 451-461. Copyright 2000 by the Society for the Experimental Analysis of Behavior. Reprinted with permission.

ternate the conditions *rapidly* and *randomly* to obtain the multielement effect.

In drug trials, the goal is to conceal any discriminative stimuli associated with the treatment, so the observers, parents, and teachers are made unaware of medication status while the multielement design is in place. Northup et al. (1999) used the multielement design in this way to evaluate the effects of methylphenidate (MPH) versus a placebo under various contingencies. Their results are intriguing and warrant replication and further study because there seems to be a clear interaction between MPH effectiveness and analogue contingencies. Another interesting study (Ardoin & Martens, 2000) used the multielement design to test whether children on MPH and placebos (in a double-blind placebo-controlled multielement design) could accurately report the effects of the medication on their behavior. Kennedy and Meyer (1996) also used a multielement design to good effect to determine if biological factors such as sleep deprivation and allergy reactions could affect student behavior.

Limiting Conditions of the Multielement Design

The multielement design is basically a rapidly changing reversal design. One limiting condition, then, involves the extent to which rapidly changing from one condition to another is feasible. Comparing MPH and placebos is feasible because MPH has a rapid onset and washes out in a relatively short period of time, but with other medications this might not be the case, and the alternation might have to be across weeks rather than days.

Another consideration is whether one condition might affect another in a "carryover" effect (Barlow & Hayes, 1979). This is especially likely if the treatment sessions are short (e.g., 10 minutes) and several occur each day; if, for example, while testing the B condition you might also be seeing the effects of the prior A condition that occurred just 15 minutes ago. A related problem involves a possible "contrast" effect between conditions. That is, if Condition A was presented alone it might produce 50% off-task behavior and if Condition B were presented alone it might produce 10% off-task behavior, but when A and B are rapidly alternated, they might give much different results, as shown in Figure 2.7-30, where one measure is increased and the other decreased as a result of their being alternated.

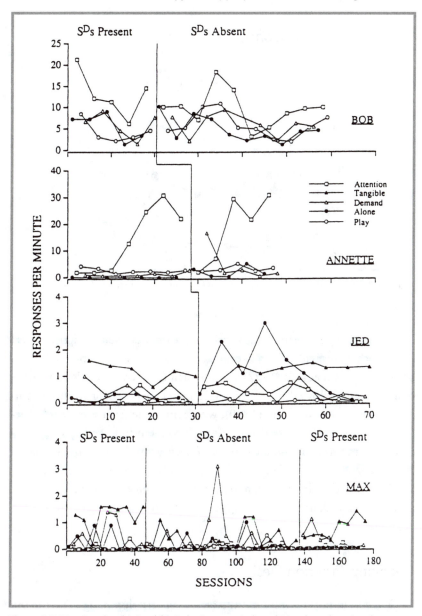

Figure 2.7-29. Results obtained for Bob, Annette, Jed, and Max from functional analyses conducted in the presence and absence of S^Ds

SOURCE: From "Differential Responding in the Presence and Absence of Discriminative Stimuli During Multielement Functional Analyses," by J. Conners, B. Iwata, S. Kahng, G. Hanley, A. Worsdell, and R. Thompson, 2000, *Journal of Applied Behavior Analysis, 33,* pp. 299-308. Copyright 2000 by the Society for the Experimental Analysis of Behavior. Reprinted with permission.

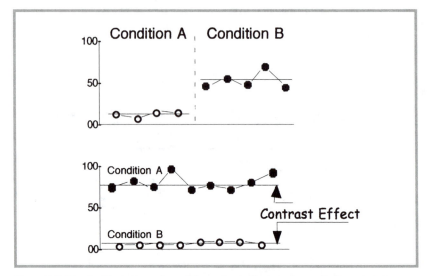

Figure 2.7-30. An illustration of possible contrast effects in the multielement design

The only way to be sure if the results of the multielement design are valid is to test them individually in a reversal design. A good example of this can be seen in Piazza et al.'s (1997) study, which ran a two-part design with a multielement followed by a reversal design. This is similar to the recommendation of Wacker et al. (1990), who coined the term *sequential alternating treatment design* to describe a multielement followed by one treatment in a multiple baseline to correct for any contrast effects that might have occurred. Higgins-Hains and Baer (1989) have discussed this and related issues in detail; if you plan to use the multielement design, it would be good to review their article for suggestions on some necessary control procedures.

Changing-Criterion Design

One design not often used is the changing-criterion design (Hartmann & Hall, 1976). It was apparently first used in applied work by Weiss and Hall (1971), although a somewhat similar strategy was described by Sidman (1960, pp. 254-256) for coping with the problem of irreversibility of behavioral effects in animal operant research. Basically, the design shows experimental control by demonstrating that changes in the level of a behavior occur only when the criterion (usually for the delivery of reinforcers or escape) changes. Once stability at the criterion is met, a new one is set, and the behavior must then conform to this *new* criterion. A study by Foxx and Rubinoff (1979) shows one of the best examples of this design (see Figure 2.7-31). In this study, participants earned $14 per treatment phase for reducing their daily caffeine intake. Experimental control is shown because behavior changes only when a new criterion is established.

A useful variation on the design is to occasionally reverse the contingency, as was done by Fitterling, Martin, Gramling, Cole, and Milan (1988) in their use of the changing-criterion design to shape adherence to an aerobic exercise program to reduce vascular headaches.

When to Use the Changing-Criterion Design

The primary use of the changing-criterion design would appear to be in cases where the target behavior is unidimensional (otherwise you could use a multiple baseline) and where the intervention involves changing some contingency, also along one dimension. We assume that the behavior is irreversible or should not be reversed (except perhaps for very short periods for demonstrations of experimental control) and that the changes to be made will occur in small increments. Presumably, any treatment program that seeks a stepwise reduction in, for example, weight or drinking, or a similar increase in, for example, exercise (DeLuca & Holborn, 1992) or problems solved, would be appropriate.

Limiting Conditions of the Changing-Criterion Design

We do not have many published examples of the changing-criterion design, but it is clear that it is a rather limited-use design. There must be a baseline of sufficient length to allow prediction of behavior if no changes are made, and the first criterion change intervention must produce a visually significant change, as with a reversal design. In addition, each criterion must be significantly different from the previous one to allow for a visual detection of a difference, and each must be kept in force until stability has been reached; any trending will destroy the usefulness of the design.

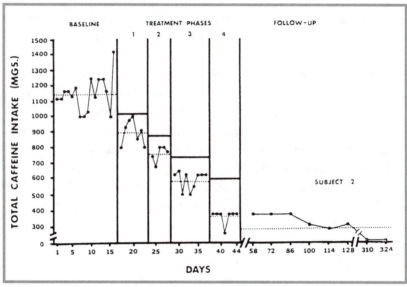

Figure 2.7-31. Subject 2's daily caffeine intake (in mg) during baseline, treatment, and follow-up. The criterion level for each treatment phase was 137 mg of caffeine less than the previous treatment phase. Solid horizontal lines indicate the criterion level for each phase. Broken horizontal lines indicate the mean for each condition.
SOURCE: From "Behavioral Treatment of Caffeinism: Reducing Excessive Coffee Drinking," by R. Foxx and A. Rubinoff, 1979, *Journal of Applied Behavior Analysis, 12,* pp. 335-344. Copyright 1979 by the Society for the Experimental Analysis of Behavior. Reprinted with permission.

Group Designs

The superiority of single-subject designs for examining the relationship between environmental changes and individual behavior has been discussed at length by Sidman (1960) and more indirectly and briefly by Kendall (1973). Behavior analysts are by definition interested in the behavior of individuals, and we believe that we can learn the most about them by studying them over some considerable period of time, making systematic changes in the environment, and replicating the results using each person as their own control. Behavior analysts, by and large, are not interested in the types of questions that are typically answered by group-statistical designs. Nonetheless, there are occasional circumstances under which the only way to demonstrate experimental control for the question being asked is by using groups of participants.

When to Use Group Designs

As behavior analysts begin operating on a larger scale, it is inevitable that they will begin to ask questions about groups of participants who have received some treatment that has been previously worked out in minute detail using single-subject designs (Baer, 1975). In some cases, the nature of the "intervention" is such that the application is long term (e.g., college instruction), and to break it down would be to lose the face validity of the independent variable. For some other types of research, the experimenter may wish to know about the comparative effects of several treatments, but the available single-subject designs, if employed, would not rule out order or sequence effects (Jason, Billows, Schnopp-Wyatt, & King, 1996). Finally, one simply may wish to collect the data on one behavior of a number of persons to establish norms for the occurrence of certain responses. Clearly, as the field of applied behavior analysis develops, and larger applications are made, greater use of group designs is likely.

Examples of Group Studies
Used in Applied Behavior Analysis

A few examples of the uses of groups and group designs may help illustrate the circumstances under which they may be appropriately used. Bostow and his colleagues (Kritch & Bostow, 1998; Kritch, Bostow, & Dedrick, 1995; Tudor & Bostow, 1991), for example, have evaluated the effects of college-level programmed instructional material and have often involved hundreds of college students as participants. Data often involve a comparison of pre- and posttest scores of at least two different groups of students, and the results are analyzed with an analysis of variance (ANOVA) or some other appropriate statistic. This is a perfectly appropriate use of group designs that widens the scope of behavior analysis in an area where it is much needed—college instruction. Neef and her colleagues (Neef, Lensbower, Hockersmith, DePalma, & Gray, 1990; Neef, Trachtenberg, Loeb, & Sterner, 1991) have worked in another important area, the training of respite care providers and mentally retarded adults. They use a within-subjects Latin square design nested in a multiple-baseline design to evaluate instructional materials and training strategies. One final type of inquiry is exemplified by Kazdin's (1980) research on the acceptability of various treatments for deviant child behavior. In this work, he used a 4 x 4 Replicated Latin square design to present clinical cases to students taking undergraduate college courses. They were asked to rate the acceptability of four different treatments: differential reinforcement of incompatible behaviors (DRI—that is, reinforcement of a behavior that is incompatible with the behavior that the analyst is trying to eliminate), time-out, drug therapy, and electric shock. His finding that DRI is more acceptable than the other treatments is important information for researchers concerned with social validity, and it would be difficult to obtain this information in any other way than through a group design.

Limiting Conditions of Group Designs

The use of group designs and statistical analyses thereof has a long history dating back to Fisher's early (1925, 1926) work in agriculture. One inherent weakness in all group designs is their inability to allow a direct statement of causality. Rather, an estimate of the probability of a given finding occurring by chance is stated. In addition, because the use of groups obscures the scores for individual participants, it is impossible to make any estimate of the effects of the treatment for any given person (unless individual data were taken and presented, as in Neef et al., 1991). Thus, an *average* increase of 10 points from a pre- to a posttest may mean that a few participants did very well while others got worse or that most got a little better and a few did very well, and so on. Beginning researchers who have research questions that will clearly require some sort of group statistical design are advised to *consult with a statistician well in advance of the study*. Determining group sizes and selecting experimental variables require expertise usually well beyond that which may be acquired in the classroom, and having a statistical expert guide you through this maze will ensure that your study is suitable for publication when you are done.

This completes our discussion of research designs that are most commonly used in behavior analysis. There are other variants on these basic designs that may be discovered in reviewing the literature. As you begin to develop your research procedures, you will want to incorporate the variants on basic designs where it seems appropriate. In addition, there will no doubt be new research designs emerging with which to demonstrate experimental control under different circumstances. Just as the multiple-baseline design arose out of a need to show experimental control without the reversal of behaviors, it is anticipated that other designs will be developed to permit a demonstration of control as more sophisticated research questions arise.

The next step that must be taken by the researcher, just prior to the actual beginning of the experiment, is a careful examination of issues related to possible legal and ethical questions. These questions are presented in Step 8.

8

CONDUCT AN ETHICS CHECK

MAIN TOPICS

The Role of Ethics in Behavior Analysis Research
Guidelines for Responsible Conduct in Applied Research
Developing a Responsible Research Design
Working With the Institutional Review Board
Preventing the Abuse of Behavioral Research Findings
The Ethics of Publishing Your Work

LEARNING OBJECTIVES

In Step 8, we consider the importance of conducting your study in an ethically responsible way. You will review the "Guidelines for Responsible Conduct" adopted by the Behavior Analyst Certification Board as this document relates to applied behavior analysis research, learn how to work with your institutional review board (IRB), and learn what you can do to

193

prevent the misuse of your findings. When you have finished with this step, you should be able to

▶ Discuss the role of ethics in the development of your research plan.

▶ Describe how to work successfully with your IRB.

▶ Give examples of ways you can prevent the abuse of your research findings.

▶ Explain the ethics of publishing your work.

Behavior analysis researchers have special responsibilities for the conduct of their work, primarily because it *is* socially significant. We work with populations that are often ignored by other professionals in settings that frequently see no other researchers operating. And we work with human behaviors, such as aggression, self-injury, pica, and running away, that can be harmful if not handled absolutely appropriately. As a field, we have a tarnished history of which we should be ashamed. This is a history that involves abusing and mistreating "subjects" who were in our care. We are fortunate that in recent years, we have seen the emergence of human rights committees and peer review committees to provide oversight for behavior analysts. University-based institutional review boards (IRBs) oversee *all* researchers. The abstract term *ethics* has been replaced by the more behavioral *responsible conduct* as a way of describing our role as researchers. Finally, we have a set of Guidelines for Responsible Conduct (www.BACB. com) that have been adopted by the Behavior Analyst Certification Board™ (BACB; G. Shook, personal communication, 2001). This document includes recommendations for professional behavior analysts as well as behavior analysis researchers.

BACB Guidelines for Responsible Conduct

The guidelines relevant to researchers are shown in Table 2.8-1. These guidelines, as you can see, are very extensive and cover every aspect of research, from the design of responsible research (7.3) and avoiding harm to participants (7.1) to preventing the misuse of their work by others (7.1). Furthermore, they require you to obtain informed consent from all partici-

Table 2.8-1   Behavior Analyst Certification Board™ Guidelines for Responsible Conduct

7.0   **The Behavior Analyst and Research.** Behavior analysts design, conduct, and report research in accordance with recognized standards of scientific competence and ethical research. Regarding research with nonhuman subjects, the behavior analyst accepts the code of ethics approved by the American Psychological Association in 1992. Behavior analysts conduct research with human and nonhuman research participants according to the proposal approved by the local human research committee, and Institutional Review Board.

Behavior analysts plan their research so as to minimize the possibility that results will be misleading.

Behavior analysts conduct research competently and with due concern for the dignity and welfare of the participants. Researchers and assistants are permitted to perform only those tasks for which they are appropriately trained and prepared.

Behavior analysts are responsible for the ethical conduct of research conducted by them or by others under their supervision or control.

Behavior analysts conducting applied research conjointly with provision of clinical or human services obtain required external reviews of proposed clinical research and observe requirements for both intervention and research involvement by client-participants.

In planning research, behavior analysts consider its ethical acceptability under these Guidelines. If an ethical issue is unclear, behavior analysts seek to resolve the issue through consultation with institutional review boards, animal care and use committees, peer consultations, or other proper mechanisms.

7.1   **Scholarship and Research.** The behavior analyst engaged in study and research is guided by the conventions of the science of behavior including the emphasis on the analysis of individual behavior and strives to model appropriate applications in professional life.

Behavior analysts take reasonable steps to avoid harming their clients, research participants, students, and others with whom they work, and to minimize harm where it is foreseeable and unavoidable. Harm is defined here as negative effects or side effects of behavior analysis that outweigh positive effects in the particular instance, and that are behavioral or physical and directly observable.

Because behavior analysts' scientific and professional judgments and actions affect the lives of others, they are alert to and guard against personal, financial, social, organizational, or political factors that might lead to misuse of their influence.

Behavior analysts do not participate in activities in which it appears likely that their skills or data will be misused by others, unless corrective mechanisms, i.e., peer or external professional or independent review, are available.

Behavior analysts do not exaggerate claims for effectiveness of particular procedures or of behavior analysis in general.

(continued)

Table 2.8-1   Continued

If behavior analysts learn of misuse or misrepresentation of their individual work products, they take reasonable and feasible steps to correct or minimize the misuse or misrepresentation.

7.2   **Using Confidential Information for Didactic or Instructive Purposes.** Behavior analysts do not disclose in their writings, lectures, or other public media, confidential, personally identifiable information concerning their individual or organizational clients, students, research participants, or other recipients of their services that they obtained during the course of their work, unless the person or organization has consented in writing or unless there is other ethical or legal authorization for doing so.

Ordinarily, in such scientific and professional presentations, behavior analysts disguise confidential information concerning such persons or organizations so that they are not individually identifiable to others and so that discussions do not cause harm to participants who might identify themselves.

7.3   **Conformance With Laws and Regulations.** Behavior analysts plan and conduct research in a manner consistent with federal and state law and regulations, as well as professional standards governing the conduct of research, and particularly those standards governing research with human participants and animal subjects.

7.4   **Informed Consent.** Using language that is reasonably understandable to participants, behavior analysts inform participants of the nature of the research; they inform participants that they are free to participate or to decline to participate or to withdraw from the research; they explain the foreseeable consequences of declining or withdrawing; they inform participants of significant factors that may be expected to influence their willingness to participate (such as risks, discomfort, adverse effects, or limitations on confidentiality, except as provided in Standard 7.5 below); and they explain other aspects about which the prospective participants inquire.

For persons who are legally incapable of giving informed consent, behavior analysts nevertheless (1) provide an appropriate explanation, (2) discontinue research if the person gives clear signs of unwillingness to continue participation, and (3) obtain appropriate permission from a legally authorized person, if such substitute consent is permitted by law.

7.5   **Deception in Research.** Behavior analysts do not conduct a study involving deception unless they have determined that the use of deceptive techniques is justified by the study's prospective scientific, educational, or applied value and that equally effective alternative procedures that do not use deception are not feasible.

Behavior analysts never deceive research participants about significant aspects that would affect their willingness to participate, such as physical risks, discomfort, or unpleasant emotional experiences.

Any other deception that is an integral feature of the design and conduct of an experiment must be explained to participants as early as is feasible, preferably at the conclusion of their participation, but no later than at the conclusion of the research.

7.6   Behavior analysts inform research participants of their anticipated sharing or further use of personally identifiable research data and of the possibility of unanticipated future uses.

7.7   In conducting research, behavior analysts interfere with the participants or milieu from which data are collected only in a manner that is warranted by an appropriate research design and that is consistent with behavior analysts' roles as scientific investigators.

7.8   Behavior analysts take reasonable measures to honor all commitments they have made to research participants.

7.9   In presenting research, the behavior analyst ensures participant anonymity unless specifically waived by the participant or surrogate.

7.10   The behavior analyst informs the participant that withdrawal from the research may occur at any time without penalty except as stipulated in advance, as in fees contingent upon completing a project.

7.11   The behavior analyst informs the participant that debriefing will occur on conclusion of the participant's involvement in the research.

7.12   The behavior analyst answers all questions of the participant about the research that are consistent with being able to conduct the research.

7.13   The behavior analyst must obtain the written consent of the participant or surrogate before beginning the research.

7.14   If the behavior analyst recruits participants from classes and the participants are provided additional credit for participating in the research, nonparticipating students must be provided alternative activities that generate comparable credit.

7.15   In presenting research, the behavior analyst acknowledges the contributions of others who contributed to the conduct of the research by including them as coauthors or footnoting their contributions.

7.16   The behavior analyst who pays participants for research involvement or uses money as a reinforcer must obtain Institutional Review Board or Human Rights Committee approval of this practice and conform to any special requirements that may be established in the process of approval.

7.17   The behavior analyst who withholds part of the money earned by the participant until the participant has completed their research involvement must inform the participant of this condition prior to beginning the experiment.

7.18   The behavior analyst who serves on grant review panels avoids conducting any research described in grant proposals that the behavior analyst reviewed, except as replications fully crediting the prior researchers.

7.19   **Research With Animals.** Behavior analysts who conduct research involving animals treat them humanely and are in compliance with the Federal Animal Welfare Act.

pants, including permission from a legally authorized person to work with someone who might be incapable of giving informed consent.

The Institutional Review Board

All research conducted in any setting must pass muster with the IRB in the researcher's area. Because most research is done at universities, this will be handled on your campus. If you are not connected with a university—if, for example, you are working in a school or state facility—you will need to check with your administration to determine the protocol for presenting your proposal to the nearest IRB. These committees are made up of active researchers and often members of the community whose duty it is to represent the best interests of the participants and the research community. They usually meet once per month on a regular schedule and will have standard forms for you to fill out to have your work reviewed. It is a good idea to check with other students and professionals about the process and to ask for copies of submissions they have made to determine the proper format. When you find out that a date has been set for the review of your proposal, it is advisable (although not usually required) for you to attend. The members of the board often work in areas far removed from behavior analysis and may have questions that could hold up your proposal for a month or more if you are not present.

The IRB is seen as a troublesome and unnecessary hurdle by some, but in actuality, it is a godsend for researchers. By setting high standards for the responsible conduct of research, these committees do in fact protect the participants we work with. Experience has shown that recommendations coming from the board often strengthen applied proposals and offer protections not previously thought of by the researcher. In addition, by gaining IRB approval, you can be assured that if you follow closely all the approved protocols, you will not be accused of misconduct or wrongdoing. Prior to the advent of the IRB approval framework, researchers were on their own and put themselves at great risk for possible charges that they were operating unethically or irresponsibly.

Developing a Responsible Research Design

The nature of controlled research experiments is such that ethical issues can easily be raised about the use of certain designs under certain circumstances. Although these issues were alluded to in Step 7, a more detailed discussion is warranted at this juncture. It may be noted at the outset that withholding, withdrawing, or delaying a treatment in order to demonstrate experimental control may represent a breach of ethics. This is primarily the case when the researcher proposes to reverse a behavior (even for a short time) that is clearly not in the best interest of the participant. Such examples would presumably include a situation where the participant causes serious injury to himself or others (i.e., self-injurious or severe aggressive behavior). In most settings where you are working with participants who have dangerous behaviors, you will very likely have a nurse or physician who checks them each day and may even be present when the research is under way. Other protections include having an advocate or guardian for the participant either observe or be close by to make a determination if the person needs to be removed from the experimental setting. Research protocols often call for the session to be terminated if there is *any sign* of stress on the part of the participant.

In other cases where the behavior is chronic but is not considered critical (e.g., nail biting or being off task), a reversal design may be acceptable to the parties involved. Note that the issue of informed consent comes into play here: Teachers and parents have to be informed of this aspect of the study in advance and give their approval. Thus, in instances where the critical nature of the behavior precludes the use of a reversal design, one of the other designs should be used (e.g., cumulative-treatment multiple-baseline-across-subjects or across-behavior design). In other instances, the acute nature of the behavior under study may preclude a long baseline; again, ethical considerations demand that thought be given to, perhaps, a multielement or changing-criterion design as alternatives to a multiple baseline. Using an experimental group-control design may be seen as a desirable option in other cases where arrangements can be made to apply the treatment to the control group at the end of the experiment.

The importance of *matching the experimental design to the problem being studied in such a way that no harm comes to the participant* is paramount.

Careful consideration must be given to the ethical issues involved in demonstrating experimental control; this seems so apparent that little more need be said at this point. The creative, responsible researcher who is in close touch with these legal and ethical issues should have no trouble complying with the ever-increasing standards for responsible conduct of applied behavioral research.

Prevention of Abuse of Behavioral Research Findings

A second major obligation incumbent upon the applied researcher is for the development of procedures that, by their nature or their deployment, have a low risk of being abused by workers in the field. The ubiquitous *time-out* readily suggests itself as a procedure that has been widely abused. The early applied work with time-out (Tyler & Brown, 1967; Wolf et al., 1964) showed that removal of a child from a reinforcing situation to one where no reinforcement was available could be used as a nonharmful but effective punishment procedure. In those particular cases, the time-out area was a room void of furnishings but where monitoring of the subject was possible, and the duration of time-outs was relatively short (i.e., approximately 15 minutes). In an extension of this work, Bostow and Bailey (1969) showed that an even shorter (2-minute) time-out could be used to effectively reduce severely aggressive and destructive behavior if an incompatible behavior was reinforced at the same time (i.e., differential reinforcement of other behaviors [DRO]of 2-30 minutes).

Unfortunately, in none of these studies was a heavy emphasis placed upon (a) the need for almost *constant monitoring* of the subject, (b) a time-out area that was *well lighted and ventilated,* and (c) the fact that the client had to be removed from a *reinforcing* state of affairs. In addition, this work was done prior to the furor over patients' rights, and thus no discussion regarding informed consent can be found in these early studies. Subsequently, abuses of the grossest kind were to take place. In the Miami Sunland (an institution for developmentally disabled persons in Florida), a punishment procedure was used where residents were stripped of their clothes and placed naked in darkened rooms; often, more than one would be placed in the same "time-out" room. Being left overnight was not uncommon! This example turned out to be representative of several other distorted and inhumane forms of "behavior modification" that resulted in an investigation by a blue-ribbon committee (May, Risley, Twardosz, Friedman, Bijou, & Wexler, 1975) and the formalization of guidelines for the management of behavior problems of the mentally retarded (Risley & Twardosz, 1974).

In another incident that received wide press coverage, two teachers in Butte, Montana, who had formerly been employees at an institution for the mentally retarded, used a "homemade time-out box" as a punishment procedure in a class for emotionally disturbed children. The small box had no lighting or ventilation in it and was used in a classroom. When the mother of an asthmatic child found out that her child was being put in the box, she protested vigorously; the teachers were fired, the principal was demoted (they were all later reinstated), and the box was removed (Martin, 1975). It may be mere speculation at this time, but probably if the original time-out procedure been described as (a) the brief removal of the subject from a reinforcing activity, (b) to a well-ventilated and lighted but neutral space where (c) the child could be easily and regularly monitored, and if it was specified that (d) informed consent was required before the procedure could be used, most of these and other abuses could have been totally avoided. What *has* happened is that the courts have established guidelines and restrictions on the use of time-out (*Morales v. Turman*, 1974; *Gary W. and the United States v. Stewart et al.*, 1976). Thus, researchers who misuse time-out do not simply breach ethical and moral standards; they also violate federal law.

The abuses of time-out exemplify the need for researchers to be responsible in developing the conditions and circumstances under which a procedure may be employed. One way that this can be achieved today is by specification of all of the monitoring devices required (i.e., human rights committee, peer review committee, and IRB approval) before a restrictive procedure can be implemented. Another strategy is for the applied researcher to actively devise and develop unabusable procedures at the outset.

The "contingent observation" technique reported by Porterfield, Herbert-Jackson, and Risley (1976) is an excellent example of a humane and socially acceptable way of reducing misbehavior by removing a child from his or her playmates for short periods. Basically, the child is required to "sit and watch" the other children engage in their play until he or she is ready to rejoin the group. For our purposes, it is important to notice first that the procedure is described as *appropriate for a restricted setting and population:* namely, "in a day care center with very young normal children" (Porterfield et. al., 1976, p. 56) rather than being described in more global, all-inclusive terms (e.g., "This procedure is used to reduce inappropriate behavior"). Second, the contingent observation procedure is *described in great detail,* including how the child is to be handled and what should be said to the child in the process. In addition, a behavioral specification with a criterion for returning to the group is included. Finally, the researchers took the extra effort to do a social validation on the acceptability of the procedures by caregivers and parents as well. The behavior analysis researcher cannot, of course, take complete responsibility for potential abuse of their procedures by others. Like any tool, the contingent observation technique can be abused by those who are not sensitive to the ethical requirements of the field and the society. However, the obligation to anticipate potential abuses and to correct for them by building in controlling mechanisms (i.e., restriction, specification, and social validation) is clearly with us. This sequence, as so well illustrated in the Porterfield et al. (1976) study, would appear to establish a model for the development of humane, effective, and socially acceptable procedures for modifying human behavior.

The Ethics of Publishing Your Work

New researchers are often excited about their work and want to see it in print. Making a contribution to the literature in your field can bring you fame and, every now and then, fortune. When researchers are eager to see their names in print, there is sometimes a temptation to submit to several journals at once. This practice is strictly forbidden by the American Psychological Association (APA) Code of Ethics and by the BACB Guidelines (9.4) because it "distorts the knowledge base by making it appear there is more information available than really exists" (APA, 1994, p. 295). Additionally, researchers "must not submit to an APA journal a manuscript describing work that has been published in whole or in substantial part elsewhere" (p. 296). Although this principle is adhered to by the vast majority of authors, there are occasional lapses. Chhokar and Wallin (1984a, 1984b), for example, published two versions of the same study, including the same graphs, within the same year in the *Journal of Applied Psychology* and the *Journal of Safety Research*.

CARRY OUT YOUR RESEARCH PROJECT

Daily and Weekly Checklists for Success

MAIN TOPICS _____

Preparing Your Contact Person for the Start of the Study
Preparing Your Observers for Their Research Debut
Final Preparations for Days 1, 2, 3, and 4
Designing a Checklist for Week 2 and Beyond
Planning for Your First Intervention
Managing the Rest of Your Study
Wrapping Up Your Research

LEARNING OBJECTIVES _____

In Step 9, we provide you with tips and checklists for actually carrying out
your research project. You will learn how to prepare your contact person
and your observers and how to construct operations checklists for the first

day through the end of your study. After you have completed this step, you should be able to

- Describe how you will prepare your contact person for the start of your research project.

- Tell how you will prepare your observers for their big first day.

- Discuss your final preparations and make checklists for Day 1 and the rest of the first week.

- Develop checklists for the succeeding weeks of your study.

- Describe how you will prepare for your first intervention.

- Depict scenarios for managing the rest of your study.

- State how you will wrap up your study successfully, leaving no loose ends.

The big moment of your research career is about to arrive. You have planned everything carefully and are now ready to actually carry out your research project. You should have a rough time line for running your project in mind at the outset of the study. This is important, even though with behavioral research we never really know until the data start rolling in exactly how long a study will take. You will develop your time line and add to this number of weeks 2 or 3 additional weeks to cover any problems that might arise. Once you have an estimate of how long your study will take, you should inform your observers of the length of their commitment.

Preparing Your Contact Person

By now you should be well established with your contact person in the setting where you will be working, and that person should be very clear about the research that is about to take place. There is nothing worse than surprises for contact persons—especially if the surprise somehow reflects negatively on them. This means that your contact knows each of your observers. He or she should have been introduced a week or two earlier when you were doing your pilot work and should know where he or she will be located when observing, how long he or she will be on site, and so on. This is just in case a staff person or someone else asks questions about the observers. Your contact should know roughly how long the study will run and should be aware of the research question you are asking and something about your data collection system.

Preparing Your Observers

You are responsible for your observation team and need to make sure that they are accountable for their time at the research location. You may need to have them sign in and out or at least have them check in with your contact person when they arrive on site. This is especially true in some settings, such as schools, nursing homes, and residential facilities. Remember, in a sense you are intruding on someone else's turf. You must be respectful of their setting, whether it is an office, business, classroom, or home. Your observers should have been trained to be unobtrusive in all respects, including voice loudness, movements, and appearance. They should be aware of the need for them to be polite at all times. They should arrive at the setting on time and with little fanfare, have all their observation sheets or computer data collection devices ready, and know where to go to begin their observations.

Final Preparations

At this point, you should have received all your necessary permissions from your committee, the institutional review board (IRB), and any other research review committees. You should have completed your social validation interviews or surveys and have confidence in the findings. Your pilot work should be complete, and you should have worked out all the bugs in your data collection system. Because most studies begin with a baseline, you should not be putting any interventions in place right away. However, you should have tested interventions in your pilot work and determined the necessary parameters to make them effective. Your observers should be well trained and producing high reliabilities with you and with each other. By now you should have selected your primary observer and designated your reliability checkers. Observation schedules for at least the first couple of weeks should have been handed out. Any equipment that you will need should have been thoroughly checked.

Getting Ready for Day 1

Other things being equal, it is a good idea to start your study on a Tuesday or Wednesday; this will give you the Monday before to work out any last-minute details. It is not a good idea to start on a Friday because you will only have 1 day's data, and if there are glitches, which there always are, you will have to work on them over the weekend when the setting may be closed and your observers unavailable.

Table 2.9-1 shows a checklist for Day 1.

Days 2, 3, and 4

Table 2.9-2 shows a checklist for Day 2. Table 2.9-3 shows a checklist for Days 3 and 4.

Week 2

Table 2.9-4 shows a checklist for Week 2.

Week 3 and Beyond

By Week 3, you will be an old hand at running your study. You will have made all the necessary adjustments in your data collection and perhaps fired an observer or done some retraining with others. You should be very familiar to the stalwarts in the setting and may be warmly greeted with a "How's it going?" This is not a serious invitation to discuss your findings (which are very premature at this point and should never be discussed at the setting with anyone but your contact person except under very unusual circumstances). You should be in the habit of graphing your data every day. You can begin showing them to your research colleagues or presenting them at research meetings to get the reaction of your friends and associates. They may have some valuable thoughts or suggestions. Continue to meet

Table 2.9-1   Checklist for Day 1

❑ Plan to arrive at the setting a good hour before data collection begins.

❑ Have your observer schedule and extra data sheets ready.

❑ Meet your observers outside, and have a brief pep talk about the importance of being professional, show them where to sign in, and escort them to the observation area.

❑ Find an unobtrusive place to observe the first data collection and take notes.

❑ When the session is over, gather up the data sheets (or computerized data collection recorders).

❑ Have a debriefing with the observers. Give them feedback (hopefully all positive) on how they did, answer any questions, and prompt them about their next assignment.

❑ Meet with your contact person and tell him or her how it went. Mention any problems and troubleshoot them for the next day. Tell your contact person how important he or she is to your study.

❑ Retreat to a quiet place, breathe a deep sigh of relief, and pull out your first day's data.

❑ Graph your data (note: working graphs are still often prepared with pencil on blue-lined graph paper).

❑ Call your major professor or whoever is helping you with the project and give this person a briefing.

❑ Make a list of any modifications or adjustments that need to be made for the next day.

Table 2.9-2   Checklist for Day 2

❑ Arrive 30 minutes before the data collection session.

❑ Meet your observers and give them any new instructions based on Day 1.

❑ Observe unobtrusively and take notes.

❑ Collect your data at the end of the session.

❑ Meet with your observers, show appreciation, answer any questions, and give feedback and suggestions.

❑ Meet with your setting's contact person and tell him or her how it went.

❑ Retreat to a quiet place, breathe a deep sigh of relief, and pull out your second day's data and graph them.

with your observers weekly to answer any questions and to show appreciation—bring food occasionally.

Table 2.9-3   Checklist for Days 3 and 4

❑ Repeat Day 2 for the rest of the first week.

❑ Meet with your major professor or whoever is helping you with the project and present the data. Take notes on any adjustments or modifications that need to be made. Get ready for Week 2.

❑ Meet with your observers as a team, buy them pizza, and celebrate the completion of the first week's data collection. Show appreciation to each one individually.

Table 2.9-4   Checklist for Week 2

❑ In Week 2, you will be able to thin out your brief meetings with your contact person; two times in the second week should be enough to let him or her know that all is going well and that you will not need to bother him or her so much. Depending upon the circumstances, you may want to show your contact person the data with assurances that he or she will not make any changes to the operation of the site.

❑ You will also be able to let your observers operate more independently, but you should still be on site when the data are being collected.

❑ Meet with your major professor or research supervisor and show the data. Discuss plans for the next week.

❑ It may be time to start preparing for your first intervention, which could be coming up soon.

❑ Meet with your observers as a team, bring snacks, and show appreciation for all their hard work.

Preparing for the First Intervention

When you are ready to carry out your first intervention, you should go back to your Week 1 schedule of arriving early and preparing the setting. Those involved, whether teachers, nursing staff, parents, or others, will need some precise training on how to carry out the first intervention, and you should be prepared to do role playing and criterion-based training to make sure it comes off without a hitch. Table 2.9-5 provides a short checklist for this phase of your research.

Table 2.9-5 Intervention Checklist

❏ Prepare a training checklist for those who will be involved in the intervention. You will want the training to be efficient and effective, and you will need to take data on it for your Method section. How long did the training take? How quickly did the performers reach criterion? What did they think of the training?

❏ Prepare an independent-variable data collection form for independent variable integrity and have a protocol ready, including designated observers who have been specifically trained on this and who can show high reliability.

❏ Make ready any special equipment or supplies that will be necessary for the intervention. Test it out to make sure it works properly.

❏ Meet with your contact person to remind this person of the intervention and talk through the details so there are no surprises.

❏ Observe the first day of intervention; take notes.

❏ Give feedback (hopefully positive) to those involved in the intervention.

❏ Meet with your major professor or research supervisor. Present the data and discuss any adjustments or modifications that might need to be made.

Managing the Rest of Your Study

After you complete your first intervention successfully, you will *really* feel like an old hand at behavioral research. By this time, you will have encountered most of the problems that *can* come up, and you will have solved them handily. This is no time to lighten up, however. After the third or fourth week, you will need to watch out for behavior drift with your observers and possibly with those who are doing the intervention. To counter this, you may need to have additional training or booster sessions to bring them back up to speed. Remember, no one on your project will be as highly motivated as you. You will need to be the one to provide *them* the motivation to stick to the protocol and maintain the quality of the research. You will need to continue your independent variable integrity measures, your reliability checks, and your social validity measures. You will also have to work diligently with your contact person to make sure that he or she is not getting tired of having you and your observers around: It may be time to take some people to lunch to show your appreciation. Particularly watch out for observer problems if you are working with undergraduates and are nearing the midterm exam portion of the semester.

As you move through your interventions, make sure you are taking good notes. These will be useful when you are writing up your Method section. You may have had to make minor modifications in procedures, and these changes will have to be noted.

Wrapping Up Your Study

At some point about 6 to 9 weeks into your study, you will begin to see the proverbial "light at the end of the tunnel." You and your major professor or research supervisor may be able to talk about a time line for finishing your project. *Do not rush to finish*. Take the necessary time to do this right the first time. As things begin to wind down, you will want to schedule some time with your contact person and let this person know your study is winding down. Some contacts will want you to do a presentation for others in the setting, and some will not. Your job is to cooperate fully with their wishes. It is a good idea to prepare an Executive Summary of your work (1-2 pages with bullet points for the key findings) for your contact person. If things have gone well and the person is interested in adopting your new procedures, you must offer to help with any training or transition meetings that will be necessary to make it happen. Ideally, you will have found the research worthwhile and will want to continue this line of research. Even better, your contact person and perhaps others in the setting will also be interested in having you or some of your associates back to continue the work. This is the highest compliment that can be paid to a behavioral researcher. This is the reinforcer that makes all of the hard work worthwhile.

ANALYZE AND
GRAPH YOUR DATA

MAIN TOPICS

The Virtues of Visual Analysis

Should I Analyze My Data Statistically?

Guidelines for the Design of Graphs in Applied Behavior Analysis

LEARNING OBJECTIVES

In Step 10, we consider issues related to graphing the data from your study so you can analyze it effectively. You will confront issues related to the possible statistical analysis of your data, and we will provide you with guidelines for designing graphs for your findings. After studying this step, you should be able to

- Discuss the virtues of visual analysis.

- Describe the pros and cons of analyzing your data statistically.

- Prepare sample graphs using recommended guidelines from the *Journal of Applied Behavior Analysis (JABA)* and other sources.

One beauty of behavior analysis research is that it is designed in such a way that the experimenter is "on line" with the data as it is collected. If you are using computerized data collection, the data can be graphed almost as soon as they are tabulated. If you are using observers and hand-tabulating your data, it might be an hour or so before you can plot the data for the day and begin to analyze them. In any event, by looking at the data every day, you will see your experiment unfold before your eyes. Graphing your data provides a graphic display of the results of all your hard work. So how do you analyze your data, and what happens next?

The Virtues of Visual Analysis

The analysis of single-participant design data has a long tradition of being done visually. The tradition began with B. F. Skinner (1938), who initially promoted the concept of the long-term operant analysis of the behavior of a few organisms, and the analysis of cumulative records. The cumulative record data came straight off the cumulative recorders of the time. Skinner and his followers (Ayllon & Michael, 1959; Parsonson & Baer, 1978; Sidman, 1960; Wolf et al., 1964) refined the analysis and adapted it to applied human behavior, and the tradition continues to this day. This method may not be perfect, and any two professionals looking at the same data may not agree on what they see or may draw different conclusions from time to time. However, it is a time-tested method that does have some advantages. First, the data that the person is viewing are basically very nearly raw data, untouched by statistical "cooking." What you see is what you get when it comes to behavioral data. The only manipulation that seems to be of much concern involves the scale of the y axis. In judging data visually, it pays to check this to make sure it does not distort the data in any systematic way. Second, graphing data and analyzing them visually appears to be a conservative way of making judgments. If you make a mistake in judgment, it is likely to be in the direction of saying there was no effect rather than identifying one. To conclude that an intervention had an effect, it has to be fairly sizable. Statistics on the other hand, appear to magnify small effects and lead people to be impressed with very small effects that actually could have happened by chance. Statistics show when an intervention is statistically significant. But in behavior analysis, we have to be concerned with clinical significance. The presentation of behavioral data is of utmost importance in determining if clinical significance has been achieved.

In reading a graph and drawing conclusions, you will note that essentially two decisions have to be made. Is there a cause-effect relationship between the independent and dependent variable? And, if there is, is it of sufficient size to be of interest to anyone? On the next page, Figure 2.10-1 shows (in the top panel) a clear cause-effect relationship but an effect size so small as to be trivial.

Two possible factors make drawing any conclusion difficult in analyzing graphic data: amount of variability and trending. If there is too much variability in either the baseline or the treatment conditions, it may be difficult to determine if there was a cause-effect relationship. Furthermore, if there is any significant trending during baseline or during an intervention, it may be difficult to tell if you had an effect. It should be noted that these are true effects. That is, if you were looking at variable data and could not decide whether or not there was an effect, having statistical "proof" that there was should be of little comfort. Figure 2.10-2 illustrates both points.

Should I Analyze My Data Statistically?

Statistical analyses are often applied to data such as those shown in Figure 2.10-2's top panel in an attempt to "save" the data. Because there is a difference in the mean, there is some chance that the data are statistically significant. The data shown in Figure 2.10-3 provide a good example of this approach. The data are from a de facto analysis of a change in prison policy that went into effect at the end of July in 1968. This change in policy was designed to reduce the frequency of behavioral offenses. The data are fundamentally weak because the "design" is nothing more than a baseline followed by a treatment. Looking closely at the data, you will see a clear downtrend starting in January 1968 and extending through February 1970 that completely negates any argument that the change of policy was responsible for the apparent drop in daily offenses. Nonetheless, a complicated statistical analysis "yielded a T ratio . . . which is significant at the 0.05 level" (Schnelle & Lee, 1974, p. 488). The trick, of course, is that the "significant change" is in the "level of offenses." In this case, it seems obvi-

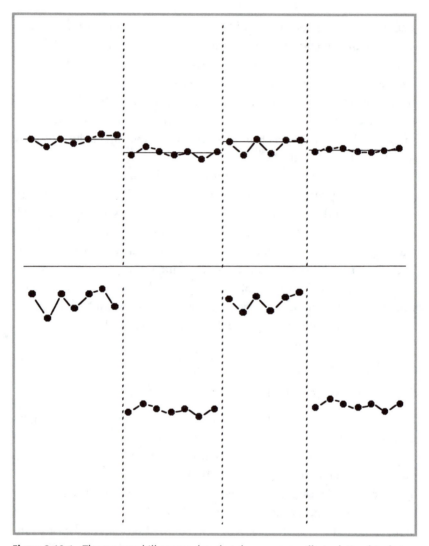

Figure 2.10-1. The top panel illustrates data that show a cause-effect relationship, but the effect size is unlikely to be of much interest. The bottom panel shows data where the effect size is likely to be socially significant.

ous that a visual analysis of the data is superior to a statistical analysis. From examining the data from January 1970 through July 1971, it seems pretty clear that the conclusion that there was a "significant" change as a result of the change in policy was premature. Basically, it would appear that "behav-

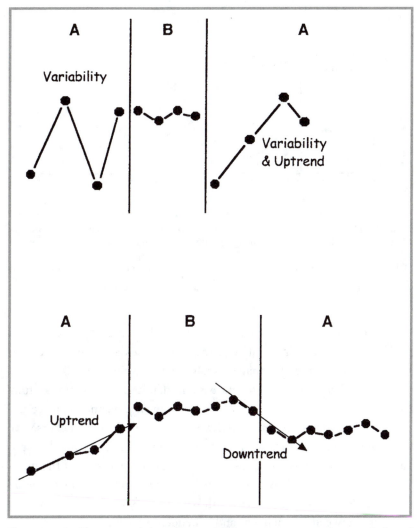

Figure 2.10-2. The top panel shows how variability can prevent any clear conclusion of an effect from Treatment B. Confounding this is the variability and uptrending in the return to baseline condition. The bottom panel shows the effect that trending in data can prevent unambiguous conclusions from being drawn.

ioral offenses" are part of a very large cycle of change controlled by variables of which we are unaware. Note, for example, the uptrend from January through April 1970, followed by a long downtrend that lasts for 13 months, followed by the beginning of a new uptrend in the data.

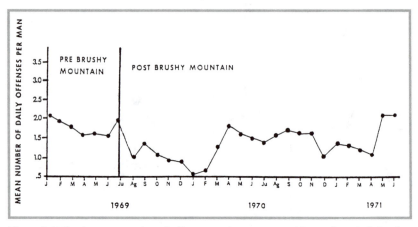

Figure 2.10-3. Average number of offenses per inmate over a 30-month period. Brushy Mountain policy introduced July 28, 1969. Monthly data multiplied by a constant of 1,000.

SOURCE: From "A Quasi-Experimental Retrospective Evaluation of a Prison Policy Change," by J. Schnelle and J. Lee, 1974, *Journal of Applied Behavior Analysis, 7,* pp. 483-496. Copyright 1974 by the Society for the Experimental Analysis of Behavior. Reprinted with permission.

Furthermore, it is clear that an AB design should rarely be used to draw any firm conclusions. The only way to "save" these data would have been to run this as a study rather than by analyzing then after it was all over. Any good researcher would want to take baseline data and watch them carefully to determine when they were stable, then put the intervention in place and run the condition again until stability was achieved. Finally, of course, we would need to return to baseline—again watching for stability and a replication of the previous condition—followed by a replication of the intervention. The statistical analysis of time-series data such as those shown in Figure 2.10-3 does little service for those who are seeking functional relationships between independent and dependent variables.

You may find yourself under some pressure to analyze your data statistically. Be aware that there is considerable debate as to the value of this approach. Whole books have been written on the topic (Haccou & Meelis, 1992) and many chapter-length treatises as well (Elashoff & Thoresen, 1978; Gorman & Allison, 1996; Matyas & Greenwood, 1996). Certainly, if you have planned and carried out what amounts to a group-design study, statistics are the relevant tool. Bear in mind the earlier recommendation to consult a statistician at the planning stage of your study and have that person describe explicitly how to design the study. If, on the other hand, you have carefully designed a thoroughly behavioral study, inferential statistics may not be relevant.

Basically, there are two questions to be asked in any behavioral study: (a) Is there a cause-effect relationship shown between my intervention and the behavior I am interested in? and (b) If there was a cause-effect relationship, was it *important* to the individuals involved? Note that we did not use the term *significant*. The first question is always answered through quality single-participant design (Step 7), and the second is always answered through social validity (Step 4). If you have carefully designed your study according to the suggestions in this book and executed it with meticulous attention to detail, then there should be little reason to use inferential statistics. Behavior analysts have always used descriptive statistics to talk about mean differences and other changes in their data—there is little question about this practice.

One issue that does seem relevant to the analysis of your data is how you prepare your graphs for your colleagues to view. After all, if you are doing a visual analysis of data, it makes sense to present the data in a way that is easy to understand. In the next section, we will provide a few suggestions for designing and displaying your data.

Guidelines for the Design of Graphs in Applied Behavior Analysis

The graphic or pictorial representation of data collected in the course of carrying out a behavior analysis study usually represents the culmination of long hours of preparation, observation, and manipulation of independent variables, the purpose of which is to discover functional relationships between the changes in the environment and socially significant behaviors. Unfortunately, many researchers do *not* take an equally intense interest in a careful, clear, and concise presentation of their finished work. All too often, an Excel spreadsheet is simply converted directly to a preformatted graph. The result is that the reader, even the sophisticated and interested one, can decipher the study only with great difficulty; the less well-prepared

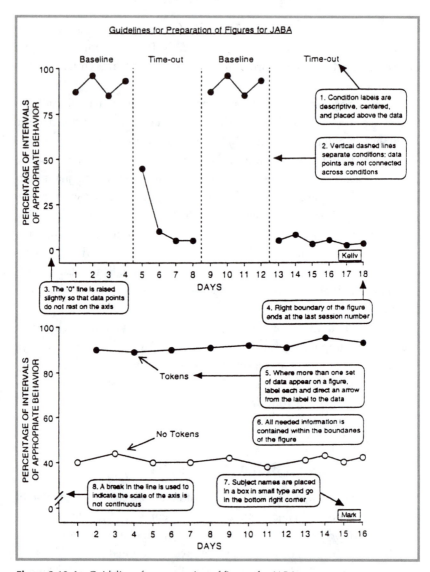

Figure 2.10-4. Guidelines for preparation of figures for *JABA*
SOURCE: "Guidelines for Preparation of Figures for *JABA*," 2000, *Journal of Applied Behavior Analysis, 33*, p. 399. Copyright 2000 by the Society for the Experimental Analysis of Behavior. Reprinted with permission.

or less motivated reader may simply give up trying to discern the results of the study.

The purpose of this section is to present some guidelines regarding the graphic representation of data that should result in a much more aesthetically pleasing, efficient, and unambiguous presentation of your results. Prior to designing the graphs of your data, you will want to consult the fourth edition of the *APA Publication Manual* (APA, 1994), Items 3.76-3.81, for their standards for figures and suggestions for the preparation of figures. Then you will need to review the "Guidelines for Preparation of Figures for *JABA*" (2000, p. 399) shown in Figure 2.10-4. These guidelines differ somewhat from those of the *APA Publication Manual* because they have been specially developed to meet the special needs of the behavior analyst researcher. By following the steps outlined by Carr and Burkholder (1998), you can fairly easily enter your raw data into a spreadsheet and format a line graph that will be fairly close to the standards suggested below. However, experience has shown that additional modifications will be necessary to produce a quality graph.

For a thorough treatment of the importance of understanding the visual aspects of graphics, we strongly recommend "Part II: Theory of Data Graphics" in Edward R. Tufte's tour de force book *The Visual Display of Quantitative Information* (1983).

Probably the first rule of data presentation is that every attempt should be made to *make the task of the reader as easy as possible*. This means that the graph should present a clear, uncluttered picture so that the reader does not have to learn idiosyncratic codes for conditions, behaviors, and special events occurring at certain times during the study (Tufte, 1983). Tufte also recommended that we "maximize the data-ink ratio" and reduce redundant or "nondata"ink to a minimum. Three other conventions are also suggested to improve the aesthetics and readability of behavior analysis graphs.

1. *Ratio of ordinate to abscissa.*   Graphs are easiest to read if the data points are not too close together on either the vertical (ordinate) or the horizontal (abscissa) axis. Also, a balanced ratio of the ordinate to abscissa of about 1:2 (i.e., wider than tall) enhances legibility. Figure 2.10-5 illustrates the "cramped" effect when data are presented on a 2:1 ratio versus the same data presented on a graph with a 1:1.6 ordinate-to-abscissa ratio as recommended by Tufte (1983).

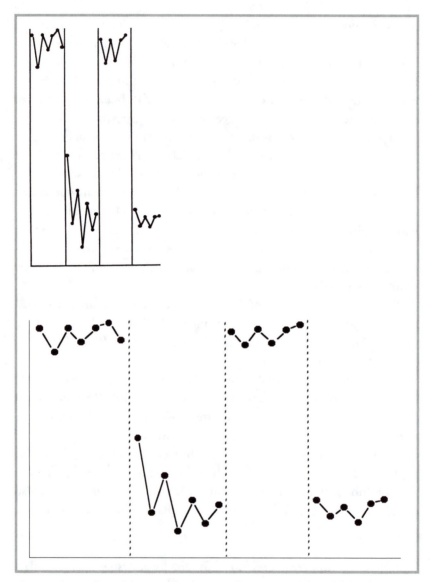

Figure 2.10-5. Effect of the ratio of ordinate to abscissa on graph readability. The top panel shows the "cramped" effect seen in graphing data on a 2:1 ratio. The same data presented with Tufte's recommended 1:1.16 are shown in the bottom panel.

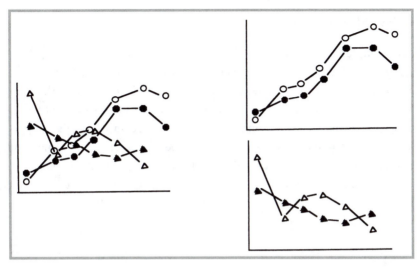

Figure 2.10-6. Effects of having too much data on one graph

2. *Connecting the data points.* Next, as shown in the bottom panel of Figure 2.10-5, a line should be drawn between data points that almost touches each point. To emphasize the individual data points, the use of relatively large dots with a connecting line (1 pt) slightly heavier than the ordinate or abscissa (hairline) is recommended.

3. *Amount of data presented per graph.* Researchers invariably take more than one measure of behavior (e.g., they may measure the effects of some independent variable(s) on four or five dependent variables). A frequent error in graphing is attempting to present all of the data on one graph, as shown in Figure 2.10-6; a preferred strategy is to divide the data and put them on at least two graphs. A good rule of thumb, then, is to avoid putting more than two sets of data on any one graph. The symbols for each should be discriminably different, for example, solid black circles and solid lines for one behavior and open triangles and dashed lines for a second behavior. Note that with multielement designs, particularly with studies of functional analysis, it is common to have all data lines on one graph because the overlapping appearance is useful for determining functions.

What Next?

This completes the 10 steps of our venture into research in applied behavior analysis. We hope you have been successful and "enjoyed the ride" and that you will want to do more. For now, though, it is time to start thinking about presenting your findings to others. You will probably start with your colleagues by giving an informal presentation at a research meeting or perhaps a colloquium in the department. Your next step involves sharing your work at a local or national conference and after that submitting your work for possible publication in a journal. All of this is covered in Part 3, "Going Public."

PART

3

GOING PUBLIC

MAIN TOPICS

Giving a Data or Other Presentation
The Components of Effective Public Speaking
Using Audiovisual Aids
Presenting a Poster
Publishing Your Research

LEARNING OBJECTIVES

In Part 3, "Going Public," we provide suggestions for presenting your find-ings in various venues and formats. You will learn the essentials of effective public speaking, how to use visual aids, and how to prepare a poster for a conference. You will also learn how to select an appropriate journal for sub-mission and how to prepare your manuscript. After studying this step, you should be able to

- Describe how you would prepare a data or other presentation.

- List the components of effective public speaking.

▶ Illustrate how you would use audiovisual aids to enhance your presentation.

▶ State how you would prepare a poster for a conference.

▶ Discuss the issues related to publishing your work, including the selection of the right journal for submission and how to prepare your manuscript.

The purpose of doing applied behavior research is to make a contribution to our understanding of human behavior. This goal implies two separate components in the research endeavor: (a) carrying out a definitive and well-controlled study and (b) *disseminating* those findings to others in the field. Research done for the idle amusement of the researcher that is neither communicated to nor evaluated by consumers and colleagues may be difficult to justify.

Dissemination of findings to the scientific community can take several forms, the most usual of which is a presentation at regional and national professional meetings and publication in peer-reviewed journals. You should be aware that your audience has become accustomed, through the Internet, television, and print media, to expect technically well-produced presentations that are concise, accurate, interesting and easy to understand. In going public, you must take the responsibility of seeing to it that your work is organized in such a way that it will have these qualities.

The purpose of this section is to suggest some guidelines for the successful presentation and dissemination of research findings. We will first provide some suggestions on giving an oral presentation for a conference or other group, followed by some suggestions for preparing a poster. Next, we will share some thoughts on submitting manuscripts to a journal for review and publication. Finally, we will offer some guidelines for the design and preparation of graphs for publication and presentation.

Giving a Data or Other Presentation

One of the most frequent ways that behavior analysts communicate with one another and the public is through talks, lectures, and workshop presentations. Unfortunately, few of us have a natural bent for public speaking, and even fewer have tried to remedy the problem through courses that are readily available at most colleges and universities. The failure to communicate effectively can result in bored audiences who only half understand the point of your research and who may be disinclined to pursue your area of research. Depending upon the audience and the circumstances, your presentation could result in your graduate school application not being well received if a member of the admissions committee is in the audience, or in a job interview being canceled at the last minute. With potentially so much at stake, the need to develop a pleasing speaking style that is suited to the audience and gets the message across would seem of utmost importance to the behavior analyst. The discussion that follows is not meant to substitute for a course on public speaking; rather, it is designed to point out some key skills required in good public speaking. We will concentrate on the most frequent form of speaking, that which involves a presentation of data from a research study.

Determination of Audience Makeup and Time Allotment

Before you do anything else, it is important to find out who your audience will be. For behavior analysis, your audience will, of course, consist of colleagues and graduate students who expect a high-level technical presentation on the topic. As a graduate student, you may be required to address three distinctly different audiences: your master's or doctoral committee (as in a prospectus defense), colleagues at a paper session at the Association for Behavior Analysis (ABA) annual meeting, or a meeting of professionals in the setting where you conducted your research. Also, bear in mind that some talks are "just the facts," as in a data presentation at a conference. Others are more to persuade or to serve as casual background or general information sessions. Make sure you know what the purpose of the talk is before you step in front of the audience.

In those cases where you are not so familiar with your audience, it is best to inquire from the person arranging the talk as to the makeup of the audience. Be particularly aware that a lay audience, or one made up of persons not in your specialty area, will often be unreceptive to a complex technical presentation involving all the jargon of the field. For such an audience, it is best to use nontechnical language, add anecdotes and personal experiences to make a point, and allow plenty of time for them to ask questions. If you were speaking to the parent-teacher organization, you could inquire directly, "How many parents are there here tonight? Could you hold up your hands, please? Good, thank you. Now, how many teachers are there?" and so on.

It is also important to know the size of the group to which you will be speaking. It is usually appropriate to be more informal if there is a small gathering than if you are speaking to several hundred people. The size of the group will also affect the audiovisual equipment you will need, if any. For a small group, the original poster with your data on it may be more appropriate than the use of an overhead or computer projector. Computer projectors are available in the LCD (liquid crystal display) or DLP (digital light processing) formats. There are advantages and disadvantages to each type of computer projector, and you are most likely to have access to the LCD format at conferences.

Another key consideration is the length of time that you will be allowed to speak. For papers presented in a paper session at the ABA or the American Psychological Association (APA), the standard length of time is about 15 minutes. For papers presented as part of a symposium, your talk may be 20 minutes. It is important to know how much time you have available so you can narrow the focus of your topic. For data presentations, this usually means that the introduction and review of the literature is quite short— generally less than 2 minutes in a 15-minute talk. The part on methods will usually be the longest part of any presentation, taking 7 or 8 minutes. The results and conclusions then will have to be given in 3 to 4 minutes. When the allotted time is broken down this way, it becomes clear that the shorter the presentation, the tighter the scripting must be. In addition, the use of visual aids becomes almost essential because so much more information can be presented.

Components of Effective Speaking

Effective public speakers engage in several behaviors that have been identified by experts in the field (Fawcett & Miller, 1975). These will be briefly listed, and the interested reader is referred to the previously cited literature for a complete discussion of public speaking.

1. *Eye contact.*   Scan your audience every few seconds and make eye contact with different individuals. By doing so, you will convey your interest in them as listeners. Do not look only at your script, at your feet, the wall, or one particular person from the audience. Also, do not turn your back on the audience, even when you are pointing to certain aspects of a graph on the screen.

2. *Voice loudness.*   You should adjust your voice to the size of the audience, the room, and any amplification system that may be available. Overpowering your listener is just as bad as speaking too softly.

3. *Speaking rate and tone.*   Dull monotone speakers are the most deadly of all. Try to speak in a conversational tone and at a normal rate. If you talk too fast, your audience will be confused and may lose interest. One suggestion if you are brand-new to public speaking is to ask a colleague to sit on the front row and give you prompts (e.g., "Speak louder" or "Slow down") via cue cards.

4. *Movement.*   A speaker who appears to be interested and enthusiastic in a topic seems to have greater movement. Hand or arm gestures may be used effectively as long as they are not overused. If you are using a portable microphone that will allow you to move back and forth to the screen or to approach the audience rather than being barricaded behind the podium, you will gain more attention from your listeners. Warning: Do not do this to excess. Speakers who pace from one end of the room to the other wear out their audiences.

5. *Irritating verbal and motor "tics."*   Exceedingly nervous and inexperienced speakers are most easily identified by their repetition of "you know," "uumm," "aaahh," and other verbal tics that can grate on the ears and be a major distraction to your audience. Other irritating mannerisms include buttoning and unbuttoning one's jacket, jangling keys in a pocket, touching a part of the face repeatedly, pacing, licking of the lips, and so on. The only cure for such distracting behavior is to practice your talk several times before your big day.

6. *Handling questions.*   Even an excellent speaker can destroy the effects of a talk by mishandling any questions that might follow. The most frequent error is seen in the speaker who tries to "put down" a questioner with a smart remark or who otherwise conveys a condescending attitude toward the audience. A hostile question or one meant to embarrass the speaker can often be defused by saying, "I'm sorry you feel that way. Let me see if I can explain my view. . . ." Avoid letting one person dominate the questioning. If a question is asked to which you don't know the answer, be humble. Admit you don't know, and try to provide whatever information you can. You can refer the person who has asked the question to another person, or indicate that you can look up the needed information and will e-mail or write with the answer.

Using Audiovisual Aids

Generally, the purpose of your talk will be to explain to the audience the nature of the subjects and behavior dealt with, the method of data collection, the type of research design used, the kind of independent variables studied, and, of course, the results of the study. Because you must pack so much information into so little time, audiovisual aids obviously can speed up the transmission of information. The use of audiovisual equipment is no substitute for reducing the content of a speech to the bare essentials, however. It is of the utmost importance that you match your need to explain or describe some event with the audiovisual equipment that will do this best.

Overhead Projector

The overhead projector is a versatile piece of equipment that is readily available at most conventions. Overhead projectors fit nicely with stand-up presentations when you want to point to various aspects of your overlay display while still facing your audience. Perhaps the greatest advantage of using an overhead projector is that the plastic acetate overlays are so easy to make. Basically, you generate the text or graphics you want on your computer, put the appropriate transparency in your printer, and select the "Print" icon. It is not a bad idea to pick up a pen (such as a Vis-à-Vis pen) that can be used to mark on transparencies from an office supply. The most frequent error that is made in the use of transparencies is having too small an image. If you are word-processing an outline of a set of procedures or the definition of behavior, for example, use at least a 12-point font. It is important in the use of an overhead projector to check out the arrangement between the microphone, screen, projector, and podium ahead of time. To fill a standard screen, an overhead projector must be approximately 6 to 8 feet in front of the screen. If the overhead is too far from the screen (the most common error of placement), your image will exceed the boundaries of the screen. Take the time to move it closer until there is a tight fit between the outer edges of your transparency and the screen. If there is a podium with a fixed microphone to the side of the screen, either you must have someone else put the transparencies on for you or you must walk back and forth to the projector to change the transparencies. One option is to hold a portable microphone in your hand, wear a lavalier microphone around your neck, or attach a wireless mike to your shirt or blouse and stand at the projector so you can make your own changes.

Producing an E-Slideshow Using Microsoft PowerPoint

PowerPoint is rapidly becoming the most popular way to give a presentation. This easy-to-use software can give a professional look to almost any talk. Here are a few tips. First, use a nongarish template—one that has muted colors without excess starbursts, comets, or grid lines running through the text. Second, resist the temptation to put too much information on one slide. Generally, there should be no more than six words per line and no more than six lines of text per page. It is always a good idea to "animate" your text by having the key points come in one at a time, but do not go overboard. It is very distracting to have lines of text flying in and around the screen finally landing in position to the sound of clattering typewriter keys. Third, when showing data, "program" the sequence that your audience sees by showing the baseline first, followed by the baseline *and* first intervention, and so on. This is easily done by making as many duplicates of the slide as there are conditions and then masking the parts you do not want to be seen. It is a good idea to include digital slides or video clips of your actual experiment. It heightens the interest of your audience if they can see the setting where the study was done, get a look at the participants (make sure you have signed permissions for all photos), and possibly see the interventions in action. Finally, you can lighten up your presentation with a few pieces of clipart, but do not go overboard. Put an ending slide with something like "Can I answer any questions?" on it so your audience will know you are done.

Making Last-Minute Arrangements for PowerPoint Presentations

Making sure that your computer and LDC projector work perfectly is your primary concern with this type of presentation. Be sure that you can make all the cable connections and have memorized the keystroke sequence for the image to be transferred to the LCD projector. Practice this over and over until you can do it in the dark if necessary. Bring your own laptop and LCD projector; it is risky to think that someone else will bring one or that you will be easily able to make the necessary connections with their equipment. Include a 15-foot extension cord in your case, and bring a backup set of transparencies of your talk in case of laptop or LCD failures. It is best to check the room where you will be speaking well in advance of your talk. Be sure to note the location of the screen, projector, podium, and microphone. Although not exercised by most speakers, it is your prerogative to move the equipment and furniture around to best suit your style of presentation. Be sure to test your slideshow on the screen to make sure it fits. If it does not, move the screen or projector to give a perfect image on the screen. One final item to check is the lighting in the room. Ideally, you should be able to dim the lights slightly so that the PowerPoint slides will show up bright and colorful on the screen.

Presenting a Poster

Presenting a poster at a conference is the most likely way you will make your debut with the public. At the annual meeting of the Association for Behavior Analysis (ABA), there are literally hundreds of posters presented each year, many of them by first-time students presenting their research.

The Poster Environment

The natural tendency on the part of the viewers is to stroll along the "avenue" of posters, stopping briefly before those whose titles can be read from about 10 to 12 feet. If the title sounds interesting, viewers will move up to about 5 feet for more information, and if something catches their attention, they move directly up to the poster for details. To create some "flow" of viewers past the board, one suggestion might be to arrange the display in such a way that one proceeds through the study from left to right from the abstract through the results. If you stand at the far right of the poster, you will be able to answer questions or provide some discussion for those who find the poster of interest.

Because you will have only 15 minutes or so to set up your poster, it is obvious that no actual preparation at the site is possible; only the assembly and attachment of the predesigned elements can be done. As with public speaking, you may practice a poster session prior to attending a convention by assembling it under similar conditions and determining audience reactions: whether it catches their attention, whether it "flows" properly, whether the different sections can be read from the appropriate distances, and so on.

Each association to put on conferences will have its own specifications and recommendations for preparing a poster. First, make sure you know whether you should bring your poster in pieces and pin them to a backboard or whether your poster will be freestanding on a table. Find out how much space you will have. The biggest problem with posters is that the presenters try to put too much information in one small space. Remember that the person stopping by for a visit will only be there 3 to 5 minutes and that you will need to convey your most important points in that span of time. Start with a great title for your poster to draw people in. It should be carefully worded to sound interesting and to convey something of the population you worked with and perhaps something about the intervention. A title with a question can often intrigue people who will want to find the answer. Make sure that the title is in very large letters (at least 3 inches high) at the top of your poster. Any text you have on the poster must be read from 3 to 5 feet away, so use at least a 14-point font with 24-point header titles. Design your poster so that it can be "read" from left to right as you would read a book. That is, put the abstract and method on the left panel and the results and discussion on the right. Make a large version of your primary graph, and put it right in the middle in a prominent place. Adding pictures of your setting and participants brings life to a poster and makes it more interesting. Bring 25 copies of a one- or two-page handout giving a brief description of the study and one or more graphs of your data. Be sure to indicate on the handout where you can be reached.

Publishing Your Research

The Functions of a Journal

Journals for publication of original research serve several important functions in the operation of any scientific enterprise. Whether sponsored by professional societies or organizations (e.g., the Society for the Experimental Analysis of Behavior, the American Psychological Association, the Association for the Advancement of Behavior Therapy) or publishing companies (e.g., Sage Publications), a journal serves as a quality control mechanism, an information dissemination device, a data bank for future historians, a reinforcement function for those who participate, and, finally, a tool for shaping on the research skills of those who serve the role of author, reviewer, and editor.

Selection

In most scientific fields, there is a great deal more research being done than is economically feasible to publish. Thus, the journal serves as a mechanism by which standards are set for the acceptability (according to current standards) of research. Those manuscripts that do not meet the minimum standards are filtered out by the editorial process. Those accepted are implicitly given the stamp of approval of the journal. That a given manuscript has passed the close scrutiny of those members of the profession held in highest regard by the field gives some assurance to the reader that the research is reliable and valid. Similarly, research not submitted for examination by the peer review process remains an unknown quantity. It is for that reason that relying on data described in papers delivered at conventions (but never published) or articles listed in Dissertation Abstracts (but never subsequently published) to support or refute a position may be a questionable practice.

Dissemination

The sharing of the most recent findings of a field with all interested members is one journal function that is most readily recognized. Unfortunately, this function is not as easily fulfilled as might be desired. There are two primary problems. First, because of the cost of publishing, the length of manuscripts must be kept to minimum. Editors will very frequently insist that certain paragraphs, charts, tables, or other parts of a manuscript be deleted in the interest of saving space. Thus, a Method section, which presumably will be written in such a way as to allow for the replication of findings, is often missing critical details. Reviews of the literature are greatly condensed and the Discussion section is usually limited. An instruction to cut the length of a manuscript by a third is frequently given by an associate editor at the same time that more information about some aspect of the manuscript is requested for inclusion in the next draft. This produces "journal-induced anxiety" on the part of the authors.

The second major drawback to the dissemination function is publication lag time. From the time that an article first reaches an editor (which may be 3 months to 1 year *after* the research was actually completed), it may be 1½ to 2 years to actual publication. By the time an article appears, the authors may be involved in a completely new line of research. By the time readers have been able to review and adopt a particular method or procedure, it could well be obsolete. To be current on research methodology, one must either attend conventions regularly or participate in the peer review process, or both. The primary drawback to keeping current via attending conventions is that the peer review process does not always operate to screen out low-quality research.

Preservation of the History of the Field

Once an article is published, it becomes part of the archives for future historians to examine. Having an archival record of the field will allow historians to react to long-term trends and perhaps predict where new areas of research will develop.

Reinforcement for Scientific Achievement

Because most research, even applied research, is likely to have a major impact upon the culture only after a long period of time, the role of the journal as a source of intermediate conditioned reinforcement for scientific behavior seems critical. Because of the highly selective nature of the reviewing process (e.g., 70% to 80% rejection rate), having an article published in an important journal carries considerable prestige. Social reinforcement to authors may also come in the form of requests for more information and occasionally invitations for speaking engagements at workshops, conventions, and departmental colloquia or seminars. Other reinforcers include occasional requests to reprint an article in a textbook or collection of readings.

Needless to say, publication of one's work in a peer-reviewed journal is one of the primary criteria used in making decisions regarding promotion and tenure at most colleges and universities. Some departments have codified this process to the point where a *fixed* number of publications is necessary for a promotion to associate and full professor—for example, 15 for associate and 30 for full. With such pressure to publish, it is little wonder that publication per se, regardless of the social or scientific contribution it might make, becomes an end, in and of itself, for many people.

Shaping and Education

Perhaps the most important but least appreciated (even by some journals) functions of a journal is to serve as a vehicle for shaping upon the field. Since editors, associate editors, and members of the editorial boards of behavioral and psychological journals are chosen because of their acknowledged expertise, the person sending in a manuscript for review has an opportunity to participate in what amounts to a personalized postdoctoral seminar on research methodology—by correspondence. If properly instructed, reviewers (sometimes called referees) will provide considerable feedback to an author about the adequacy of the research design, methodology, subject selection procedures, data analysis techniques, and so on.

With the probability of being rejected so high, many people will either avoid sending their research in for review or will try once, receive a rejection, and be so punished that they stop submitting their work altogether.

Actually, of course, this decision is counterproductive because if they do not receive feedback on their methodology there is little chance that they will be able to keep up with the rapidly changing field. Viewed objectively, there is nothing to lose in having a manuscript reviewed even if it is rejected. As a general rule, one would be well advised to seek as much feedback from peers as possible: When in doubt, send it in.

Finding the Right Journal

Once the decision to try and publish a piece of research has been made, the next step, that of selecting a potentially receptive journal, should be taken carefully. Basically, you will want to survey several potential journals to determine what kind of research they generally seem to accept. By closely studying the most recent issues of each journal, you should develop a feel for whether they publish primarily experimental or theoretical articles, how much detail they want, how many graphs they usually publish, and so on. In maximizing your chances for having your manuscript accepted, you must decide whether the presumed criteria for accepting any given journal article approximate the quality of your research. That is, you will discover that some journals accept case studies and AB designs and others do not; if your research equals or exceeds the type of study usually accepted, then you may have found a potential outlet for your work. It would probably be a mistake, on the other hand, to submit an AB design or a case study to a journal that obviously requires greater experimental control. In addition to determining these criteria, it is also important to note whether a journal is more likely to accept papers on a particular type of problem or subject population. Some journals, for example, are obviously interested in special disabilities or settings (e.g., *Journal of Learning Disabilities, Exceptional Children, Mental Retardation*) and others in special problems (e.g., *Environment and Behavior);* still others will publish articles on many topics concerning applied behavior analysis or behavior modification if an advance in the science of behavior can be demonstrated (e.g., the *Journal of Applied Behavior Analysis* and *Behavior Modification).*

Once the field of possible journals has been narrowed to one or two, it is necessary to examine closely any written editorial policy statements regarding manuscript submission. These may include statements about specific categories of articles that are published or special criteria for certain categories. At this point, you should finally select the journal that seems most appropriate and most likely to accept your manuscript. Note that an article may *not* be submitted to more than one journal at a time. (If you get a rejection, you are of course free to submit to another journal.)

Preparing the Manuscript

The way in which a manuscript is prepared no doubt makes a difference in the way in which it is received by reviewers and editors. If the manuscript is hastily slapped together, has not been spell-checked or proofread, has poorly prepared graphs, and follows none of the accepted guidelines for organization, use of headings, and so on, it is more likely to be rejected than if it shows signs of careful preparation. If questions come up about how to handle a certain section (e.g., how the research design should be explained), refer to a recent issue of the journal to which you are submitting the manuscript for some guidance from articles already published. As a general rule, you should prepare the original manuscript so that as many details as possible are included because a failure to document how a study was carried out could well result in a rejection. That is, it is better to submit an original manuscript that is slightly longer rather than one that is abbreviated; an editor can easily ask you to shorten an overly long but otherwise acceptable paper but may simply reject a paper that is incomplete. Be sure to include a cover letter indicating that you will be the corresponding author, where you can be reached in the next 2 to 3 months, and a clear statement that the paper has not been previously published and has not been submitted to any other journal.

Manuscript Processing

Under normal circumstances, an editor or associate editor will send a manuscript out to several reviewers and ask each for his or her feedback and recommendations on the manuscript. Depending upon the backlog of manuscripts, you should expect to hear from the journal in 2 to 3 months. (It is not appropriate to bother the editor during this time.) If your manuscript is accepted for publication, you should *anticipate considerable revision* of it before it will finally be accepted. Generally, this will mean shortening some parts (e.g., the Discussion section) and possibly lengthening others (e.g., Method or Results section). The editor or associate editor will typically spell out in some detail the changes to be made and perhaps refer you to the reviewers' comments for further additions, clarifications, or other changes in the manuscript. To assist the editor in determining whether you have met all the objectives, it is advised that you send a *detailed cover letter* along with the revised manuscript. This letter should itemize each reviewer's comments in one column, and beside each should be *your response,* for example, "A more complete description of the reliability assessment has been included and can be found on page 14." The final step in processing an accepted manuscript comes when you receive galley proofs of the article. These must be checked *very carefully* for typographical errors and usually must be returned within 48 hours to guarantee rapid publication. No changes beyond corrections are possible at this stage except at a cost to the authors.

If your manuscript is rejected, study the editor's letter and the comments of the reviewers closely to see how their feedback can be used in preparing a revision that may be sent to another journal. Note that the new journal selected may have slightly different requirements for the format in which the manuscript is to be submitted so that a complete retyping will almost certainly be required. A natural reaction upon receiving a rejection is to put the manuscript away and forget about it. However, if you can overcome this tendency and *be persistent,* you should eventually find some outlet for your research. Remember that applied research can easily become dated and that waiting too long to submit a manuscript elsewhere can greatly decrease the chances of finding a publisher.

It is hoped that these hints and suggestions will greatly increase your repertoire as a researcher in two ways. First, by participating as an author, you will keep in close touch with the current standards within your field. Second, if you are successful in having your manuscript published, your scientific repertoire should be sufficiently strengthened so as to eventually result in new research findings that will enhance our understanding of human behavior.

REFERENCES

Allen, K. D. (1998). The use of an enhanced simplified habit-reversal procedure to reduce disruptive outbursts during athletic performance. *Journal of Applied Behavior Analysis, 31,* 489-492.

Allen, K. D., Loiben, T., Allen, S. J., & Stanley, R. T. (1992). Dentist-implemented contingent escape for management of disruptive child behavior. *Journal of Applied Behavior Analysis, 25,* 629-636.

Allen, K. D., & Warzak, W. J. (2000). The problem of parental nonadherence in clinical behavior analysis: Effective treatment is not enough. *Journal of Applied Behavior Analysis, 33,* 373-391.

Allen, K. E., Hart, B. M., Buell, J. S., Harris, F. R., & Wolf, M. M. (1964). Effects of social reinforcement on isolate behavior of a nursery school child. *Child Development, 35,* 511-518.

American Psychological Association. (1994). *Publication manual of the American Psychological Association* (4th ed.). Washington, DC: Author.

Ardoin, S. P., & Martens, B. K. (2000). Testing the ability of children with attention deficit hyperactivity disorder to accurately report the effects of medication on their behavior. *Journal of Applied Behavior Analysis, 33,* 593-610.

Asmus, J. M., Wacker, D. P., Harding, J., Berg, W. K., Derby, K. M., & Kocis, E. (1999). Evaluation of antecedent stimulus parameters for the treatment of self-maintained aberrant behavior. *Journal of Applied Behavior Analysis, 32,* 495-573.

Austin, J., & Carr, J. E. (2000). *Handbook of applied behavior analysis.* Reno, NV: Context Press.

Austin, J., Kessler, M. L., Riccobono, J. E., & Bailey, J. S. (1996). Using feedback and reinforcement to improve the performance and safety of a roofing crew. *Journal of Organizational Behavior Management, 16,* 49-75.

Ayllon, T., & Michael, J. (1959). The psychiatric nurse as a behavior engineer. *Journal of Experimental Analysis of Behavior, 2,* 323-334.

Azrin, N. H., Bugle, C., & O'Brien, F. (1971). Behavioral engineering: Two apparatuses for toilet training retarded children. *Journal of Applied Behavior Analysis, 4,* 249-253.

Azrin, N. H., & Foxx, R. M. (1971). *Toilet training in less than a day.* New York: Simon & Schuster.

Azrin, N. H., Holz, W. C., Ulrich, R., & Goldiamond, I. (1961). The control of the content of conversation through reinforcement. *Journal of the Experimental Analysis of Behavior, 4,* 25-30.

Azrin, N. H., & Nunn, R. G. (1973). Habit reversal: A method of eliminating nervous habits and tics. *Behavior Research and Therapy, 11,* 619-628.

Azrin, N. H., & Powell, J. R. (1968). Behavioral engineering: The reduction of smoking behavior by a conditioning apparatus and procedure. *Journal of Applied Behavior Analysis, 1,* 193-200.

Azrin, N. H., Rubin, H. B., O'Brien, F. J., Ayllon, T., & Roll, D. L. (1968). Behavioral engineering: Postural control by a portable operant apparatus. *Journal of Applied Behavior Analysis, 1,* 99-108.

Bachrach, A. J., Erwin, W. J., & Mohr, J. P. (1965). The control of eating behavior in an anorexic by operant conditioning techniques. In L. P. Ullmann & L. Krasner (Eds.), *Case studies in behavior modification.* New York: Holt, Rinehart & Winston.

Baer, D. M. (1975). In the beginning, there was a response. In E. Ramp & G. Semb (Eds.), *Behavior analysis: Areas of research and application.* Englewood Cliffs, NJ: Prentice Hall.

Baer, D. M., Wolf, M. M., & Risley, T. R. (1968). Some current dimensions of applied behavior analysis. *Journal of Applied Behavior Analysis, 1,* 91-97.

Bailey, J. S. (1991). Marketing behavior analysis requires different talk. *Journal of Applied Behavior Analysis, 24,* 445-448.

Barker, M. (2001). *Reversing the trend: Using behavioral strategies to prevent shopping cart related injuries.* Unpublished master's thesis, Florida State University, Tallahassee, FL.

Barlow, D. H., & Hayes, S. C. (1979). Alternating treatments design: One strategy for comparing the effects of two treatments to a single subject. *Journal of Applied Behavior Analysis, 12,* 199-210.

Barnette, J. L. (1999). *The effects of goal setting and group feedback on safety behaviors in the workplace: An investigation of response generalization.* Unpublished doctoral dissertation, Florida State University, Tallahassee, FL.

Berman, B. (2000). The academic children's hospital primary care clinic: Responding to the challenge of a changing health care environment. *Clinical Pediatrics, 39,* 473-478.

Bijou, S. W. (1961). Discrimination performance as a baseline for individual analysis of young children. *Child Development, 32,* 163-170.

Bijou, S. W., & Baer, D. M. (1961). *Child development: A systematic and empirical theory.* New York: Appleton-Century-Crofts.

Bijou, S. W., & Orlando, R. (1961). Rapid development of multiple schedule performances with retarded children. *Journal of Experimental Analysis of Behavior, 4,* 7-16.

Bijou, S. W., Peterson, R. F., & Ault, M. H. (1968). A method to integrate descriptive and experimental field studies at the level of data and empirical concepts. *Journal of Applied Behavior Analysis, 1,* 175-191.

Bijou, S. W., & Sturges, P. T. (1959). Positive reinforcers for studies with children: Consumables and manipulatives. *Child Development, 30,* 151-170.

Birkimer, J. C., & Brown, J. H. (1979). Back to basics: Percentage agreement measures are adequate, but there are easier ways. *Journal of Applied Behavior Analysis, 12,* 535-543.

Bosch, S., & Fuqua, R. W. (2001). Behavioral cusps: A model for selecting target behaviors. *Journal of Applied Behavior Analysis, 34,* 123-125.

Bostow, D. E., & Bailey, J. S. (1969). Modification of severe disruptive and aggressive behavior using time-out and reinforcement procedures. *Journal of Applied Behavior Analysis, 2,* 31-37.

Boyce, T. E., & Geller, E. S. (2001). A technology to measure multiple driving behaviors without self-report or participatory reactivity. *Journal of Applied Behavior Analysis, 34,* 39-55.

Briscoe, R. V., Hoffman, D. B., & Bailey, J. S. (1975). Behavioral community psychology: Training a community board to problem solve. *Journal of Applied Behavior Analysis, 8,* 157-168.

Budney, A. J., Higgins, S. T., Delaney, D. D., Kent. L., & Bickel, W. K. (1991). Contingent reinforcement of abstinence with individuals abusing cocaine and marijuana. *Journal of Applied Behavior Analysis, 24,* 657-665.

Burch, M. R. (2000). Program evaluation and quality assurance in animal-assisted therapy. In A. Fine (Ed.), *Handbook of animal-assisted therapy: Theoretical foundations and guidelines for practice* (pp. 129-148). San Diego, CA: Academic Press.

Burch, M. R., & Bailey, J. S. (1999). *How dogs learn.* New York: Howell Book House, Macmillan.

Burns, P. C., & Wilde, G. J. S. (1995). Risk taking in male taxi drivers: Relationships among personality, observational data and driver records. *Personality and Individual Differences, 18,* 267-278.

Campbell, D. T., & Stanley, J. C. (1970). *Experimental and quasi-experimental designs for research.* Chicago: Rand McNally.

Carnegie, D. (1981). *How to win friends and influence people* (3rd ed.). New York: Simon & Schuster.

Carr, E. G., Yarbrough, S. C., & Langdon, N. A. (1997). Effects of idiosyncratic stimulus variables on functional analysis outcomes. *Journal of Applied Behavior Analysis, 30,* 673-686.

Carr, J. E., & Burkholder, E. O. (1998). Creating single-subject design graphs with Microsoft Excel. *Journal of Applied Behavior Analysis, 31,* 245-251.

Chhokar, J. S., & Wallin, J. A. (1984a). A field study of the effect of feedback frequency on performance. *Journal of Applied Psychology, 69,* 524-530.

Chhokar, J. S., & Wallin, J. A. (1984b). Improving safety through applied behavior analysis. *Journal of Safety Research, 15,* 141-151.

Conners, J., Iwata, B. A., Kahng, S. W., Hanley, G. P., Worsdell, A. S., & Thompson, R. H. (2000). Differential responding in the presence and absence of discriminative stimuli during multielement functional analyses. *Journal of Applied Behavior Analysis, 33,* 299-308.

Cooper, J. O., Heron, T. E., & Heward, W. L. (1987). *Applied behavior analysis.* Columbus, OH: Merrill.

Dahlquist, L. M., & Gil, K. M. (1986). Using parents to maintain improved dental flossing skills in children. *Journal of Applied Behavior Analysis, 19,* 255-260.

DeLeon, I. G., Iwata, B. A., Conners, J., & Wallace, M. D. (1999). Examination of ambiguous stimulus preferences with duration based measures. *Journal of Applied Behavior Analysis, 32,* 111-114.

DeLuca, R. V., & Holborn, S. W. (1992). Effects of a variable-ratio reinforcement schedule with changing criteria on exercise in obese and nonobese boys. *Journal of Applied Behavior Analysis, 25,* 671-679.

Ducharme, D. E., & Holburn, S. W. (1997). Programming generalization of social skills in preschool children with hearing impairments. *Journal of Applied Behavior Analysis, 30,* 639-651.

Dunlap, G., Kern-Dunlap, L., Clarke, S., & Robbins, F. R. (1991). Functional assessment, curricular revision, and severe behavior problems. *Journal of Applied Behavior Analysis, 24,* 387-397.

Elashoff, J. D., & Thoresen, C. E. (1978). Choosing a statistical method for analysis of an intensive experiment. In T. Kratochwill (Ed.), *Single subject research: Strategies for evaluating change* (pp. 287-311). New York: Academic Press.

Ellingson, S. A., Miltenberger, R. G., Stricker, J. M., Garlinghouse, M. A., Roberts, J., Galensky, T. L., & Rapp, J. T. (2000). Analysis and treatment of finger sucking. *Journal of Applied Behavior Analysis, 33,* 41-52.

Engelman, K. K., Altus, D. E., & Mathews, R. M. (1999). Increasing engagement in daily activities by older adults with dementia. *Journal of Applied Behavior Analysis, 32,* 107-110.

Engerman, J. A., Austin, J., & Bailey, J. S. (1997). Prompting patron safety belt use at a supermarket. *Journal of Applied Behavior Analysis, 30,* 577-580.

Fawcett, S. B. (1991). Social validity: A note on methodology. *Journal of Applied Behavior Analysis, 24,* 235-239.

Fawcett, S. B., & Miller, L. K. (1975). Training public speaking behavior: An experimental analysis and social validation. *Journal of Applied Behavior Analysis, 8,* 125-135.

Ferster, C. B., & Skinner, B. F. (1957). *Schedules of reinforcement.* New York: Appleton-Century-Crofts.

Fisher, R. A. (1925). *Statistical methods for research workers.* London: Oliver & Boyd.

Fisher, R. A. (1926). The arrangement of field experiments. *Journal of the Ministry of Agriculture, 33,* 503-513.

Fitterling, J. M., Martin, J. E., Gramling, S., Cole, P., & Milan, M. A. (1988). Behavioral management of exercise training in vascular headache patients: An investigation of exercise adherence and headache activity. *Journal of Applied Behavior Analysis, 21,* 9-19.

Foxx, R. M., & Rubinoff, A. (1979). Behavioral treatment of caffeineism: Reducing excessive coffee drinking. *Journal of Applied Behavior Analysis, 12,* 335-344.

France, K. G., & Hudson, S. M. (1990). Behavior management of infant sleep disturbance. *Journal of Applied Behavior Analysis, 23,* 91-98.

Fuller, P. R. (1949). Operant conditioning of a vegetable human organism. *American Journal of Psychology, 62,* 587-590.

Gallagheer, S. M., & Keenan, M. (2000). Independent use of activity materials by the elderly in a residential setting. *Journal of Applied Behavior Analysis, 33,* 325-328.

Garcia, D., Starin, S., & Churchill, R. M. (2001). Treating aerophagia with contingent physical guidance. *Journal of Applied Behavior Analysis, 34,* 89-92.

Gary W. et al. and the United States v. Stewart et al. (No. 74 2412, E.D. La., 1976).

Geller, E. S. (Ed.). (1991a). Social validation [Special issue]. *Journal of Applied Behavior Analysis, 24*(2).

Geller, E. S. (1991b). War on the highways: An international tragedy. *Journal of Applied Behavior Analysis, 24,* 3-7.

Gena, A., Krantz, P. J., McClannahan, L. E., & Poulson, C. L. (1996). Training and generalization of affective behavior displayed by youth with autism. *Journal of Applied Behavior Analysis, 29,* 291-304.

Gibbs, M. (2001). *Effects of differential reinforcement of other behavior in decreasing mouthing behavior in the domestic dog.* Unpublished master's thesis, Roosevelt University, Chicago.

Goetz, E. M., Holmberg, M. C., & LeBlanc, J. M. (1975). Differential reinforcement of other behavior and noncontingent reinforcement as control procedures during the modification of a preschooler's compliance. *Journal of Applied Behavior Analysis, 8,* 77-82.

Gorman, B. S., & Allison, D. B. (1996). Statistical alternatives for single-case designs. In R. D. Franklin, D. B. Allison, & B. S. Gorman (Eds.), *Design and analysis of single-case research* (pp. 159-214). Mahwah, NJ: Lawrence Erlbaum Associates.

Green, C. W., Gardner, S. M., & Reid, D. H. (1997). Increasing indices of happiness among people with profound multiple disabilities: A program replication and component analysis. *Journal of Applied Behavior Analysis, 30,* 217-228.

Green, C. W., & Reid, D. H. (1996). Defining, validating, and increasing indices of happiness among people with profound multiple disabilities. *Journal of Applied Behavior Analysis, 29,* 67-78.

Green, C. W., & Reid, D. H. (1999). Reducing indices of unhappiness among individuals with profound multiple disabilities during therapeutic exercise routines. *Journal of Applied Behavior Analysis, 32,* 137-148.

Gresham, F. M. (1996). Treatment integrity in single subject research. In R. D. Franklin, D. B. Allison, & B. S. Gorman (Eds.), *Design and analysis of single case research* (pp. 93-117). Mahwah, NJ: Lawrence Erlbaum Associates.

Gresham, F. M., Gansle, K. A., & Noell, G. H. (1993). Treatment integrity in applied behavior analysis with children. *Journal of Applied Behavior Analysis, 26,* 257-264.

Guidelines for preparation of figures for *JABA*. (2000). *Journal of Applied Behavior Analysis, 33,* 399.

Gulley, V., & Northup, J. (1997). Comprehensive school-based assessment of the effects of methylphenidate. *Journal of Applied Behavior Analysis, 30,* 627-638.

Haccou, P., & Meelis, E. (1992). *Statistical analysis of behavioural data: An approach based on time-structured models.* Oxford, UK: Oxford University Press.

Harding, J. W., Wacker, D. P., Berg, W. K., Barretto, A., Winborn, L., & Gardner, A. (2001). Analysis of response class hierarchies with attention-maintained problem behaviors. *Journal of Applied Behavior Analysis, 34,* 61-64.

Harris, F. R., Johnston, M. K., Kelley, C. S., & Wolf, M. M. (1964). Effects of positive social reinforcement on regressed crawling of a nursery school child. *Journal of Educational Psychology, 55,* 35-41.

Harris, F. R., & Lehey, B. B. (1978). A method for combining occurrence and nonoccurrence interobserver agreement scores. *Journal of Applied Behavior Analysis, 11,* 523-527.

Harrop, A., & Daniels, M. (1986). Methods of time sampling: A reappraisal of momentary time sampling and partial interval recording. *Journal of Applied Behavior Analysis, 19,* 73-77.

Hart, B. M., Allen, K. E., Buell, J. S., Harris, F. R., & Wolf, M. M. (1964). Effects of social reinforcement on operant crying. *Journal of Experimental Child Psychology, 1,* 145-153.

Hartmann, D. P. (1977). Considerations in the choice of interobserver reliability estimates. *Journal of Applied Behavior Analysis, 10,* 103-116.

Hartmann, D. P., & Hall, R. V. (1976). The changing criterion design. *Journal of Applied Behavior Analysis, 9,* 527-532.

Hawkins, R. P. (1991). Is social validity what we are interested in? Argument for a functional approach. *Journal of Applied Behavior Analysis, 24,* 205-213.

Hawkins, R. P., & Dotson, V. A. (1975). Reliability scores that delude: An Alice in Wonderland trip through the misleading characteristics of interobserver agreement scores in interval recording. In E. Ramp & G. Semb (Eds.), *Behavior analysis areas of research and application.* Englewood Cliffs, NJ: Prentice Hall.

Higgins-Hains, A., & Baer, D. M. (1989). Interaction effects in multielement designs: Inevitable, desirable, and ignorable. *Journal of Applied Behavior Analysis, 22,* 57-69.

Horner, R. D., & Baer, D. M. (1978). Multiple-probe technique: A variation on the multiple baseline. *Journal of Applied Behavior Analysis, 11,* 189-196.

Hughes, C., Lorden, S. W., Scott, S. V., Hwang, B., Derer, K. R., Rodi, M. S., Pitkin, S. E., & Godshall, J. C. (1998). Identification and validation of critical conversational social skills. *Journal of Applied Behavior Analysis, 31,* 431-446.

Issacs, W., Thomas, J., & Goldiamond, I. (1960). Application of operant conditioning to reinstate verbal behavior in psychotics. *Journal of Speech and Hearing Disorders, 25*, 8-12.

Iwata, B. A., Dorsey, M. F., Slifer, K. J., Bauman, K. E., & Richman, G. S. (1982). Toward a functional analysis of self-injury. *Analysis and Interventions in Developmental Disabilities, 2*, 3-20.

Iwata, B., Dorsey, M., Slifer, K., Bauman, K., & Richman, G. (1994). Toward a functional analysis of self-injury. *Journal of Applied Behavior Analysis, 27*, 197-209. (Original work published 1982)

Iwata, B. A., Pace, G. M., Kissel, R. C., Nau, P. A., & Farber, J. M. (1990). The Self-Injury Trauma (SIT) Scale: A method for quantifying surface tissue damage caused by self-injurious behavior. *Journal of Applied Behavior Analysis, 23*, 99-110.

Iwata, B. A., Smith, R. G., & Michael, J. (2000). Current research on the influence of establishing operations on behavior in applied settings. *Journal of Applied Behavior Analysis, 33*, 411-418.

Jackson, D. A., & Wallace, R. F. (1974). The modification and generalization of voice loudness in a fifteen-year-old retarded girl. *Journal of Applied Behavior Analysis, 7*, 461-471.

Jason, L., Billows, W., Schnopp-Wyatt, D., & King, C. (1996). Reducing the illegal sales of cigarettes to minors: Analysis of alternative enforcement schedules. *Journal of Applied Behavior Analysis, 29*, 333-344.

Johnson, S. M., & Bolstad, O. D. (1973). Methodological issues in naturalistic observation: Some problems and solutions for field research. In L. A. Hamerlynk, L. C. Handy, & E. J. Mash (Eds.), *Behavior change: Methodology, concepts, and practice* (pp. 7-67). Champaign, IL: Research Press.

Johnston, J. M., & Pennypacker, H. S. (1993). *Strategies and tactics of behavioral research.* Hillsdale, NJ: Lawrence Erlbaum Associates.

Jones, R. J., & Azrin, N. H. (1969). Behavioral engineering: Stuttering as a function of stimulus duration during speech synchronization. *Journal of Applied Behavior Analysis, 2*, 223-229.

Jordan, J., Singh, N. N., & Repp, A. C. (1989). An evaluation of gentle teaching and visual screening in the reduction of stereotypy. *Journal of Applied Behavior Analysis, 22*, 9-22.

Kahng, S. W., & Iwata, B. A. (1998). Computerized systems for collecting real-time observational data. *Journal of Applied Behavior Analysis, 31*, 253-261.

Kahng, S. W., Tarbox, J., & Wilke, A. E. (2001). Use of a multicomponent treatment for food refusal. *Journal of Applied Behavior Analysis, 34*, 93-96.

Kamps, D. M., Leonard, B. R., Vernon, S., Dugan, E. P., Delquadri, J. C., Gershon, B., Wade, L., & Folk, L. (1992). Teaching social skills to students with autism to increase peer interactions in an integrated first-grade classroom. *Journal of Applied Behavior Analysis, 25*, 281-288.

Kazdin, A. E. (1980). Acceptability of alternative treatments for deviant child behavior. *Journal of Applied Behavior Analysis, 13*, 259- 273.

Kazdin, A. E. (2001). *Behavior modification in applied settings* (6th ed.). Belmont, CA: Wadsworth Thomson Learning.

Keeney, K. M., Fisher, W. W., Adelinis, J. D., & Wilder, D. A. (2000). The effects of response cost in the treatment of aberrant behavior maintained by negative reinforcement. *Journal of Applied Behavior Analysis, 33*, 255-258.

Kendall, M. G. (1973). Hiawatha designs an experiment. *Journal of Applied Behavior Analysis, 6*, 331-332.

Kennedy, C. H., & Meyer, K. A. (1996). Sleep deprivation, allergy symptoms, and negatively reinforced behavior. *Journal of Applied Behavior Analysis, 29*, 133-135.

Kent, R. N., Kanowitz, J., O'Leary, K. D., & Cheiken, M. (1977). Observer reliability as a function of circumstances of assessment. *Journal of Applied Behavior Analysis, 10,* 317-324.

Kneringer, M. J., & Page, T. J. (1999). Improving staff nutritional practices in community based group homes: Evaluation, training, and management. *Journal of Applied Behavior Analysis, 32,* 221-224.

Kritch, K. M., & Bostow, D. E. (1998). Degree of constructed-response interaction in computer-based programmed instruction. *Journal of Applied Behavior Analysis, 31,* 387-398.

Kritch, K. M., Bostow, D. E., & Dedrick, R. F. (1995). Level of interactivity of videodisc instruction on college students' recall of AIDS information. *Journal of Applied Behavior Analysis, 28,* 85-86.

Kubany, E. S., & Sloggett, B. B. (1973). A coding procedure for teachers. *Journal of Applied Behavior Analysis, 6,* 339-344.

Lavelle, J. M., Hovell, M. F., West, M. P., & Wahlgren, D. R. (1992). Promoting law enforcement for child protection: A community analysis. *Journal of Applied Behavior Analysis, 25,* 885-892.

Lindberg, J. S., Iwata, B. A., Kahng, S. W., & DeLeon, I. G. (1999). DRO contingencies: An analysis of variable-momentary schedules. *Journal of Applied Behavior Analysis, 32,* 123-136.

Lowndes, L. (1998). *Talking the winner's way.* Chicago: Contemporary Books.

Lucker, K. (1998). *The effects of a lesson plan intervention on teacher and student behavior in an extended clay enrichment program.* Unpublished master's thesis, Florida State University, Tallahassee, FL.

Ludwig, T. D., & Geller, E. S. (1991). Improving the driving practices of pizza deliverers: Response generalization and moderating effects of driving history. *Journal of Applied Behavior Analysis, 24,* 31-44.

Ludwig, T. D., & Geller, E. S. (1997). Managing injury control among professional pizza deliverers: Effects of goal-setting and response generalization. *Journal of Applied Psychology, 82,* 253-261.

Ludwig, T. D., & Geller, E. S. (2000). An organizational behavior management approach to safe driving intervention for pizza deliverers [Monograph]. *Journal of Organizational Behavior Management.*

Lumley, V. A., Miltenberger, R. G., Long, E. S., Rapp, J. T., & Roberts, J. A. (1998). Evaluation of a sexual abuse prevention program for adults with mental retardation. *Journal of Applied Behavior Analysis, 31,* 91-102.

Magee, S. K., & Ellis, J. (2000). Extinction effects during the assessment of multiple problem behaviors. *Journal of Applied Behavior Analysis, 33,* 313-316.

Maglieri, K. A., DeLeon, I. S., Rodriguez-Catter, V., & Sevin, B. M. (2000). Treatment of covert food stealing in an individual with Prader-Willi syndrome. *Journal of Applied Behavior Analysis, 33,* 615-618.

Marchand-Martella, N. E., Martella, R. C., Agran, M., Salzberg, C. L., Young, R., & Morgan, D. (1992). Generalized effects of a peer-delivered first aid program for students with moderate intellectual disabilities. *Journal of Applied Behavior Analysis, 25,* 841-851.

Martin, G., & Pear, J. (1999). *Behavior modification: What it is and how to do it* (6th ed.). Upper Saddle River, NJ: Prentice Hall.

Martin, R. (1975). *Legal challenges to behavior modification: Trends in schools, corrections and mental health.* Champaign, IL: Research Press.

Mathews, J. R., Hodson, G. D., Crist, W. B., & Laroche, G. R. (1992). Teaching young children to use contact lenses. *Journal of Applied Behavior Analysis, 25,* 229-235.

Matyas, T. A., & Greenwood, K. M. (1996). Serial dependency in single-case time series. In R. D. Franklin, D. B. Allison, & B. S. Gorman (Eds.), *Design and analysis of single-case research* (pp. 215-243). Mahwah, NJ: Lawrence Erlbaum Associates.

May, J. G., Risley, T. R., Twardosz, S., Friedman, P., Bijou, S. W., & Wexler, D. (1975). Guidelines for the use of behavioral procedures in state programs for retarded persons. *M. R. Research*, Volume 1 (entire issue).

McGee, J. J. (Producer). (1986). *Gentle approach.* [A four-part video series]. (Available from Media Resource Center, Meyer Children's Rehabiliation Unit, Omaha, NE).

McKenzie, T. L., Sallis, J. F., Nader, P. R., Patterson, T. L., Elder, J. P., Berry, C. C., Rupp, J. W., Atkins, C. J., Buono, M. J., & Nelson, J. A. (1991). BEACHES: An observational system for assessing children's eating and physical activity behaviors and associated events. *Journal of Applied Behavior Analysis, 24,* 141-151.

McMichael, J. S., & Corey, J. R. (1969). Contingency management in an introductory psychology course produces better learning. *Journal of Applied Behavior Analysis, 2,* 79-83.

Michael, J. (1982). Distinguishing between discriminative and motivational functions of stimuli. *Journal of the Experimental Analysis of Behavior, 37,* 149-155.

Miltenberger, R. G. (2001). *Behavior modification: Principles and procedures* (2nd ed.). Belmont, CA: Wadsworth Thomson Learning.

Miltenberger, R. G., Rapp, J. T., & Long, E. S. (1999). A low-tech method for conducting real-time recording. *Journal of Applied Behavior Analysis, 32,* 119-120.

Minkin, N., Braukmann, C. J., Minkin, B. L., Timbers, G. D., Timbers, B. J., Fixsen, D. L., Phillips, E. L., & Wolf, M. M. (1976). The social validation and training of conversational skills. *Journal of Applied Behavior Analysis, 9,* 127-139.

Morales v. Turman, 383 F. Supp. 53 (E.D. Tex. 1974).

Morgan, D. L., & Morgan, R. K. (2001). Single participant research design: Bringing science to managed care. *American Psychologist, 56,* 119-127.

Mudford, O. C., Beale, I. L., & Singh, N. N. (1990). The representativeness of observational samples of different durations. *Journal of Applied Behavior Analysis, 23,* 323-331.

Neef, N. A., Lensbower, J., Hockersmith, I., DePalma, V., & Gray, K. (1990). In vivo versus simulation training: An interactional analysis of range and type of training exemplars. *Journal of Applied Behavior Analysis, 23,* 447-458.

Neef, N., Parrish, J., Hannigan, K., Page, T., & Iwata, B. (1989). Teaching self-catheterization skills to children with neurogenic bladder complications. *Journal of Applied Behavior Analysis, 22,* 237-243.

Neef, N. A., Trachtenberg, S., Loeb, J., & Sterner, K. (1991). Video-based training of respite care providers: An interactional analysis of presentation format. *Journal of Applied Behavior Analysis, 24,* 473-486.

Nicolson, A. (2000). *A behavioral intervention for shaping the resumption of exercise after drop-out: Implications for practice and theory.* Unpublished doctoral dissertation, Florida State University, Tallahassee, FL.

Niemeyer, J. A., & McEvoy, M. A. (1989). *Observational assessment of reciprocal social interaction: Social Interaction Code (SIC).* Nashville, TN: Vanderbilt/Minnesota Social Interaction Project, Vanderbilt University and the University of Minnesota.

Noell, G. H., Witt, J. C., LaFleur, L. H., Mortenson, B. P., Ranier, D. D., & LeVelle, J. (2000). Increasing intervention implementation in general education following consultation: A comparison of two follow-up strategies. *Journal of Applied Behavior Analysis, 33,* 271-284.

Northup, J., Fusilier, I., Swanson, V., Huete, J., Bruce, T., Freeland, J., Gulley, V., & Edwards, S. (1999). Further analysis of the separate and interactive effects of methylphenidate and common classroom contingencies. *Journal of Applied Behavior Analysis, 32,* 35-50.

Northup, J., Wacker, D. P., Berg, W. K., Kelly, L., Sasso, G., & DeRaad, A. (1994). The treatment of severe behavior problems in school settings using a technical assistance model. *Journal of Applied Behavior Analysis, 27,* 33-47.

O'Brien, F., & Azrin, N. H. (1970). Behavioral engineering: Control of posture by informational feedback. *Journal of Applied Behavior Analysis, 3,* 235-240.

O'Leary, K. D., & Kent, R. D. (1973). Behavior modification for social action: research tactics and problems. In L. A. Hamerlynk, P. O. Davidson, & L. E. Acker (Eds.), *Critical issues in research and practice.* Champaign, IL: Research Press.

O'Leary, K. D., Kent, R. N., & Kanowitz, J. (1975). Shaping data collection congruent with experimental hypotheses. *Journal of Applied Behavior Analysis, 8,* 43-51.

Oliver, C., Oxener, G., Hearn, M., & Hall, S. (2001). Effects of social proximity on multiple aggressive behaviors. *Journal of Applied Behavior Analysis, 34,* 85-88.

Olmsted, J. M. D., & Olmsted, E. H. (1952). *Claude Bernard and the experimental method in science.* New York: Henry Schuman.

Pace, G. M., & Toyer, E. A. (2000). The effects of a vitamin supplement on the pica of a child with severe mental retardation. *Journal of Applied Behavior Analysis, 33,* 619-622.

Parsonson, B. S., & Baer, D. M. (1978). Training generalized improvisation of tools by preschool children. *Journal of Applied Behavior Analysis, 3,* 363-380.

Piazza, C. C., Fisher, W. W., Hanley, G. P., Remick, M. L., Contrucci, S. A., & Aitken, T. L. (1997). The use of positive *and* negative reinforcement in the treatment of escape-maintained destructive behavior. *Journal of Applied Behavior Analysis, 30,* 279-298.

Porterfield, J. K., Herbert-Jackson, E., & Risley, T. R. (1976). Contingent observation: An effective and acceptable procedure for reducing disruptive behavior of young children in a group setting. *Journal of Applied Behavior Analysis, 9,* 55-64.

Powell, J., & Azrin, N. H. (1968). The effect of shock as a punisher for cigarette smoking. *Journal of Applied Behavior Analysis, 1,* 63-71.

Powell, J., Martindale, A., & Kulp, S. (1975). An evaluation of time-sample measures of behavior. *Journal of Applied Behavior Analysis, 8,* 463-469.

Quinn, J. M., Sherman, J. A., Sheldon, J. B., Quinn, L. M., & Harchik, A. E. (1992). Social validation of component behaviors of following instructions, accepting criticism, and negotiating. *Journal of Applied Behavior Analysis, 25,* 401-413.

Ragnarsson, R. S., & Bjorgvinsson, T. (1991). Effects of public posting on driving speed in Icelandic traffic. *Journal of Applied Behavior Analysis, 24,* 53-58.

Rapport, M. D., Murphy, H. A., & Bailey, J. S. (1982). Ritalin vs. response cost in the control of hyperactive children: A within subject comparison. *Journal of Applied Behavior Analysis, 15,* 205-216.

Richman, D. M., Wacker, D. P., & Winborn, L. (2001). Response efficiency during functional communication training: Effects of effort on response allocation. *Journal of Applied Behavior Analysis, 34,* 73-76.

Ringdahl, J. E., Vollmer, T. R., Borrero, J. C., & Connell, J. E. (2001). Fixed-time schedule effects as a function of baseline reinforcement rate. *Journal of Applied Behavior Analysis, 34,* 1-15.

Risley, T. R. (1997). Montrose M. Wolf: The origins of the dimensions of applied behavior analysis. *Journal of Applied Behavior Analysis, 30,* 377-381.

Risley, T. R., & Twardosz, S. (1974). *Suggested guidelines for the humane management of the behavior problems of the retarded.* Unpublished manuscript.

Robinson, P. W., Newby, T. J., & Ganzell, S. L. (1981). A token system for a class of under-achieving hyperactive children. *Journal of Applied Behavior Analysis, 14,* 307-315.

Romanczyk, R. G., Kent, R. N., Diament, C., & O'Leary, K. D. (1973). Measuring the reliability of observational data: A reactive process. *Journal of Applied Behavior Analysis, 6,* 175-184.

Roscoe, E. M., Iwata, B. A., & Goh, H. L. (1998). A comparison of noncontingent reinforcement and sensory extinction as treatments for self-injurious behavior. *Journal of Applied Behavior Analysis, 31,* 635-646.

Rosenthal, R. (1966). *Experimenter bias in behavioral research.* New York: Appleton-Century-Crofts.

Sarokoff, R. A., Taylor, B. A., & Poulson, C. L. (2001). Teaching children with autism to engage in conversational exchanges: Script fading with embedded textual stimuli. *Journal of Applied Behavior Analysis, 34,* 81-84.

Saudargas, R. A., & Zanolli, K. (1990). Momentary time sampling as an estimate of percentage time: A field validation. *Journal of Applied Behavior Analysis, 23,* 533-537.

Schepis, M. M., Reid, D. H., Behrmann, M. M., & Sutton, K. A. (1998). Increasing communicative interactions of young children with autism using a voice output communication aid and naturalistic teaching. *Journal of Applied Behavior Analysis, 31,* 561-578.

Schmidt, G. W., & Ulrich, R. E. (1969). Effects of group contingent events upon classroom noise. *Journal of Applied Behavior Analysis, 2,* 171-179.

Schnelle, J., & Lee, J. (1974). A quasi-experimental retrospective evaluation of a prison policy change. *Journal of Applied Behavior Analysis, 7,* 483-496.

Schroeder, S. R. (1972). Automated transduction of sheltered workshop behaviors. *Journal of Applied Behavior Analysis, 5,* 523-525.

Schwartz, I. S., & Baer, D. M. (1991). Social validity assessments: Is current practice state of the art? *Journal of Applied Behavior Analysis, 24,* 189-204.

Shirley, M. J., Iwata, B. A., Kahng, S. W., Mazaleski, J. L., & Lerman, D. C. (1997). Does functional communication training compete with ongoing contingencies of reinforcement? An analysis during response acquisition and maintenance. *Journal of Applied Behavior Analysis, 30,* 93-104.

Shore, B. A., Lerman, D. C., Smith, R. G., Iwata, B. A., & DeLeon, I. G. (1995). Direct assessment of quality of care in a geriatric nursing home. *Journal of Applied Behavior Analysis, 28,* 435-448.

Sidman, M. (1960). *Tactics of scientific research.* New York: Basic Books.

Skinner, B. F. (1938). *The behavior of organisms.* New York: Appleton-Century-Crofts.

Skinner, B. F. (1950). Are theories of learning necessary? *Psychological Review, 57,* 193-216.

Skinner, B. F. (1953). *Science and human behavior.* New York: Free Press.

Skinner, B. F. (1966). Operant behavior. In W. K. Honig (Ed.), *Operant behavior: Areas of research and application.* New York: Appleton-Century-Crofts.

Skinner, B. F. (1969). *Contingencies of reinforcement.* Englewood Cliffs, NJ: Prentice Hall.

Skinner, B. F. (1974). *The technology of teaching.* New York: Appleton-Century-Crofts.

Strang, H. R., & George, J. R. (1975). Clowning around to stop clowning around: A brief report on an automated approach to monitor, record, and control classroom noise. *Journal of Applied Behavior Analysis, 8,* 471-474.

Stricker, J. M., Miltenberger, R. G., Garlinghouse, M. A., Deaver, C. M., & Anderson, C. A. (2001). Evaluation of an awareness enhancement device for the treatment of thumb sucking in children. *Journal of Applied Behavior Analysis, 34,* 77-80.

Switzer, E. B., Deal, T. E., & Bailey, J. S. (1977). The reduction of stealing in second graders using a group contingency. *Journal of Applied Behavior Analysis, 10,* 267-272.

Tate, B. G. (1968). An automated system for reinforcing and recording retardate work behavior. *Journal of Applied Behavior Analysis, 1,* 347-348.

Thompson, R. H., Iwata, B. A., Conners, J., & Roscoe, E. M. (1999). Effects of reinforcement for alternative behavior during punishment of self-injury. *Journal of Applied Behavior Analysis, 32,* 317-328.

Thomson, C., Holmberg, M., & Baer, D. M. (1974). A brief report on a comparison of time-sampling procedures. *Journal of Applied Behavior Analysis, 7,* 623-626.

Thurkow, N. M. (2001). *Using behavioral technology in a total quality management environment: A systems level analysis.* Unpublished doctoral dissertation, Florida State University, Tallahassee, FL.

Tudor, R. M., & Bostow, D. E. (1991). Computer-programmed instruction: The relation of required interaction to practical application. *Journal of Applied Behavior Analysis, 24,* 361-368.

Tufte, E. R. (1983). *The visual display of quantitative information.* Cheshire, CT: Graphics.

Tyler, V. O., & Brown, G. D. (1967). The use of swift, brief isolation as a group control device for institutionalized delinquents. *Behavior Research and Therapy, 5,* 1-9.

Ulman, J. D., & Sulzer-Azaroff, B. (1975). Multi-element baseline design in educational research. In E. Ramp & G. Semb (Eds.), *Behavior analysis areas of research and application.* Englewood Cliffs, NJ: Prentice Hall.

Ullmann, L. P., & Krasner, L. (1965). *Case studies in behavior modification.* New York: Holt, Rinehart & Winston.

Vollmer, T. R., Roane, H. S., Ringdahl, J. E., & Marcus, B. A. (1999). Evaluating treatment challenges with differential reinforcement of alternative behavior. *Journal of Applied Behavior Analysis, 32,* 9-23.

Wacker, D. P., McMahon, C., Steege, M., Berg, W., Sasso, G., & Melloy, K. (1990). Applications of a sequential alternating treatments design. *Journal of Applied Behavior Analysis, 23,* 333-339.

Wallace, M. D., & Iwata, B. A. (1999). Effects of session duration on functional analysis outcomes. *Journal of Applied Behavior Analysis, 32,* 175-183.

Weiss, L., & Hall, R. V. (1971). Modification of cigarette smoking through avoidance of punishment. In R. V. Hall (Ed.), *Managing behavior: Behavior modification applications in school and home.* Lawrence, KS: H & H Enterprises.

Werts, M. G., Caldwell, N. K., & Wolery, M. (1996). Peer modeling of response chains: Observational learning by students with disabilities. *Journal of Applied Behavior Analysis, 29,* 53-66.

Wilder, D. A., Masuda, A., O'Connor, C., & Baham, M. (2001). Brief functional analysis and treatment of bizarre vocalizations in an adult with schizophrenia. *Journal of Applied Behavior Analysis, 34,* 65-68.

Williams, C. (1959). The elimination of tantrum behavior by extinction procedures. *Journal of Abnormal and Social Psychology, 59,* 269.

Wilson, W. W., & Hopkins, B. L. (1973). The effects of music on the intensity of noise in junior high home economics classes. *Journal of Applied Behavior Analysis, 6,* 269-275.

Winett, R. A., Moore, J. F., & Anderson, E. S. (1991). Extending the concept of social validity: Behavior analysis for disease prevention and health promotion. *Journal of Applied Behavior Analysis, 24,* 215-230.

Witt, J. C., Noell, G. H., LaFleur, L. H., & Mortenson, B. P. (1997). Teacher use of interventions in general education settings: Measurement and analysis of the independent variable. *Journal of Applied Behavior Analysis, 30,* 693-696.

Wolf, M. M. (1978). Social validity: The case for subjective measurement or how applied behavior analysis is finding its heart. *Journal of Applied Behavior Analysis, 11,* 203-214.

Wolf, M. M., Risley, T. R., & Mees, H. (1964). Application of operant conditioning proce-dures to the behavior problems of an autistic child. *Behaviour Research and Therapy, 1,* 305-312.

Wood, D. K., Frank, A. R., & Wacker, D. P. (1998). Teaching multiplication facts to students with learning disabilities. *Journal of Applied Behavior Analysis, 31,* 323-338.

Woods, D. W., Miltenberger, R. G., & Lumley, V. A. (1996). Sequential application of major habit-reversal components to treat motor tics in children. *Journal of Applied Behavior Analysis, 29,* 483-493.

Worsdell, A. S., Iwata, B. A., Conners, J., Kahng, S. W., & Thompson, R. H. (2000). Relative influences of establishing operations and reinforcement contingencies on self-injurious behavior during functional analyses. *Journal of Applied Behavior Analysis, 33,* 451-461.

Yelton, A. R., Wildman, B. G., & Erickson, M. T. (1977). A probability-based formula for cal-culating interobserver agreement. *Journal of Applied Behavior Analysis, 10,* 127-131.

Index

Behavioral definitions, in observation protocol, 112–113 (table), 114 (table), 134

Behavioral focus, of applied behavior analysis, 12–13

Behavior modification, ix–x, 147–148

Behavior product, 91

Behaviors of Eating and Activity for Children's Health Evaluation System (BEACHES), 112

Behrmann, M. M., 169, 172, 173 (figure), 174

Believability, 14

Berg, W. K., 78, 80, 92, 112, 159, 186

Berman, B., x

Berry, C. C., 112

Bias, observer, 13, 121, 123

Bickel, W. K., 66

Bijou, S. W., 7, 127, 128

Bijou, Sidney, 6, 9

Billows, W., 189

Biological variable, 49, 73

Birkimer, J. C., 128

Bjorgvinsson, T., 75

Bolstad, O. D., 122, 128

B-only (treatment) research design, 148, 149 (figure)

Bootleg reinforcer, 47

Borrero, J. C., 161

Bosch, S., 46

Bostow, D. E., 189, 200

Boyce, T. E., 67, 95, 110

Braukmann, C. J., 83

Briscoe, R. V., 31

Brown, G. D., 200

Brown, J. H., 128

Bruce, T., 76, 184

Budney, A. J., 66

Buell, J. S., 6, 7 (figure), 8 (figure), 119

Bugle, C., 96

Buono, M. J., 112

Burch, M. R., 143

Burkholder, E. O., 221

Burns, P C., 67

Caldwell, N. K., 172–173

Camcorder, 57

Campbell, D. T., 143

Carnegie, D., 37

Carr, E. G., 53

Carr, J. E., 221

Case study, in early behavior modification, 147–148

Cause-effect relationship, 215, 216 (figure), 219

Changing-criterion research design, 187–188

Cheiken, M., 121, 122

Chhokar, J. S., 203

Child behavior, 10-second interval observation on, 6–7 (figure)

Churchill, R. M., 66, 74, 160, 162 (figure)

Clarke, S., 85

Cold calling, 34–35

Cole, P., 187

Comparative treatment research, 79

Computerized data collection, 97, 100, 214

Computer projector, 228

Conceptual system, of applied behavior analysis, 15

Conditioned emotional response, 49

Confidential information, 196 (table)

Connell, J. E., 161

Conners, J., 92, 100, 179, 182, 183 (figure)

Consensual observer drift, 121

Consequent event, 73

Consequent stimulus variable, 73–74

Contact person, preparing, 206–207

Contingency variable, 49

Contingent observation, 201–202

Contrucci, S. A., 186

Cooper, J. O., xi

Corey, J. R., 83

Crist, W. B., 66

Critical conversation skill study, 86

Culturally conditioned behavior, 50

Cumulative treatment, in multiple baseline research design, 167

Dahlquist, L. M., 94

9780761925569

ABOUT THE AUTHORS

Jon S. Bailey, PhD, is Professor of Psychology at Florida State University. He is a Board Certified Behavior Analyst™, a past editor of the *Journal of Applied Behavior Analysis,* and the author of over 100 scholarly research articles. He was listed in the *Behavior Analyst* as the second most widely published author in applied behavior analysis. He is an internationally recognized speaker on the topic of applied behavior analysis. He has given major addresses at conferences throughout the United States, Canada, and Europe.

Mary R. Burch, PhD, is a Board Certified Behavior Analyst™. She is also a Certified Applied Animal Behaviorist. She is an award-winning writer; she has published five books and over 100 articles. Her behavioral research has been published by the U.S. Department of Education. She is a member of the American Society of Journalists and Authors.